Just Keep Shooting

My Youth in Manhattan

Memoir of a Midwestern Girl
In the 1950s and 1960s

Judy McConnell

Acknowledgements

I am indebted to the following people: Ingrid Lund and
Mary Swanson for their invaluable input, Marvin
Walowitz for providing photos and other materials, and
editors Nancy Raeburn and Patti Frazee.

The experiences related in this book are products of my own
perception, based on diaries, journals, letters, and memory. The
names of some characters have been changed to protect the guilty
and expose the innocent.

Dedication

To my children Libby and David
who survived

Published by Yorkford Press
Printed in the United States of America

SAVE THE LAST DANCE FOR ME

by Doc Pomus and Mort Shuman, 1960

You can dance
Every dance with the gal
Who gave you the eye
Let her hold you tight

You can smile
Every smile for the girl
Who held your hand
'Neath the pale moonlight

Oh I know
That the music is fine
Like sparkling wine
Go and have your fun

Laugh and sing
And while we're apart
Don't give your heart
To anyone

But don't forget who's taking you home
And in whose arms you're gonna be
So darlin'
Save the last dance for me, mmm

Frontispiece photo of author by Krishna Singh
Photo of NYC on page 230 by Frank Oscar Larson

Author, 1957

Part 1
Eastern Exposure

Chapter 1   Minneapolis Hiatus

The world was out there, vast as a celestial ocean, all I had to do was pick a star and lift off. With a fresh college degree from the University of Southern California packed with cinema credits tucked in my pocket, I was ready to conquer the film world. I counted on the esteem focused on college graduates—a premium for a female in 1956—with the whole of society primed and waiting.

The first weeks back home in Minneapolis I preferred to remain closeted, seeing no one, basking in a future of unlimited possibilities. But it soon became clear I couldn't remain at home listening to echoes float through the big Kenwood house. My life's work lay ahead—and it was up to me to plot a direction.

Meanwhile, determined to continue the non-conformist life of bohemian resistance I'd embraced in Los Angeles, I enrolled in Howard Nemerov's creative writing class at the University of Minnesota and began to work on a short story. Afternoons I hopped on a bus to Larson's Photo Studio off Lake Street, where I developed prints in the darkroom. The idea was to accumulate enough money to move with my big fat degree to New York City by Christmas.

*Dad, Harold, Granddad Fought, Mother, back
Jamie (Hal's daughter), Susan, front*

Living at home was a novelty at first. I found myself swallowed in a round of socializing: tea at Gamma Phi luncheons with Mother, donned in my worsted wool suit; family dinners at the Minikahda Club dining room overlooking the silver-green waters of Lake Calhoun; visits to friends of my parents in homes awash with colorful Christmas streamers, mint juleps, and hearty cheer, where I was acclaimed as a newly minted college graduate. My brother and sister were mere shadows drifting like vaguely familiar cutouts through the house, with Harold often off with his law school buddies and Susan buried in an eighth-grade underworld of Northrop activities.

Harold, Susan, Judy in Minneapolis

It didn't take long for the differences between me and my surroundings to contaminate the atmosphere. I didn't fit in. My ideas were diametrically opposed to those around me. All those material things, rich and initially satisfying, ended up lying dead in my lap. There was nothing here I wanted. It was all meaningless. What good was all of this to me?

The old patterns of conflict soon began to reappear. Mother and I were at odds, you might say in dire conflict. First of all, I rejected in one swoop her existence and everything that touched it. She epitomized all I abhorred. The senseless small talk, the same phrases over and over, the identical reactions to the paltry concerns of the household, the fuss over details that were uninteresting and trivial.

Mother had eschewed a college degree in favor of marriage. She gloried in building a family and the rise in position created by Dad's

3

transfer from West Virginia to Minnesota and his subsequent rise up the career ladder. She held no interest whatsoever in the business and political world—"don't bother me with these dull matters." But with her children now throwing their educated viewpoints into the dinner conversation, she wanted to be involved. "What does GNP mean?" she asked, repeating *Gross National Product* aloud over and over. But her attention was soon averted to a lighter subject. She tried, but her heart wasn't in it.

I was aware that my attitude, my very presence undermined and irritated her. A subtle competition grew between us. When she noticed that I replaced the vacuum cleaner bag, a chore usually handled by my father, all of a sudden she was doing it herself. She got herself a 35 mm camera and was instantly a photographer. Activities once scorned she now undertook; evidently if I could do it so could she, so could anybody. Women with her background traditionally benefited by assuming an unskilled, dependent role, and maybe she was now grateful to find small avenues of independence, but it made me feel small and insignificant.

She was not impressed with my aloof airs and high-toned ideas. I had no friends—except Margo—and no prospects. There I was home again, age 21, back to square one. And disdaining everything. Who did I think I was? What call had a freeloader to be so persnickety? Although Margo was required to pay room and board, Dad wouldn't hear of me paying a cent. To Mother this was unreasonable, I should be pulling my weight. She didn't think they should buy me anything and stiffened when I used her car and smoked her cigarettes. They had fulfilled their duty, she said, and I should be making my own way.

I wanted nothing more than to lift my foot and take the first step, if only I knew where to plant it. True, I had been procrastinating for some time. Her stance made sense, seen in the light of reason, but all I saw then was the cool air of dismissal and her deep-seated antagonism.

I performed jobs around the house dutifully, but continually perceived that she felt I no l longer belonged. She wanted me out. I had long given up hope of penetrating her armor of containment and learned to match her dislike, even outdo it.

I shuffled around in a state of muted defiance.

Tension permeated the house. Mother hid her animosity toward me when Dad was around, but when alone we dug at each other with subtle

4

jabs. Both of us, in a gallant effort to smooth things over, kept up a pleasant chatter as we worked in the kitchen. But it was impossible to sustain the hypocritical niceness. I determined to stay out of her way as much as possible.

Journal Entry

> There is no meeting ground. It's hard to write about, as I find I have no understanding of what is transpiring between my parents and me. But it isn't pretty.
> I stare out my bedroom window. A cold November sun covers into the lawns and a few stubborn leaves dangle from the trees. There are no signs of life; the ground is a dull nether land, waiting for the onslaught of winter.

I had to leave, but how? Up until now my life had been plotted in educational phases and all I had to do was drift with it and nurse my dissatisfactions. Now I was called on to rely on my own initiative, talent, and self-possession, of which I held very little. How was I to attach my dreams to the finite world of opportunity stretching across the continent?

One evening Mother called me up to her room and closed the door. This was unusual, as it was Dad who took me aside for little talks, persuasive litanies on the values of life that I ignored. (Years later his words would break into my head out of nowhere, with new significance.)

What in heaven's name was wrong? Mother wanted to know. "There is to be no unpleasantness in the house," she said emphatically, before I could think of what to say. "Your attitude is poisoning the household. What is it that is bothering you?"

Seated on the four-poster bed, I glanced at her. A telltale flake of impatience flashed from her eyes. "Nothing is wrong," I said. I felt a familiar dread rising in my throat and struggled to conquer the feeling of childhood shame that blocked all thought. That I was under the gun was evident. I searched for ammunition with which to defend myself. "I am just—confused about life."

I didn't trust her. Such direct confrontation was rare, but now finally she was willing to talk—on her terms, I was sure.

"Your dad and I are very concerned. What exactly is it that you expect?"

I decided to punt. "Nothing, just to be left alone. There is so much pressure to be a certain way. I need to find my own way." I looked down at my lap and started picking at the green malachite ring on my finger.

She regarded me steadily. "I don't know what you're talking about. You're *not* here alone. You must consider others. Why are you always so negative? Can't you just get along?"

"I'll try," I sighed. I couldn't open my heart to her. I could say nothing that she could conceivably comprehend. Her only concern was that peace be maintained. She was looking for some tight answer to believe in so she could put the whole ordeal out of her mind.

At my assurance that nothing was wrong she looked relieved. "Well, I'm glad everything is all right. Lord knows I've made every effort to make you comfortable. We have supported you, entertained you, fed you, and backed your wishes. My conscience is entirely clear."

I hated her.

"I am thinking of your happiness. If things don't improve I think it best for you to move out." The finality in her tone signaled that she had played her final card. But she hit me with one last blow. She had procured the name of someone—a psychiatrist—highly recommended. I needed to get myself straightened around. For my own good.

The idea hit my skin and veered off like a bullet, without penetrating. Something was wrong with *me?* You've got to be kidding!

I stood up abruptly as a crush of anger flared into every fiber of my body. "You know nothing about me!" It was a ridiculous thing to say, she knew the vicissitudes of my temperament better than anyone, my little turns of habit. But to my inner being she was blind, she neither investigated nor understood what went on in the heart and mind of a little creature struggling to make sense of growing up. So many nights alone in a corner of the house watching her and my father sweep out of the house to a party or to catch a flight to Hilton Head Island; so many times watching her slip from the room as my brother shoved me into the pitch-dark basement. Bitterly I recalled the times when I had slunk upstairs, mortified at the ridicule she heaped on my latest scrape; the

6

scorn in her tone as I attempted to trace the trip to my summer camp on a map—the hundred ways she displayed her dislike of my foibles, my emotions, me. With Dad absorbed in getting ahead and my brother and sister off in their private enclaves, the house I grew up in was devoid of human comfort. And to my young mind it was all the cause of the imperial person who seemed to be always floating like a ghost in the next room—my mother.

After four years of college independence, living in the house was stifling. I had to get out, but where, how—the vastness was too wide, too imprecise. I could view no perch to grab on to.

"Judy, can you come over tonight?" It was my best friend from high school Margo. "A guy from Blake will be here. You probably know him, he played the lead role in *Sense and Sensibility* during our senior year. He's bringing a friend." The excitement in Margo's voice was catching. My mind veered back to our Northrop days, trying to visualize the boys from our male-equivalent high school who had flickered in the background during my teen-age years. Boys with bright assurance and quick minds who rushed to open doors and told amusing stories that sent listeners howling. With these boys in shiny loafers and V-necked tennis sweaters I associated the word smashing.

"We'll watch the game, with beer and popcorn and all. You must come."

The game. I had never been a fan of the yelling, knock-out ritual of football. All noise, bluster, and conquer without an ounce of artistry. It didn't interest me. On the other hand, two boys of the sort I had gazed at with longing during my Northrop years did. I was not doing anything else, my days were free as flying kites and just as aimless. I was treading water, waiting for my life to begin. I agreed.

Since Margo had flown out East to attend Colby College in Maine and I out West to complete my degree in Los Angeles, our paths had veered in different directions. I sought self-expression, to develop my artistic talents, and repudiated all thoughts of convention and domesticity. On the other hand, the search for dates and fun times was prominent in Margo's twenty-one-year-old mind. She also needed a job, the route to independence from smothering home life, and floundered in the same quandary of indecision as I did. Both of us faced an undefined future.

7

After an evening of TV and popcorn at Margo's, the four of us became something of a team. We lounged in my basement amusement room, exchanging stories of college life and discussing wistful dreams of post-graduate fulfillment. Gordon Malloy, a business finance major, was dissatisfied with his bank teller position at a neighborhood bank. Gordy was the good-looking one, with soft brown eyes and a calm demeanor that suggested a conservative, cautious nature. He had a penetrating gaze and a way of leading light conversation into commentaries on life. There was something different about him, and I was intrigued by the way he studied me and made oblique comments on what he considered my bizarre ideas.

His sidekick Luke Cumberland, in contrast, with his tall lumbering build and bland complexion, exuded easygoing simplicity. He lounged back on the couch with hearty cheerfulness and obtained tickets for us to the latest community theater productions.

One night we attended a costume party at Theater in the Round Playhouse, where Gordy occasionally acted in productions. Gordy and I, photography buffs, brought our cameras and captured Margo dressed as a Chinese coolie, Luke in a pinchfront cowboy hat wiping beer foam from his mouth, and I in a Count of Monte Cristo cape sucking on a pipe. One photo shows Gordy in a Douglas Fairbanks pirate pose, staring straight into the lens, looking handsome and impenetrable.

As the weeks passed, we continued to mingle without paring up—the mood alternated between friendly distance and subtle flirting. Buoyed by Margo's bubbly personality and Luke's goofy antics, no one seemed inclined to move into more serious waters, as if not quite sure which direction to take.

The estrangement between Mother and me continued. Dad was unhappy about it. He worried that I was spending too much time alone in the house. When we were together he uttered pleasantries and chattered on in one long breath as if afraid something uncomfortable would insert itself. He laughed too often. He offered me money.

One afternoon the two of us descended to the amusement room for a serious talk. Dad began by asking me how I was and if something was wrong. I had no answer. To unravel the mass of undefined pain that swirled inside me in dark confusion would be like trying to pick the end of a ball of twine from a tangled mass.

"You appear...unhappy. Is there anything you'd like to talk about? Is there any way I can help?"

We sat alone. The door at the top of the stairs was shut. The narrow casement window let in just enough light to detail his figure across from me, leaning back in the leather recliner with his arms stretched along the frame, worry etched across his face. He looked more weary and gray than I'd ever seen him. I gathered my thoughts, uncertain how many of the jumbled explanations running through my head to reveal; that was, if I could make sense of them.

I shook my head, unable to come up with a response. I had long ago learned to smother my emotions—the source of perpetual anxiety on the part of my parents—replaced by a cautious reticence. Since nothing I ever did had been right, best to retreat and do nothing. All was hidden, even from myself.

"Material things are not the most important. Its people that count in the world," my father went on in a patient voice. "We have to get out and meet people and have friends. This not seeing anyone is not healthy." He continued on this theme for some time.

As I heard his concern, wrapped in the usual guise of parental advice that up to now I discounted, it came to me that he might be able to understand. "People in Minneapolis are nice," I said, "but they're not interesting, there's no variety, no deviation, no exploration. Everything is routine and based on presentation. It's stifling. There's no tolerance for anything different. I have nothing in common with anyone here."

"You judge people at first sight," he said, "and will have nothing to do with them. Think how much you miss. And remember," he went on in a deep, reasonable voice, "Your family is the most solid base you have. Only your family will stick by you no matter what." It was clear he would do that for me. No matter what, no matter, I guessed, how much grief I caused, he would stick by me.

I softened at his attempt to put me straight. But putting my family first was not where I was going.

Journal Entry

It's getting worse. I am unsteady and avoid eye contact. It is impossible to sit next to someone in silence without my throat clutching. My swallowing makes everyone uncomfortable. I stay holed up in my room.

If only I knew what to do!

Once I know what to do about Dad I will have one answer I care about.

I was overpowered by the feeling that something was drastically wrong with me. And that it was all the fault of my parents, who epitomized the impenetrable superficiality of family life. I had little contact with my siblings. During the six months of my stay at home, my older brother Harold had nothing to say to me. I did not allow my sister Susan, eight years younger, to infringe on the privacy I coveted. It was not until we were in our twenties and Susan was studying at the University of California Berkeley that we started talking. It is peculiar how people can grow up in the same house and be strangers, with no alliance or charity, linked by only narrow, adversarial bonds.

Journal Entry

The family is supposed to be a haven but instead seems to be a microcosm of the rough and tumble life of the outside world. Retreating into the supposed safety of the family, members find only more of the same, with each person prey to the others' impulses and drives, with the same battles perpetuated generation after generation. Maybe it's in our genes. Maybe we are driven by an irrepressible animal instinct for self-preservation in the face of a life-threatening jungle environment to seek refuge in the family group. But in the Twentieth Century the family as a productive, caring unit is a failure. While claiming to furnish the ideal conditions for raising and shaping young lives, it produces the very dangers it claims to protect against. Parents exert god-like control. Even with the intentions of all the saints, parents are filled with untamed instincts that lash through the household. Those who have suffered from poor parenting themselves can hardly do any better than the model they follow.

What are the qualifications for parenthood? Mates are not selected on their abilities to be a good mother, father, or helpmate—the drive of attraction predominates.

While waiting in limbo for the future to reveal itself, the mail became my lifeline. Every day I ran downstairs to the front hall to pick up letters: a Delta Gamma named Marnelle I'd met at the University of Minnesota wanted me to join her in Venezuela; a friend from the University of Southern California suggested I accompany her on a trek through Mexico; several guys from the USC Cinema Department planned to move to Manhattan after graduation; Joan Aquino, my neighbor in Los Angeles, was thinking of returning to New York; Jean Paul, the handsome French boy I'd met in Paris during the 1954 European tour with Margo. Jean Paul wrote from his military post in Algeria pleading for letters—I spent hours translating and analyzing his every word.

I dashed off responses to friends and acquaintances from all parts, long epistles on life and the significance of artistic expression, every ounce of energy focused on the course of the postal system.

The New Year was not far off. The atmosphere in the house was acerbic and I was smothered in an environment that sucked all creative energy out of the air.

In December the Minnesota temperature dropped to zero and snow transformed the landscape into an ocean of white swells. Stretched out in her attic room one afternoon, Margo and I heard the slow, lowering sound of the Winchester chime of the grandfather clock drifting from the downstairs hall.

"I wonder," I said, looking up from an oversized hardcover of Margaret Bourke-White photographs, "if we are going to see the boys on New Year's Eve?"

Margo shrugged. Luke would be spending the New Year with his parents in La Crosse. That left Gordy—what would he do for a date? Both Margo and I considered Gordy seductively attractive. But he was so devilishly vague! Up until now we'd drifted, each secretly hoping that Gordy would declare a preference. But he continued to present a noncommittal front.

We wondered long we were going to chum around as a foursome. We finally agreed that if he did call one of us, whoever it was would turn him down—friendship came first.

It was a useless pledge, never put to the test. By the next time Gordy called me I already had my plane ticket to the East Coast in my pocketbook and was fastened on more distant shores.

Journal Entry

1956. I'm off to New York. I don't think I'm afraid any longer. This time I'm gone for good. Dad is still trying. "Why don't you stay an extra week—month?" Mother speaks of my leaving to others, making sure the plan is irrevocable.

There is a fresh breeze emanating from the year 1957. It's time to go.

2   *New York City*

The clerk at the YWCA was indifferent. You've been here two days, you say? he repeated in a dry monotone. Yes, he supposed he could direct me to some cheap rooms. He pulled a ruffled book of listings onto the counter and I jotted down several phone numbers. I walked outside to a corner phone booth, pulled out some dimes and started dialing. On the third call a woman answered, speaking in a soft Irish brogue.

Yes, she had a vacant room, and yes, I could come right over.

As I waited for the bus, a grip of excitement throbbed through my lungs as I breathed in the crisp January air and felt the bustle and energy of the city that pressed on all sides. Honking vehicles clogged the streets, nose-to-nose, and skyscrapers raced each other to the sky, surrounding the city in a circle of architectural splendor. Life beat everywhere, behind flickering windows, in scuffled doorways, around canopied sidewalk stalls, people hurrying along the streets in every direction like colonies of bees preparing for frost. A burnished energy spiced the air—this place was alive, here things got done.

I jumped off the bus at 76th Street, pulled my wool scarf tight around my neck, and headed for the address clasped in my hand. Climbing the stairs of the dim third-floor walkup, I was intoxicated with the freedom of being completely on my own in the big city where teeming avenues harbored legions of possibilities.

The woman who answered the door looked relieved when she saw me. She smiled crisply, patted down her apron with one hand, and ushered me through the apartment hall and into a living room full of dark furniture covered with doilies and brick-a-brack. She told me her name was Mrs. Murray and she and her husband had lived here for twenty-three years. Mr. Murray stood up and held out his hand. He looked scruffy, with bushy eyebrows and a reddish flush across his face, but he wore an amiable, cheerful expression.

Mrs. Murray brought in tea, placed a blue porcelain cup and saucer on the coffee table in front of me, then settled into a rocker and smoothed her hands on her cotton print housedress. I noticed she had removed her apron in the kitchen and wore a pink rosebud pin clipped to her breast.

I sketched my background, a brief version: how I was brought up in Minnesota, obtained my college degree in Los Angeles, and now on my own for the first time I was anxious to break into the high-powered New York scene. I planned to search for a job with a film production company. I didn't mention my dream of exploring the globe and experiencing everything out there, except to say that I wanted to travel. Ireland? Oh yes, certainly on my list. They couldn't speak too highly of the old country, although they never planned to return themselves. Too expensive; their life was in America now.

"I don't mind telling you," Mrs. Murray confided after I had consumed two butter cookies, "We have rented our two rooms to some bad eggs. We have to be careful. That's why I'm glad to see that you seem a decent sort, college degree and all. One girl—well, too old to be called girl—"she glanced at her husband—"one woman had night visitors and they carried on..." she stopped. I nodded in understanding. Mrs. Murray pressed a hand along the back of her thick grey hair. "And one fellow stored heavy crates in his room, piled up to the ceiling. Strange men came at all times of the night and walked out with a crate or two. Of course, I'd go in there to clean, so I noticed. The fellow had no day job, was in and out at all times of day and night, and seemed to have plenty of money. The Lord help us." Mr. Murray was shaking his head. "So you see we no longer rent out to men and we have set rules. There are no men allowed in the rooms."

"Oh, I don't have boyfriends, no problem," I hastened to assure her. I felt rather proud of this ethical stance, which separated me from the crowd of giddy girls seeking domestication.

After leading me to inspect a small room that was scrubbed and stiff like monk's quarters, Mrs. Murray walked me to the front door, her rather plump, matronly figure erect and managerial. Something in the soft roll of white hair capping her face and the uplift of her mouth hinted at a warm heart and enough generosity to fill the small quarters where she and her husband spent their lives.

I moved in the next day. My new home was windowless, with sprinkled daisy and vine wallpaper, a bare maple desk along one wall, and a miniature white lamp on a small night stand. A single bed jutted into the middle of the room. Except for a copper cross affixed above a low bureau, the walls were bare. I stepped onto an oval throw rug, slipped off my loafers, and swung onto the bed. Leaning against the headboard, knees up, I opened my journal.

Journal Entry

January 1957. A new page, a new start. I can't wait! Joan Aquino will be moving here next month from Los Angeles, we will find an apartment, and I will get back to writing. I will watch my diet and sleep, get exercise, take naps, no coffee, quit smoking.

Re job hunting: I am following leads from University of Southern California buddies. Chester Sewell and Dick Malovich have furnished me with several personal contacts in the New York area, plus the names of several film studios.

It's time to make new friends—to find people in this metropolis I can relate to.

Just then footsteps sounded outside my door and disappeared into the room next to mine. Small, soft scrapes sounded through the wall. A few minutes later, more footfalls leaving the room. I stepped into the hall and found myself standing face-to-face with a tall girl whose dark hair was pulled off her face with a red hair band and flowed in dark streams around her shoulders.

"Hi there." A pair of honey brown eyes regarded me with curiosity. "I'm Barbara." She gave me a wide smile. There was the hint of a drawl in her words.

Barbara Vincent

"Hi, I'm Judy."

"Oh, I'm so glad you're here! It was getting so lonely. I don't know anyone in New York—well, one guy—but I've been here two weeks and I've been job hunting and it's a downer. Reba, that's my sister, will be coming next month, well, probably. Anyway, someone my age, how great. I don't miss Decatur one bit. It's taken me long enough to get here, but I've had it with living at home. Have you ever been to Alabama? Where're you from?"

By the end of the week we were tramping the city, classifieds in hand, with the budding idea that we would move in together. That was, if Reba and Joan failed to show up, a not unlikely prospect. Although we couldn't afford to move until we had jobs, it didn't hurt to see what was out there. After three long days of constant companionship, we had mastered the subway system, cruised the streets of the upper West Side, the lower East Side, and Chelsea, worn out our feet, and fallen into a comfy familiarity.

This was more togetherness than I was used to. Barbara and I couldn't have been more different. She took pride in her sleek model figure and fussed with every detail of her makeup. Men were attracted to her lively wide eyes, the soft Southern roundness of her words, and her way of moving in close to the person she was speaking to. Under her incessant talk, I faded into my usual quietness.

The story of her life in Decatur accompanied us on the subway, in coffee shops, and as we waited on the curb for the next bus. Her fatherless household was convoluted, painful, and consuming. Although she loved her three sisters dearly and doted on her mother, their small home in Decatur was plagued with mistrust, accusations, and reconciliations.

"My sister Reba tells horrible tales about me behind my back and we all blame each other when something goes wrong, and people are continually slamming through the house. No one says what they really mean and then words fly when they don't get what they want. Arguments, cover-ups, blame—I can't take it anymore." Nevertheless she remained committed to working out their conflicts and followed every family move, especially that of her older sister, Reba, to whom she was devoted.

We stopped for frequent breaks at coffee shops and lingered at small tables, the smoke from our cigarettes curling upwards in long strands. Barbara kept complaining of fatigue, but was never so tired she couldn't think of more to say. Her thoughts ran in an unbroken link that fed on itself, continually replenished by some mental fountain.

It was not long before our differences surfaced. To Barbara, I was recklessly independent. She didn't think children should look down on their parents and consider them backwards. She said I had a way of building myself up, making myself look special that lowered the other person's confidence. And I was always thinking lofty. In her view, the everyday pleasures of the moment were the most worthwhile. I countered that I couldn't admire those who didn't study and apply themselves to some intelligent pursuit. That I didn't give a hang for make-up and clothes—I considered all that shallow.

Barbara, on her side, was bored by my theoretical ramblings and references to higher education—which she had never aspired to—and smarted at the implication that she was dumb every time she said something obvious.

Journal Entry

Reasons to room with Barbara 1) We are in the same boat 2) She is a nice and decent person 3) She is fun and keeps things moving 4) Her lightness balances my seriousness 5) I like her 6) She is intense 7) She tries to be honest with herself 8) She seems to think I am wonderful

Reasons not to room with Barbara: 1) I would get irritable around her flightiness 2) Her continual talking would get on my nerves 3) She is concerned with surface looks 4) She has no interests 5) Sometimes she seems unscrupulous—the way she treats people is not always consistent with the way she feels. For instance, she acquiesces to your viewpoint but says the opposite when talking to someone else 7) She acts ambitious, full of drive, yet when apartment hunting she had to stop every two minutes for coffee and we sat and sat.

By our last day of tromping the streets, I couldn't wait to be free of her company.

Why can't I accept people? As soon as I get close to someone their faults flare up and that's all I can see. The good points are obliterated. Do I need to be more selective? Am I only capable of a negative approach?

The sky was overcast and the sidewalks drenched in wet snow. I angled across the streets between cars crunched nose-to-nose and sloshed along the sidewalks, propelled by the screeching of traffic. By now I was getting used to the brusque independence of the New York merchants, especially the shopkeepers who had no time or patience for hesitation or negotiation. When I stopped at a convenience store, the man towering behind the counter shot me a look of stone and tossed the package of Marlboro's on the counter as if I were dirtying his store. "You better decide how many packages you want, I haven't got all day," he snarled. People manning the street stalls and newspaper stands showed equally sour dispositions. I learned to point, drop the money, and run.

†

I hardly knew where to start the daunting round of job hunting. When I called the contacts furnished by my USC cinema buddies, they immediately cut to the core. What exactly can you do? Well—this was hard to answer. I had no prior employment in film work, no flashy credits, and no, was not a member of a motion picture film union. Sorry, we'll let you know if...

Every day I folded myself inside the red phone booth on a nearby street corner, classifieds on my lap, a coin purse full of dimes, and dialed call after call. When the temperature rose above freezing, I leaned back on the stool and watched the flakes as they splat against the panes in fat drops and dripped downwards, trailing streaks of New York dirt. Through the bleeding glass I could see the blurred outlines of the skyscrapers, smeared together like black cutouts. I experienced an unreal feeling of being caged in a small boat in a stormy sea, and I wondered what the devil I was doing here and what I thought I was going to accomplish. The coins kept slipping from my wet fingers and the phone receiver, propped by one shoulder, rubbed like pumice against my chin. It was like shooting an arrow over a dark ocean, each rejection a shaft of hope disappearing into the fog.

Just keep shooting.

I returned to the apartment shivering. Mrs. Murray served me hot tea and cookies in the living room and listened, arms folded in her lap, while I described the frustrations of working in a phone booth: running back and forth to the tobacco store for change, dropping dimes on the muddy floor of the booth, squinting to read the scrawled phone numbers on my tablet from the dim bulb overhead, and trying simultaneously to balance the receiver, hold a pen and tablet at the ready, and feed coins into the phone slot. Mrs. Murray half-smiled, shaking her head, and poured me another cup.

During these job-seeking efforts, I held little sense of how my value as an applicant fit into the demands of reality. On one hand, with my fresh diploma I considered myself well certified, on the other hand, when confronted with an actual environment in which to plug in my learning, it was hard to find a fit. To bolster my self-esteem, my parents had undertaken to pump me up with compliments about my attributes, talents, and privileges. They kept reminding me how special I was. I was only too ready to acquire an assumption of superiority. On the other hand, life kept informing me how much I lacked. Instead of the two concepts balancing out to a middle ground, I ended up not knowing which of these contradictory self-images was real.

It was hard to gauge how high I could reach. For years I leapt into jobs way above my head, thinking I could do anything, and avoided opportunities that appeared below my abilities. In this way I often missed a suitable place to belong at a realistic level.

I still carried the old anger, simmering among the coals of the past. Every time I received a letter from Mother I was overpowered by a reaction that flared through me like an explosion. It was the old resentment, hot as ever, burning through the page as I read. When I reached her closing words "I Love You" seared at the bottom of the page, rage shook my limbs and with a crushing clench of fist I flung the crumpled letter into a nearby trash can.

The conflict between my mother and me had sputtered throughout my childhood years. We were too much alike and too different. Both of us were sensitive and easily flustered, with her blithe pleasantness pitted against my earnest intensity. My neediness was constantly battering against the wall of her remoteness—I demanded entrance and she parried in a continual battle of wills.

Even up to her death at age 103, I was not able to let go of the resistance I felt in her presence. No matter how many times I'd appear before her, cloaked in my recovered, grown-up self, she always looked at me and saw the troubled kid she'd had to put up with for all those years.

Nothing could cut through the image she held of me. In her mind my definition was permanent and there was no escape.

Years later, reading James' *Washington Square*, I was struck by Catherine's response to the claim that she owed her father nothing because of his lifelong distain towards her. Her father was not, she countered, responsible for his feelings, that's how he was, he couldn't help it. We couldn't govern our affections. Did she govern hers? Lacking such astuteness, it didn't occur to me that my mother had a powerful story of her own.

†

A few weeks after my arrival, Dad flew into town on one of his IDS business trips and treated Barbara and me to dinner at the Pierre Hotel. Before leaving Minneapolis, he had lined up interviews to introduce me to several of his New York connections. Bright and early the next day we started on our rounds, Dad in a tan overcoat and fedora hat, me in my jet black wool coat, Peck and Peck suit, and matching heels. Alighting from a cab in front of a tubular glass and steel skyscraper, we circled through a revolving door, squeezed into a packed elevator and rose silently to a top floor. The waiting room was circled with leather couches and low coffee tables piled with neat stacks of *Life*, *Time Magazine*, and *The Wall Street Journal*. Outside the floor-to-ceiling window I could look down at the miniature figures scurrying like cut-outs on the sidewalks below.

No sooner had the receptionist hung up our coats than a tall thin-lipped man in a dark grey suit and silver cuff-links appeared, shook our hands and with wide smile led the way to his office. Motioning us into two leather chairs, he seated himself at his desk, beyond which we could see the peeks of glimmering skyscrapers jutting into a sapphire blue sky.

"So what can I do for you, Mr. Bradford?" asked Mr. Lane, after small talk about the weather back in Minnesota.

"Earl Brown tells me you're the man to see," Dad began. "He and I are old friends from way back and have done business together for years." And so it went. Dad was full of warm amiability, quite different from the no-nonsense authority I had witnessed in other business dealings. The executive behind the desk was friendly and relaxed. After learning that I had recently graduated from the University of Southern California, he asked me a series of pointed questions. Then he claimed he would do what he could, that he thought I would fit in very well in the company, and assured us that he would personally undertake to find something suitable. As we walked back to the elevator, Dad and Mr. Lane chattered amicably about the number of newly erected skyscrapers and the independence of New York cab drivers.

This scene was repeated several times during the next two and a-half days. The next appointment was with Mr. Ed Cashin, Vice President of BBD&O, a large advertising firm. Mr. Cashin himself met us in the lobby. He and Dad greeted each other like old friends, with hearty handshakes and inquiries about their wives. After escorting us to his carpeted office, Mr. Cashin leaned back in his chair behind the mahogany desk. His questions were friendly but pressing; he wanted specifics. What were my expectations?

Finally he stood up. My educational background did not prepare me for any slot in their firm, but he was aware that college graduates had to take a giant step to find their niche. If I were willing to start where there was an opening, without being sure where it might lead, there was always a place for someone like me. He would send out feelers and see what he could do.

"Thanks a million, Ed," said my dad. Handshakes all around. "I appreciate it. Come visit us in Minnesota. We have *real* snow there." They laughed and Mr. Cashin waved us off as the elevator door glided shut.

The following week Mr. Cashin and his wife invited me to dinner at Asti's with their nineteen-year-old daughter Mary. We discussed Mary's classes at Mount Holyoke, the space race with Russia, the smog in California, and what it was like for a girl to move alone to New York City. Once again, I was aware that my liberal arts education had not targeted me for a specific job. I was willing, I told them, to chance it, to keep on beating the career trail as long as it took. I wasn't sure if the Cashins were impressed by my daring or horrified by my ignorance.

One of the interviews Dad arranged occurred the week after he left. A crisp young executive with packed brown hair, an angular jawline, and a stiff white collar above a charcoal suit with wide lapels guided me into his office and grilled me for an hour. His manner was officious and personal at the same time. At first he wanted the facts. Then he pressed me to explain myself, to justify the evident holes in my background. He elicited minute details of my past: what type of high school I had attended, what I had liked about it, what college had been like, why I had attended three different universities, if I had been popular. How did I feel, what did I want? The adrenalin was running fast to keep my mind alert, and I sat on the edge of the chair, steeled for the next barrage.

Finally he came around the desk, sat on the rim with his legs crossed, and leaned towards me with an air of severity. Exactly what, he asked, burrowing his eyes into my mine, was my goal? What did I want from a job? What did I want out of life? Why did I want a job? Why in New York? Why did I want a job with this company? I didn't know if he was satisfying his curiosity or incensed that I had the nerve to show my face with such thin recommendations.

When he pursued, "What do you want with a bachelor's degree anyway?" I became annoyed. It seemed like I was hearing "What is a girl doing combing the streets? Do you think you're a big shot with that scrubby piece of paper?"

"What do you think, you idiot?" I wanted to yell out. "A degree prepares one for a career," I said evenly. "The study skills and discipline developed in higher education form a solid base to build on and continue learning. In my view, college develops your critical skills, you learn to observe, to think and make reasoned judgments, to explore outside the box, to analyze problems and devise solutions. You are exposed to great cultural ideas, prodded by great minds. After four years, you emerge viewing the world in a new, deeper way. Plus, of course, the competencies gained in your chosen field." Or I said something to that effect. I ended with, "Right now, I'm hoping a degree will help me land a front-level job in film or publishing, but I'm open to anything."

I was determined to say no more. My interlocutor appeared more interested in baiting me than finding me a position. But I didn't have to resist. The interview was over.

None of these leads paid off. I heard nothing. Mother wrote that Dad came home from his New York trip exhausted. Ferreting out a job among his investment associates for a green young girl with a degree in Comparative Literature from USC—this was after all the *East* Coast—was not on top of Dad's list of preferred activities. (Several months later a contact of Mr. Cashin's notified me of a film job, but by then I was already employed.)

Dad never gave up. Looking back across the years, I see him making decisions, exerting his will and drive laboring for his family. Because he took action, administered discipline, and bestowed advice, he was a more obvious target for parental blame than Mother's subtle undermining. But he never gave up on me. He used his influence on my behalf, followed my jagged path wherever it led, took an interest in my succession of jobs, and provided a modest but regular source of investment income. He showed up during my forays in France, Florida, and California with gestures of encouragement. He kept up the struggle long after Mother had stopped trying and I had left home and turned my back on the family.

†

Finally Joan arrived from Los Angeles—a familiar, welcome face! We found a small apartment on the upper west side and signed a six-month sublease. It was furnished by the primary renter, an architect, with modern white furniture, Jackson Pollock paintings, and a white worsted couch that curved around low glass tables. French doors opened onto a small back balcony with wrought iron furniture and colorful Mexican pots lined around the railing. The center yard, several stories below, was framed by three other apartment buildings, all with similar balconies. Joan and I, perched on chairs sipping Jasmine tea, watched people across the courtyard who sat on decks reading or flittering behind curtained windows. Two boys with curly black hair often sat on a terrace one story below and strummed guitars, sending the notes, we imagined, in our direction. It was New York, it was novelty and action and daring, it was the top of the world—we loved every Frank Lloyd Wright drawing on the apartment walls and every speck of black soot that settled relentlessly on the balcony furniture.

Joan Abena

Joan's only family consisted of an absent Filipino father. She managed to support herself with one meager secretarial job after another, jobs where she was continually found wanting. Having scrounged over the years entirely on her own, she appeared unscathed by hardship. Full of optimistic eagerness, she moved along in life surrounded by a bubble of security derived from her own innocent simplicity.

Living with Joan was easy. She was non-demanding, accommodating, and ready to absorb anything I put in front of her. She told me the story of her life and chattered a great deal, saying everything there was to say and more. Of course we were very different—her aspirations were astonishingly modest—but I didn't care about that. I didn't expect to be uplifted and I didn't have to give up anything. If she wasn't interested in the Alger Hiss spy case being debated in all the newspapers, it was all right with me.

Joan's sole friend in town was an East Indian named Krishna Singh, a reserved, taciturn Hindu she'd met at an interfaith symposium. Krishna visited our new apartment and invited us to a party at his Midtown Towers apartment. The following Saturday

Joan and I dressed up in black sheath dresses, heels, and pearl earrings and splurged on a taxi. We were met at the apartment door by Krishna himself, dressed in black business suit and tie. He greeted us with a soft smile and led us inside. His proper, upright carriage never flagged, but beneath the composed demeanor a spark of intelligence flickered in his dark eyes. As we became acquainted I was to learn that his inscrutable expression masked a gentle, caring nature.

The living room of Krishna's large apartment was packed with people of various sizes, costumes, and nationalities. There were colorful headdresses, flowing saris, and mandarin collars, a regular diplomatic corps representing the foreign makeup of Manhattan. The assemblage could have passed for a meeting of the U.N. Security Council. Joan sipped lemon punch while I nursed a gin and tonic. I was one of a smattering of Americans and the only Midwesterner in the group.

"Minnesota? Is that east or west of Chicago? Do you have wild buffalo?" But most were better informed. "Isn't that where 3M is located? And Honeywell? My son's friend goes camping in the Boundary Waters. I hear International Falls gets the coldest temperature in the United States. Does Governor Orville Freeman support civil rights?" One or two of the guests held diplomatic posts, but most were employees of the United Nations, where Krishna worked as a film editor.

Joan searched the room eagerly, hoping to meet a maharajah, but we didn't see a single prospect. I kept asking her what they looked like so I could help her look—she would know one, she said, when she saw one. While Joan wormed through the crowd, I sidled up to groups and thrilled at the lilting accents, the draped robes and wrapped turbans, the civilized exchanges. Given the range of transatlantic news and political opinions I heard being discussed at all sides, I was glad I read the *New York Times* and felt fairly abreast of what was going on in the world.

Krishna insisted on driving us home. A car in Manhattan was a rarity, but Krishna's position at the United Nations drew a handsome salary. Joan looked up to him and leaned into his every word. Krishna smiled at her attentions, but did not appear flattered. I will call you soon, he said, looking at me and rotating his eyes towards Joan to include her.

We began to see him regularly.

†

One Saturday I opened the letter box to find an onionskin letter from Jean Paul. Smiling, I ran upstairs, flung myself on the white couch, and ripped it open. Jean Paul Bourquin had been a flame in my mind ever since the European tour of 1954 when I sat with the young Frenchman along the Parisian boulevards sipping *café au lait* and conversing in a mixture of fractured French and English. For the past two years our letters had criss-crossed the Atlantic, each writing in our native language. Jean Paul's last letter was postmarked Algeria, where he was now serving in the French army. Jean Paul detested war and the struggle of greed between the French colonialists and the Algerian separatists that was costing many lives. He detested almost as much the remote barracks where he was stranded and where my letters, he claimed ruefully, furnished a lifeline to the outside world.

I peered at the thick layers of onionskin and read:

(1957 letter translated and condensed)

Hello old friend,

France, because of its governments each shabbier than the last, with several rare exceptions has known crushing failures. But most often the Americans have taken top place, as in the case of Indochina. Moreover, American anti-colonialism has raised extreme anger. The most modern argue thus: "Yes, we have conquered Algeria, in the same manner that your colonists conquered the west, with the same procedures. Should we, like you, create reservations for natives, etc." I am struck, here, by the resemblance that exists between the

27

Europeans established in Algeria and the Americans. Precisely, the French colonists for the most part arrived in Algeria with a sole desire to work, they succeeded in taming nature, in creating a rich agriculture, industry, commerce. Now they belong to the soil. The métropole doesn't always understand them. Most fearful is the division between the two countries that, it seems to me, have every interest in understanding one another.

Let me tell you the story that has choked people here. Senator Nixon applauded strongly the new independence of Algeria, in the name of the glorious republican and democratic virtues and the rest, and in a burst clapped the shoulder of the nearest black man and asked: "Well, you now have independence!" And the black modestly replied, "Oh, me, no, I still live in South Carolina."

Sometimes I think that my place should have been in a convent. It requires a frightful courage to consider one's humble dimension and the help of a devotion that I do not possess.

Let us leave others to fight between themselves and become heated over subjects of discord. I owe you the recognition and warmth of a friendship that is dear to me.

I believe that it will come to pass that we will speak with voices that are alive… I know a perfect place where we can talk tranquilly, and know each other, finally…

Jean Paul

(letter condensed)

Dear Jean Paul,

My good friend, I was sorry to hear how despondent you have become. You must really find a way to buck up for the months you have left in the army. Your description of the Arab country sounds exotic and you describe it so beautifully and with such enthusiasm. I don't blame you for refusing to take officer training, knowing how you hate hierarchy, but there must be a price to pay. Try not to hate the army too much.

You are an idealist, always difficult for idealists are never content with reality.

You ask what I am doing. I am looking for work, reading Camus—The Stranger—and exploring Manhattan. I still have an eye on returning to Europe—my dream.

So you are looking for American jeans—two pair, for you and another petite person 5'3" tall. Jean Paul, you did not tell me you had a sister! I thought you were an only child. I will do what I can.

I agree, deception is to be avoided at all costs. People tend to be cowardly. The worst is that such a person is likely to be self-deceptive as well, to their own detriment.

Signing off for now. Since you close by kissing my hands (baser les mains) *I will give you a kiss on the cheek—the American way.*

Judy

Chapter 3   New Job, New Roommate

A t last—a job in film! After weeks of dead-end phone calls and pounding the streets, finally an offer. It was exhilarating to be employed, to catch the bus across town every morning to the east side, to be jolted along with a mass of bodies, clinging to the overhead strap, craning my neck to catch the get-off stop, then to walk the few blocks to Unifilms, Inc., quick-stepping along with the multitudes bent on the business of purposeful employment.

Landing the job at Unifilms had been a fluke. The Unifilms offices occupied the second floor of an old brick building. One morning, résumé packet under my arm, I climbed the stairs and discovered the president and founder of the company, Chick Gallagher, alone at his desk, bent over a raft of papers. Walk-ins at the small production company were rare, and my sudden appearance must have roused his curiosity, for he invited me to sit down, perused my résumé, and quizzed me at length about the USC Cinema Department and my Midwestern background. The following Friday, I was offered a job conditionally, for two weeks. If it worked out, I would stay on.

The company was small-scale and crammed into the corner of the old building, but the large cans of 35mm roll film sitting on the shelves, the projectors, cameras, and colorful poster ads of Pream and Chase and Sanborn coffee cans spread over the walls signaled that I was in the right place.

I worked in a corner of the editing room at a long table that served for transferring, packing, and splicing film. My duties consisted of rewinding and repackaging 35 mm negatives, getting them into the mail, and providing backup assistance—meaning grunt work—wherever needed. If one of the actors in a commercial shoot asked for a Coke, I was the go-fer. Once I was asked to hold a cigarette and had the thrill of seeing three of my fingers show up in an Old Gold commercial.

During the second week, I accompanied my boss, Mr. Gallagher, on a sales presentation. When I fumbled operating the film projector he lost his temper, barked a series of angry epithets across the room, nudged me brusquely aside, and restricted me to the office for good. Nevertheless, he relented and hired me to stay on permanently, no doubt because I performed necessary tasks in the office for which he had to pay very little.

The spot ads created by Unifilms were produced and directed respectively by Lance and Terrance, a couple gifted in locating and cultivating a stream of actors and creative ad designers. They wrote the scripts, hired the graphic designers, set the staging, and operated the camera for the three-to-four-minute ads. I saw them mostly in the editing room, where they monitored takes on the Motorola at one end while I rewound and packaged large 35mm reels at the other.

One morning Lance and Terrance walked in the door raving about the new Broadway musical *My Fair Lady*, assuring me it was the smash of the season, the year, the century. When I saw it, I could see why so many men thought so. Superior man dominates lowly girl. I loathed Rex Harrison and the pitiful ending where Eliza returns, doomed to a life of fetching his slippers in devoted gratitude. But Harrison did such a good acting job and Julie Andrews' voice was so enchanting that I had to admit my co-workers were not far wrong.

The forth employee was Arlene Garson, editor and administrative assistant. Despite her remote manner I liked Arlene. She was seasoned, while I was pure green. I tried to copy her professional manner: friendly, consistent, and restrained. She seemed to find me youthful and naïve.

The majority of my tasks were insignificant. There was no getting around my lowly status, I was stuck with it. I did what I was told. I had no choice. Even at my level, the workplace was demanding. My occasional interaction with clients who came into the studio required me to dress properly. I wore matching outfits—which included shoes, gloves, hat, scarf—and had to press and mend outfits, brush eyebrows, apply creams, and undertake other personal upkeep that consumed most of my time and all my money. It was an effort to maintain such a level of civility, to have every pin in place and every seam straight.

Everyone ran on adrenaline. Mr. Gallagher was a hands-on entrepreneur. He worked at high tempo and murmured orders at me I couldn't understand, with the implication: "If you don't do this and do it quickly and right, out you go." He asked me questions I couldn't answer and told me things I could figure out myself. I was in turmoil. Since I imagined my whole future was at stake—jobs clearly didn't grow on trees—every new undertaking held a potential for failure. Since it was my first real job, that is, full-time permanent this-is-what-I-do-job, I was determined to toe the line and make it work. My slightest move was scrutinized. There were to be no slip-ups. Like a lion trainer, King Gallagher barked and we jumped into place, which I understood was the way top executives operated: It was me who had to fit into their world.

It was not acceptable to show moods. A great deal of effort had to be put into projecting a front of pleasant cooperation. Mr. Gallagher, or Mr. President, as I called him, or sometimes King Gallagher, had to be placated at all times, even if he was being a tyrant and didn't deserve it. Where to draw the line was hard to determine. At times it was necessary to be cheerful for the benefit of the others, but it was also important to know when to put your foot down. I tried to gauge when not to take guff and when to admit I was wrong, when to act like I knew something or would jolly well find out, and how to make myself clear without appearing impudent.

An ethical dilemma presented itself when Mr. Gallagher tried to persuade Arlene to falsify a document, to bend the law for the sake of the firm's profitability, but she steadfastly refused to partake of a minor dishonesty. I was sure she was right. King Gallagher capitulated.

It was like being plunged into a military squad after drifting along the balmy shores of the Mediterranean. I was a network of taut nerves. After work I arrived home exhausted. I began to mispronounce words, and my face flushed when I was confronted by the corner shopkeeper.

Every minute brought a new challenge. There was no question of resistance. All I wanted was to succeed.

†

In May a letter arrived: Margo was moving to New York. For weeks she had been shooting me a barrage of letters from Minneapolis. She was fed up with her clerical job, her dating life was going nowhere, and living with her family had become impossible as clashes with her mother grew more frequent. She had saved up from her paltry salary and was ready for a change. Could I put her up until she found a place of her own? She could squeeze into a corner and be no trouble. She was counting on me— please write your thoughts immediately!

Gordy had announced his intention to drive east to visit a friend and check out the big city. She just might catch a ride with him. It would be fun, the three of us hanging out again. She suspected that Gordy was interested in me, "I'm giving you fair warning." This didn't track. The letters I'd received from him had been taut and cool, questioning my erratic decision to relocate to Manhattan. It didn't matter—all that dwindled behind me, stale remnants of yesterday. My every breath was invested in the enthralling, unpredictable events now unrolling under my feet.

I considered. Margo and I had followed different paths in the five years since senior high. How would her college years of sorority living and partying converge with my break-away attempt to grasp new norms, to develop the life of the artist while struggling to build a career? How would Margo take to Joan? Would she treat Joan with condescension once she discovered her servility and tendency to follow everyone's inclination but her own?

These doubts dissolved the minute Margo appeared at the door. She wafted in with the buoyancy of someone discovering a new, boundless land. I had never been so glad to see a familiar face. Caught up in the excitement of her arrival, we sat on the little balcony drinking Joan's Jasmine tea and chatted and guffawed so loudly a neighbor across the courtyard, after fluttering a duster outside the window, banged it shut.

Margo's presence filled the apartment like a bouquet of fresh flowers, and there was so much to catch up on, so much to plan, to do!

That night Margo insisted on dragging the cot Joan and I had purchased at the Salvation Army outside and sleeping on the terrace. "Give you guys more room. Don't go to any trouble over me," she urged. "I can sleep anywhere. As you see, I've brought only two suitcases, which I can easily live out of—no need for drawers. Rest assured I will help out around the house and follow your routines. I won't be putting you out at all."

Margo's familiar companionship found a warm place in my heart, and our old affinity was easily reestablished. Joan was tickled to gain a new friend. We scoured Chinatown brandishing chopsticks, strolled across Central Park to attend Joseph Papp's outdoor Shakespeare Theater, and rode the ferry to Staten Island when the sun was full and the water smelled of crushed lime.

Margo learned to navigate the subway system, to ignore snarling tradesmen, and to locate atmospheric basement restaurants with wrought iron railings and dim-lit back rooms.

Margo loved it all. She became so entranced she forgot to look for work. Then the bills started coming in and Margo's share became due. Evidently a third of our modest expense wasn't enough to motivate her to seriously devise a job-hunting scheme. I was getting nervous about her prospects, given her lack of effort. Then one day she registered with an employment agency and returned to the apartment to wait for results.

"That's it?" I asked, incredulous, thinking of all the calls I'd made, the blocks tramped. "That's all you're going to do? You may not hear for weeks."

"Oh, no. They have innumerable openings coming in all the time. It's just a matter of matching me up. They assured me there was something for me and not to worry."

"Something? That sounds suspiciously like secretarial work. Are you expecting a well-paying job in your field?"

"Yes indeed."

We'll see, I thought.

†

Summer burst into Manhattan at long last. One fine Sunday in June, Margo, Joan, Krishna, and I sat on the balcony in the morning sun nibbling warm bear claws soaked with butter, kiwifruit and cherries dipped in foamy cream, and sipping Joan's green Jasmine tea. The tiny balcony was lined with yellow nasturtiums in large Mexican crocks and baskets of brilliant red geraniums hung from overhead grillwork. Above us the spikes of skyscrapers formed a jagged ridge of stone and glass against the blue sky.

Across the courtyard puppet figures bobbed obscurely behind thin curtains and sleepy faces peered out open windows. A woman in a yellow duster watered violets on a window sill from a tin can, and an elderly couple lounged on a balcony in bathrobes and slippers reading journals. From the narrow slots between the buildings came the sharp blast of a dog's bark, and the low rumble of traffic sounded in the distance. The two boys with guitars had not yet made an appearance.

Krishna sat upright in a chair, observing the scene with calm interest. "There is much to catch the attention from this balcony," he remarked in his usual measured tone.

"Yes, I love sitting out here and watching lives being played out. It's just like *Rear Window*," said Margo, biting into a warm pastry.

"It's sooo not Minneapolis," I said, a strong recommendation in my view.

"Yes, I like seeing what's going on," put in Joan, "What people's lives are like and how they argue and make up and handle everyday life and everything. How people make do. After all, life is what you make it." She often ended comments from her fund of aphorisms.

After a while Krishna lifted the napkin from his lap, folded it, and placed it on the wrought-iron table. "We must be on our way," he said. Joan leapt up and followed him through the French doors, wanting to know if there was anything else he wanted. He shook his head. There was no end to her fawning on him, although he never relinquished his look of stoic neutrality. As we filed through the living room, Krishna admired a sepia photograph of Central Park by Alfred Stieglitz that hung over the white couch. We were proud of our modern well-furnished pad, all but impossible to obtain in a city where you had to ransom the family jewels for anything modestly priced with a modicum of charm or originality.

"All the artwork in the apartment is original," Margo pointed out.

Focus on Krishna Singh

The right man in the right job: that's what our Office of Personnel likes to see. Where but in the UN could you find a professional zoologist and entomologist happily employed as a film editor?

We asked Krishna Singh (who took the photographs now exhibited on the fifth floor) for an explanation. He smiled gently.

"You might say that my two careers started in the same place. At the age of twelve I bought my first camera, a fifty-cent Brownie, in a flea market."

Krishna Singh
article from the Secretariat News

Krishna nodded approvingly. "Very nice, very nice." Coming from the mouth of a photographer whose works had garnered prizes world-wide, we considered his words high praise.

Soon we were seated in Krishna's Fiat, cruising north along the West Side Highway, caught in the congestion of automobiles streaming out of Manhattan for the day. Krishna planned to show us the cloister of medieval towers and buildings massed along the Hudson River, copied from twelfth century monasteries in southern France.

"My dad took me to the Cloisters once." Joan was perched in the front seat, knees pressed together, hands folded daintily on top of them. "You know, I never lived with him and hardly ever saw him, so I

36

remember special occasions like that. It was so beautiful. I can't wait to go there again. My dad didn't talk much. I guess he had a lot on his mind, I don't know what it was he was always dreaming about. Maybe he didn't like being alone, but then he never sought me out. Isn't that strange? I love being back in New York. I grew up in California, you know. Isn't it nice that Krishna has a car?" She came to a breathless halt, laughing and looking over at him. The corners of his mouth turned up slightly, and he kept his eyes on the road. Krishna never said much, in contrast to Joan's rambling, which he either enjoyed as balance to his quietness, or endured, I wasn't sure which. He spoke directly, to the point, no elaboration. But when he spoke everyone listened. In his understated way, he managed to produce obscure facts on just about every subject.

"What was it like growing up in California?" Margo wanted to know, directing her voice to the front of the car.

Joan turned and curled her fingers around the back of the seat. "Los Angeles was okay. I was given to foster parents when my mother died, and when I was six I was put in a boarding home. My dad—he's Filipino— moved to New York, and when I grew old enough I caught a bus to New York. But he didn't have time for me. He was living with his Filipino girlfriend—which was strange because he doesn't like Filipinos, refused to associate with them. Except for my mother, of course, but then he hadn't seemed to care for her much either. Well, he was out of work so much, his girlfriend finally left him. He used to drink Rittenhouse Rye with an old guy across the alley. He was gone a lot, but I could hardly tell the difference. Finally I got lonely and moved back to Los Angeles."

Margo was fascinated by the story of this Filipino/American girl on her own, barely any family, without siblings or tradition. She was probably wondering, like me, how Joan, on her own at the age of fourteen and forced to struggle alone in a big city, could have avoided becoming hardened and bitter. How she'd managed to maintain the naiveté and innocence of someone bred in a convent.

"Has it been hard, having to make it entirely on your own?" Margo asked.

"Yes, I suppose. But at least I have my dad." I shot a glance at Joan. Some Dad.

"What jobs have you held?" Margo continued.

"Well, I was a maid, then a waitress. None of the jobs lasted. But now I work in an office. I like that oh so much better!"

"You should get some education so you can move up," Margo encouraged.

"Oh, I can't afford it. Besides, I'm okay where I am. I don't ask for more. Peace comes from within."

Krishna aimed the Fiat through the tree-lined entrance to Fort Tryon Park and slipped into a row of parked cars next to an imposing pink- and beige-speckled brick building. The Cloisters, imported stone by stone from medieval European abbeys, lifted their majestic towers above a sea of spreading trees, indestructible, simmering with ancient secrets.

After exploring the museums and gardens, we gathered by the marble fountain in the Trie Cloister gardens and discussed the stained glass, sculptures, manuscripts, and tapestries we'd been admiring for the last hour. Then Krishna snapped shots of Margo, Joan and me in front of various structures and fountains, prodding with gentle directives. Finally he folded the tripod, tucked his camera into a leather bag and announced that he'd captured just the shot he wanted, and if he won the next Python award he would take us all to Baseras for saffron chicken.

We walked to the car alongside a line of quince trees accompanied by lingering whiffs of orange blossom and mint. My steps were light. Margo and Joan were hitting it off. I was rich with friends and a challenging job, thriving in an environment teeming with youth, vigor, and potential. At last I had a life amid the anonymous tangle of New York City. A sense of elation rose in my chest as I slipped into the back seat, folded my skirt over my knees and smiled at Margo.

Margo, Manhattan

One July evening as the air drifted warm and easy through the sunbaked streets, Margo and I climbed up the stairs of a dusty brick walk-up and rang the bell of apartment number thirty-nine. I was taking Margo to meet Barbara and her older sister Reba, who had finally abandoned the smoldering towns of Alabama for the Big City. The two now shared an apartment on the Lower East Side.

Author, Manhattan

We found Barbara listening to records in the living room, along with a dark-haired boy she introduced as Joey, who was sprawled bug-like on an oversized couch. Joey swung a skinny arm at us in greeting, along with a brief hi, and resumed peeling a yellow grapefruit.

The apartment, though faded, was large and airy. We seated ourselves on various-sized chairs circled around the room. I was wondering how the two girls could afford two bedrooms and a full kitchen, when Reba appeared in the doorway dressed in a long red bathrobe. She gazed at us sleepily. Barbara jumped up, pulling the edges of a flowery blouse down over her Capri pants.

"This is Judy. Judy, this is Reba I've told you so much about. Reba hasn't been feeling well and she's been resting in bed all day. Isn't it grand that she's here at last? Oh, and Reba this is Margo, Judy's friend from Minneapolis. I'm so glad you came to see us!"

Reba smiled at us lackadaisically, murmured a few words of welcome, and stood on the threshold as if taking stock. She held herself upright, arms folded across her stomach, with a contained air that contrasted with Barbara's outgoing enthusiasm. Margo and I resumed our seats while Joey remained lying full length on the couch. My curiosity was growing. Joey had made himself comfortable, bare feet propped on the arm of the couch, and did not behave as if he were a guest. Exactly what his role was, whom if anyone was he attached to, and how this kid came to have such a proprietary role in the apartment was unclear. I regarded his half-closed lids and he looked back at me with a lazy smile.

Soon, to my surprise, a good-looking boy emerged from the kitchen with a tray full of beers and Cokes. With his black hair and rumpled T shirt he resembled Joey, only older and more filled out. This, Barbara informed us, was José. José immediately flashed a boyish grin and nodded several times in response to our greetings.

"José got this apartment for us. He's been a gem. He's Reba's good friend and so is his buddy, Joey. They came from Puerto Rico last year and know the ropes, you know, where to find cheap apartments and where to dig out the hot music." Barbara laughed, the boys laughed with her. Reba smiled with an air of approval.

I found, as I grew to know the sisters better, that Reba's approval was often sought and not easy to obtain. Barbara clearly doted on her older sister. The two girls couldn't have been more different. Reba's full dark hair and dark eyes, along with a rather severe disposition and reticent manner, hinted of unspoken skepticism and buried thoughts. I could never figure out what she was about since she said little, kept to herself, and watched her sister while guarding her own reactions within close boundaries. In contrast, Barbara resembled a bubbly cheerleader, ready to pitch in and enjoy what blew her way without reserve.

As the evening progressed several other Puerto Rican boys appeared, friends of Joey and José. From a record player in the background, a harmony of male voices beat Mexican rhythms. Someone set a huge platter of enchiladas on the coffee table, along with bowls of tortilla chips and large packs of Dos Equis beer.

The boys sat quietly around the room, arms on their knees, and refilled their plates, talking in accented English to Margo and me. Barbara stirred stripped chicken soup on the stove in the kitchen, while Reba in her room changed from her bathrobe into something more suitable.

A new set of records was stacked on the turntable, the volume raised, and Latin music charged through the room. The boys emerged from their lethargy, transformed into whirlwinds of energy. Barbara was drawn from the kitchen, and Reba glided in dressed in a crimson thin-strapped dress. Margo, who had followed every aspect of the goings on with rapt attention, was pulled to her feet and drawn into a hip-swaying rumba. I was next.

"We teach you. Not hard. It's not all the feet. You have to move hips. Watch this." The boys had infinite patience, thoroughly enjoying my strenuous efforts—I was going to get this!—and Margo's delighted laughter as she swung her torso back and forth.

"This isn't the fox trot," I yelled at her across the room. "You have to let go. It's a little bump. And then a little grind. The hips move. The rest of you follows along."

"Who are you to talk?" she shot back. My efforts clearly did not succeed, for my partner had his hands on the two sides of my hips in a desperate effort to get them to move as the music prompted. Soon the enticing rhythm quickened my blood and my body began to respond on its own. I was just beginning to feel as if I were catching on, that my movements were matching my partner's, when he said, "It's okay. Maybe you learn someday."

Reba joined in, swaying, eyes closed, and Barbara undulated her Audrey Hepburn body in perfect sync with Joey's. This went on for some time, until to my relief a cha-cha moved to the bottom of the pile, a step I had learned during my summer in Mexico. This I could do! I threw myself into the swing of the dance, certain I would captivate these Latin boppers. Although my partner smiled, no one seemed impressed.

Margo broke away to fetch another beer, and I noticed that Reba had disappeared. When Barbara threw herself down beside me on the couch, ready for a breather, I leaned over. "Is Reba sick?"

"Oh no, she just holes up in her bedroom a lot. You know, she has to deal with a viral throat infection that keeps coming back. And her job keeps her standing for hours and she's always tired. But don't worry, José takes good care of her." I noticed that José was also absent.

"Reba has a job already? And she—dates José?" I faltered. Maybe Barbara didn't want to reveal the details.

"She works at the Sheridan Hotel, in the lounge. She's a cashier. At least we have one paycheck." She leaned closer as the music resumed. "José is her boyfriend. He lives here, you know. He and Joey. We rented this place together—it was just vacated and the two boys lived downstairs and they grabbed it. Reba and I share one bedroom and the boys the other. They have been such a grand help, they are so sweet. Joey is just a pal." Coming from someone as open and apparently without guile as Barbara, this was an easy story to accept. I repressed a pang of doubt. So what if Reba and José slept together? What was that to me? So they couldn't have known each other more than the three weeks Reba had been in town. I didn't care about any of that. I had thrown out all those judgments, those moral restrictions.

"Oh, I see," I replied nonchalantly, indicating it was no concern of mine.

"And, you see, the boys work at the hotel, and I might be getting a job there as well."

I looked across the room at Joey, who was swaying to the music, head lowered, caught up in the rhythm. Were he and Barbara really platonic friends? I struggled with an ominous feeling that something about the apartment was strange. Under the reigning Midwestern norms with which I grew up, the sexual act—"going all the way"—was strictly taboo. Colleges required eleven o'clock curfews, separate boy-girl dorms, no cleavage showing, no girls alone in bars or even at a restaurant, and no drinking until age 21. Even a girl living in an apartment alone was considered daring. Males and females sharing an apartment was the height of defiance and innocence was not presumed. A platonic live-in like this—the appearance was considered as bad as the actuality.

But I no longer adhered to those archaic norms that suppressed the independent life. Barbara, with her impulsive candor, was the last person in the world to be involved in something squalid.

Margo was oblivious to all this. She was at a party, there were boys, and she was not in her Minneapolis dungeon. That was sufficient. She turned a flushed face to me, clasped her hands together with vigor, and smiled widely.

"Hey Tony, bring me another beer." I joined her.

†

Joan and Margo had something in common: they wanted a man. Our conversations revealed secret longings for security, a comfortable nest, a husband. To me this harked of subservience and death to creativity, but I didn't protest. We were getting on well, having good times and putting effort into making our joint venture in the big city work.

It was not long, however, before cracks began to surface. Margo talked a great deal of our shared life in Minnesota—indulgent parents, clubs, private schools—subjects too remote for me to have mentioned. The close bond between Margo and me became all too apparent. Before Margo showed up, I was just like Joan, a young girl scrounging her way, getting on with it. Now differences in our backgrounds mushroomed at every turn. Joan listened with wide eyes. After a while she began to withdraw, saying little, closeting herself in the bedroom.

Widening the chasm was Joan's tendency to reveal too much of herself, exposing every thought, as well as her pat philosophies, such as her favorite, "All's well that ends well." Our differences were exposed daily. Joan became conscious of the support she never had, of the family she had missed out on, the opportunities denied her. In every conversation she was reminded of how bereft she was.

The atmosphere in our third floor walkup grew somber. Joan took to hiding what she didn't understand. She became guarded. She talked of returning to Los Angeles when the lease was up. I felt too guilty to respond. I liked Joan, but she was devoid of curiosity and drive. There was little to hold us together. My urge to fly, to plunge into the future where I imagined a paroxysm of fulfillment awaited if only I persevered

44

contrasted with her entrapment in the present moment. It was the quagmire of the present moment that I had for so long been desperate to escape. It took many years and twists in direction for me to appreciate Joan's upbeat acceptance of what one couldn't change in life and her brave concentration on the reality in front of her.

Differences with Margo also began to surface. She remained cheerful, grateful that we had scrunched a place for her in our apartment. Her enthusiasm was buoyed by the mass of career opportunities she imagined were hiding in every crevice of the city, ready for us to discover and the great quantities of males that swarmed around every block. But she had no far-reaching ambition, no interest in creative exploration or serious introspection. It appeared that, for the present, a good time was what she wanted. A diversion that I found I was more than willing to go along with. I wanted to begin writing again, but too much was going on. The time would come.

Journal Entry

Something is missing.

I am sitting in the park along the Hudson, journal propped open on my lap. I often sit here in the evening, watching the tug boats pull upstream, smoke curling up to the sky in thin puffs. Remains of summer hang in the air, the reddening of the trees, a touch of warmth and the smell of fresh grass. Night is gaining and it will be dark by the time I finish writing this.

I am sunk into an inexplicable passivity. In place of emotion I feel only an unshakable indifference. I must do something to counter the depression that seeps through my limbs, robbing them of movement.

Routine has set in. After a year, my life in New York has settled—this is the way it's going to be. The city has become humdrum. My work at Unifilms offers no opportunity for meaningful film work. Margo and Joan move on a different track than me and our conversations go nowhere.

> *It's getting dark and still I write. I don't care to return to the apartment. I have no interest in what anyone says and no energy to explain myself.*
>
> *I had so many things here in the city I meant to get done—but if I don't the world will go on just the same...*

Contemplating these passages decades later, I am unable to explain what blocked me from fully savoring life in the big city where I was able to freely indulge the independence I craved. Although I had gained initial ground in building a life in Manhattan, it didn't seem to be enough. Something inside me was askew, blocking an adaption to everyday life—but I hadn't a clue.

†

Margo was now employed as a research assistant at Compton Advertising, assigned to a bullpen for new entries. One day she'd been called to the phone, invited for an interview, and soon was rising every morning to the blare of the alarm along with Joan and me. She was elated. I was shocked. The one company she'd applied to hired her in a week after a single screening. Not only would she receive training and a promising salary, the office was full of young people. I was amazed that she found a position with so little effort. But then advertising was a hot-wired field in New York, not like *filmmaking*, for Pete's sake.

Margo determined to get her own place. She was cramped and sick of waking up on the balcony covered with black soot. The apartment was way too small and the miniature refrigerator in the Pullman kitchen barely held enough food for three people. The excitement of getting to know each other had been replaced by the struggle of having to face each other's foibles. I was cranky, Joan withdrawn, and Margo's enthusiasm submerged in a growing list of complaints. Although Margo could rarely tolerate being alone for one minute, now she clamored for independence. One dry Saturday morning she packed her suitcase and moved to a one-bedroom apartment on East 84th Street.

The apartment where Joan and I lived was now dead quiet, without spontaneity or life. It was like living in a nunnery—or morgue—with Joan hoping for a male savior to sweep in and carry her off and fill the gaps in her life and the longings of her early years. We got along all right. She fixed me orange juice in the morning and I brought home Chinese food from the corner café for dinner. But I was uncommunicative and Joan withdrawn. When her dad didn't return her phone calls I felt sorry for her, but my feeble attempts at conversation lacked enthusiasm.

I itched to make other arrangements—if only I could find a way to leave Joan. If only she had some haven, some person who wanted her, a friend. She needed a friend. There was no one in sight.

Chapter 4   The United Nations

Ｏne Saturday morning I was stretched out on the balcony with a Pepsi reading the *New York Times* when the phone rang. Lowering the paper, I heard the bedroom door open, another *ring,* and then Joan's voice, "Hello. May I help you, please?" in the artificial tone she now assumed when answering the telephone. "It's for you," she called, looking at me quizzically as I took the receiver from her outstretched hand. In a second I understood the look—it was Krishna. Why had he asked for me?

"Hello."

"Hi Judy. How are you?"

"Hi Krishna. You're back from your trip. How was Hungary?"

"Yes, it was fine. The film is completed, at least my part. They'll be sending me more footage here to the department. Judy, I have something for you." Joan had seated herself on the couch, letting the pages of a magazine ruffle through her fingers.

"What's up?"

"There is a job opening in film at the United Nations. Are you interested?"

I was speechless. What was this? "Tell me more."

"It's in the Audio-Visual Department. You will be working on raw footage sent by our film units from various parts of the world for cutting and editing in New York. We need someone to handle reproduction after the films have been edited."

"Krishna, it sounds great, but I have never handled negatives before." I flashed on my skimpy résumé—would I be up to it?

"There is no worry. You will work next door to me and I will show you how to do everything."

The job did not appear difficult, consisting of detail work that Krishna could easily teach me. It paid $200 a week, vastly more than I was making at Unifilms. Janine Hamel, the department supervisor, wanted to see me next week. Mail her your résumé right away.

It sounded too good to be true. I wasn't exactly certain what I would be doing. Nevertheless, a week later I donned my best business outfit, stuffed background papers into a manila envelope, and headed towards the United Nations, tingling with anticipation. As I waited for the elevator in the Secretariat building, I looked around. It seemed as if I had stepped off American soil and into a microcosm of international relations. The lobby was full of various-sized figures in foreign garb of all colors, designs, and head wrappings.

When I arrived at Mrs. Hamel's office on the twenty-eighth floor, I was shown into a large office where glass windows revealed a long stretch of the East River curving alongside tree-lined walkways. A chic French woman in her mid-thirties with dark cropped hair wearing a black wool jacket and a gold necklace stood up behind her desk.

"Janine Hamel," she said in a French accent and held out her hand with a friendly, self-assured smile. "Please do sit down." She was impressed, she informed me, with the cinema program at USC, along with the fact that I was employed in the film industry. She said she understood the problem of breaking through rigid union regulations. My acquaintance with Krishna—a guiding hand—was especially advantageous. Most of the hour was spent discussing France, the arrondissement in Paris where she was from, and my dreams of going there to live. Under her friendly questioning I revealed my friendship with Jean Paul, and she was amused at the hours I spent translating his ten-page handwritten letters.

49

"You must travel to Paris, attend the Sorbonne, and learn French properly," she smiled. "And when you and your Frenchman have no letters between you, you will learn French even faster."

Four days later I received word that I was hired. When my heart resumed pumping again I called Krishna. "Are you sure I can do this?"

Krishna brushed aside my concern. "Submit your two weeks' notice to Unifilms. I'll meet you the following Monday in the A-V Department."

The Audio-Visual Department occupied a windowless wing in the basement of the Secretariat. I was the youngest of a tight-knit staff of six and the only American. Janet, the secretary, a cheery English woman, took a liking to what she called my American *jeunesse*. She was full of tales about her cold flat in London and the disastrous heating system she and her husband were forced to endure. The sound mixer, John, also from England, kept to himself. I never saw him except seated over his dashboard of knobs and levers, bulbous headphones clamped over his ears.

As I became acquainted with our unit, I discovered that the head film producer, known as Leszek, was the well-known Czech film director Alexander Hammid. Tall, with a bold square face, soft dancing eyes, and a fatherly air of authority, he relished exploring contentious topics, especially with those who were willing to enter into a lengthy battle of opinions. Behind his dogmatic pronouncements, however, lay a genuine humility. If parrying with a strong opponent revealed that his own ideas were not entirely sound, he would revert to teasing, and the discussion faded into general laughter. Then he shrugged. "You see, I know nothing," he would capitulate.

Krishna and I worked side-by-side in identical offices, narrow editing rooms with a counter running along one wall. My job was to duplicate negatives from originals that had been edited in our office or sent directly from branches throughout the globe. Two spools of negatives were set up at one end of the counter and stretched across to take-up spools at the other end. I sat on a stool bent over under a blare of light and identified film numbers, then cut and spliced the copy to match the original.

Kirill Doronkin, an editor like Krishna, worked in an identical room next to mine. When Krishna led me in to meet him, a smiling, agreeable man in his thirties stood up from his stool and extended his hand in a friendly greeting. Despite his blond good looks and the appealing figure he cut, he held back modestly, almost shyly, although his blue eyes looked directly at me with an expression of openness.

He was the first Russian I had ever met, and I liked him at once. I was fascinated by the sound of his melodious Russian accent. But he didn't say much and kept to himself. Whenever I spoke to him, he responded with an air of reserve. He was always ready to help and obliged when I asked about work, but he didn't initiate conversations or make personal comments. I wanted to tease him about looking like an ad for a Slovak golfer magazine, a thought that made me chuckle as golf was the last sport he would engage in—too bourgeois. But I didn't dare.

One day as Leszek, Kirill, Krishna, and I conversed over lunch in the employee cafeteria, Leszek turned to me. "I have been in this country long enough, I know by now what Americans think. But you don't always reflect what I've learned. Are you different from the others?"

"Leszek, you generalize too much," I replied. "I am only one American. And you have to admit, you only know Americans who live in New York." But I was pleased. Secretly, I nursed the idea that I *was* different, that in some way I stood out and would be recognized.

"Americans love glitter," he went on. "They cover their land with neon lights. They run through life at the fastest pace possible. Things have to be quick. Everything has to be done yesterday. There is no time for appreciation, reflection, for breathing in the air of the sea."

"And," added Kirill, "They don't take responsibility for the present. Never mind what you can afford today, put off facing money problems until tomorrow. Americans charge everything. If they don't have money to go on vacation to Hawaii they go anyway. 'Fly Now, Pay Later.'" He smiled ironically. "Soon it will be 'Die Now, Pay Later." Everyone laughed, including me.

"Hey, I don't say you are wrong," I said, letting them know I was not an *America right or wrong* person. "I am an old hand at criticizing this country. And everything else, for that matter." I smiled at the others sitting across from me biting into their food.

"But in me you have the master," exclaimed Leszek with mock pomp. "My critical facilities are piercing as well as infallible. No one can uncover the pretentious as well as myself. My detections are endless."

"I'd say I rival you there. And nothing in the world is endless except ignorance," I said facetiously

"My dear Miss Judy, do excuse me. I have been too long in books and film and know nothing of the real world. I leave everyday scrutiny to others like yourself. I only claim to pronounce the truth."

Krishna would have no part of this nonsense and sat mute.

"Krishna," Leszek said, turning to him. "Why aren't you wearing your turban? Don't you Sikhs wear turbans back in India? Why deprive us? You would look so handsome. Judy would not be able to resist you." Since Krishna and I were the only two unmarried people in the unit, we were often the brunt of his ribbing. Krishna was up to this and smiled his reserved, inscrutable smile.

"Not only do we wear turbans, but we carry knives hidden in our belts and chain our women's feet to keep them indoors," Krishna said. "It is the only civilized way to manage. You don't believe me? I will show you pictures."

Leszek laughed. "You are a magnificent photographer. Whatever you show me in your photographs, I believe."

Occasionally, discussions took place in Leszek's office. He loved to discourse on filmmaker Alexander Korda, whom he considered a genius. Once when I announced my admiration for Hitchcock, he shook his head.

"His films are mere entertainment. Clever, but no meaning. A film must have *significance*—the world is too complex, too beleaguered. No, no, a great filmmaker must deal with humanity and its great challenges and struggles and victories. Now you take Andrzej Wajda's *Kanal*—a masterpiece! His film gets at the Truth—what really happened in those times—how it actually was. I use this as an example because I am Jewish, but it applies to all peoples."

Leszek was fond of discoursing on the Jewish role in history. "Why do you think the Jews dominate the field of finance? Because in Germany, during the First World War, they were prohibited from working in other occupations. They were limited to a job everyone else reviled: tax collecting. Do you think they are born with a monetary gene? Not at all! They were driven and became good at what they did. They became the skilled bankers of the world." None of us disagreed with him.

I attempted to show off some ideas of my own. "I hope you'll admit that the French New Wave directors are leaders in the film field. I mean *The Four Hundred Blows, Breathless...*"

"Oh those—Truffaut, Goddard, Chabrol, Rohmer, Malle, Resnais, yes indeed, they are innovative," agreed Leszek, "They revolutionized the shape of cinema."

Kirill was not so sure. "These films are very internal, individualistic. It would be better if they dealt more with society as a whole."

"But," I argued, "The whole can be understood by its parts. The New Wave films are shot in actual localities, they deal with reality, they depict people and their lives as they really are. We enter into the individual's world, feel their emotions—in contrast to the Hollywood productions of grandeur and gloss, based on big stars with phony names acting out variations of themselves. Hollywood films rely on stereotyped plots and feel-good endings. Those films won't last because they aren't real." Kirill agreed with this—he invariably ended up agreeing with almost everything.

Leszek continued. "*Kanal* is an example of great societal cinema. It shows the brutality of the German army devastating Warsaw in partnership with the Red Army. After the Polish army was destroyed by the Germans, the Soviet Union overran Poland and slaughtered 15,000 Polish officers and sent hundreds of thousands of Poles to Soviet concentration camps. That was before the Soviet Union became part of the Allied block."

Kirill looked up, but chose to ignore the reference. "In war, atrocities are inevitable," was all he said. The cold war raging outside the U.N. walls was muted in our snug department. We preferred to analyze and accept differences, veering away from the global competition and the political posturing of nations seeking power at any cost.

Krishna's favorite film was Satyajit Ray's *Panther Panchali*, while Krill praised Sergei Eisenstein. I promoted my favorite, Fellini's *La Strada*. I was never able to stump Leszek by naming a prominent film he had missed; he had seen everything and my repertoire was negligible in the sweep of his film experience.

"If I haven't seen it, it isn't worth seeing," he said. Noticing my dubious look, "I've been around a long time, my dear."

Another of Leszek's favorite topics was the physical charm and creative inferiority of women. "Note that the great achievers have been men, with very few exceptions. All outstanding authors, painters, politicians, inventors, leaders, since the beginning of time." He challenged me to explain. Men were naturally more gifted in math and sciences. Women did not have mental stamina or inventive imagination. If this were not so, why throughout history are there no great works achieved by women?

I knew something was gravely wrong with this picture, but was unable to refute it adequately. It wasn't until the seventies and the ignition of the women's liberation movement by such women as Betty Friedan and Gloria Steinem that I dug out the answer. Women were barred from any achievement whatsoever. They were restricted from owning property and directing their own finances and denied power in the workplace. They couldn't vote or make major decisions. Many didn't drive a car. If a woman wrote a book, few firms would publish it. Women were kept corralled at the hearth caring for house, babies, and husband, valued for their meekness and accommodation, and often isolated. In return, they were to be protected and relieved of the burdens of the world. The conformist woman standing behind her man was secure, in a fortress that contained everything she could ever want—except choice, except freedom and the avenues to express individual creativity and develop her own potential.

I invited everyone I knew to visit my new headquarters in the United Nations complex. When Chester Sewell from the USC Cinema Department arrived, we took the elevator to the Delegates Lounge, a lively bar above the city reserved at the time for U.N. employees. Squeezing through the crowd, we settled at a round marble table by the window. As we sipped dark lager beer, Chester recounted escapades of his recent film assignment in South America, and we caught up on the latest escapades of our friends from USC.

"I can't believe how you've changed," he said, studying me in his frank way. "Look at you: straight, black knee-length skirt, red blouse with long sleeves, nylon stockings, and high heels. Your old Beatnik look is gone—along with your Leslie Caron haircut. You are transformed into a career woman. It's incredible."

"I live in New York. I pay taxes in New York. I am now a *working New York girl*," I replied, laughing. Chester hadn't changed at all: same worsted suit and tie, same miniature goatee and run-on conversation. "Did you know," I confided, leaning closer to him, "That Dag Hammarskjold is a secret homosexual?" I relished passing on inside information to my innocent companions. Chester smiled. I looked at him fondly. He was a weird duck, I thought—a good match for me. In fact he had never looked so good—it was heaven to be with an old friend!

Dad flew into town. He was curious about my new job. I couldn't wait to show him around. We strolled the garden paths along the East River and down the halls of the Secretariat and General Assembly, and then made our way to the prestigious Delegate's Dining Room for lunch. With a glow of importance, I flashed my employee pass in front of the guard and strode into the restaurant, Dad following in my wake.

The room was full of foreign dignitaries seated at tables spread with white linen cloths and spanking white napkins the size of hand towels. We were shown to a table next to one of the square cream-colored pillars, from where we enjoyed a breathtaking panorama of Manhattan sliced by the winding loop of the East River. I was reminded of my downtown lunches with Dad at the Minneapolis Athletic club. This time I was treating him!

To our great luck, the General Assembly was in session. After lunch, we strode over to the visitor's gallery, stopping on the way in front of a yellow and purple Jean Miró painting looming high on a white wall.

"Do you like that, Dad?"

"Sure—real nice." He perused the painting. "I'd like it better if I knew whether it was upside down or not."

"There's a meaning there. You have to let it speak to you," I said.

He was already heading for the elevator with his familiar air of preoccupied impatience. "I'm not sure it speaks my language," he retorted, giving the call button an energetic poke and grinning at me.

Dad and I were met at the door of the assembly room balcony by a young uniformed usher with thin hair, who moved ahead to seat us without a sound, as if on slippered feet. As he left, he pressed a finger to his lips in a motion for silence. Several onlookers seated around us created shadow outlines in the dim light of the balcony. On the well-lit assembly floor one level below, delegates were seated in rows, wearing various-colored robes, turbans, and Wall Street suits. A figure in a white headdress emerged, a small figure shadowed against the towering wood wall, mounted the platform, and walked to the dais, where he tilted the microphone up a fraction of an inch. Earphones in front of us offered translations of the speeches, but since the speaker spoke in English, we sat back to listen. He launched into a lengthy description of hydroelectric dam construction in Sudan and the financial, economic, and political advantages of neighborhood coalitions.

The speaker paused, shuffling through a stack of papers.

I leaned towards Dad and whispered in a low voice. "Last time I was in this balcony, I was rebuked for reading the newspaper while the session was going on," I confided hastily.

"Shhh…" whispered Dad, lifting a finger. "Better not talk."

"But it was the *New York Times*," I barely breathed.

"You're supposed to pay attention to the speaker," he whispered back, scarcely audible.

"Shhh….But I was reading an article about the United Nations." The man in uniform by the door turned his head in our direction.

"Shhh…." Dad and I said simultaneously like two naughty grade-schoolers. We exchanged smiles as the speaker's heavily accented voice resumed its drone toward the ceiling.

Dad showed interest in everything. On the way out, we walked along a shelf-like walkway that curved along the wall to the floor below. I could tell Dad was impressed, and I was swelling with pride and satisfaction that I had achieved the position at the U.N. entirely on my own.

"Mother says she wants to tour the U.N. on her next visit," Dad said as he left to return to the Pierre Hotel.

That night we dined at an out-of-the way restaurant frequented by what I assured him were jazzy New-Yorkers-in-the-know. It was the liveliest dinner we'd had in a long time and the first time he left the city without my having to struggle, for at least a day afterwards, with an inexplicable wave of sadness.

With Dad gone, I focused my attention on my work in the editing room. I found myself watching Kirill from the corner of my eye, edging around on my stool to catch a glimpse of his figure just beyond the door between our rooms, head bent over the Motorola, one leg stretched in front of him. I was intrigued by my Russian colleague's prepossessing, unassuming manner and his way of looking directly at me when we talked as if nothing else existed. He kept to himself, did not complain, and was continually amiable. In fact, it was not long before I began to think he had the sweetest nature I had ever encountered.

He seemed unaware that he cut an attractive figure, with his dark blonde hair tumbling casually over one side of his forehead and marine, deep blue eyes. After he had dispatched the latest version of a completed film, I would fabricate an excuse and slip into his office where he perched at the counter dressed in a sage green shirt, open at the throat and tucked into beltless tan slacks.

I inquired about his impressions of New York and his life back in Russia. He stood up, leaned against the wall next to me and described his mother and sister in Moscow, who held jobs furnished by the state—there were no unemployed or homeless in the Soviet Union. As he opened up, I became the recipient of his good-natured rambling. When I declared the furry ear-flap caps worn in the cold ranges of Minnesota just as fine as the exceptional Russian fur hats he described, he smiled agreeably and said we had something in common.

Kirill dominated my thoughts. I knew the minute he arrived each morning and heard the swish of poplin as he removed his overcoat and looped it over the hook on the door. After a few hours, I'd stick my head in his office where he worked by himself, hoping to find him on break. "Would you like coffee?" But I was determined to keep my feelings to myself, to be on guard and not make a fool of myself. The quarters were so private, the work rooms so closeted, so intimate I was afraid he would guess. Once he knew my feelings, our cozy chats would be ruined, he would feel burdened, and I would shrivel in embarrassment. This was to be avoided at all costs. Luckily, I thought, I am pretty good at cool. But could I keep it up...?

Late one afternoon, after the rest of the staff had left, Kirill poked his head through my door. "Are you still here?" he asked.

"No, I've gone for the day."

"Ha, ha. These films have to be ready tomorrow morning first thing. I was just finishing them up." Determining that I had by now missed my regular bus, he offered me a ride home, not out of his way he insisted. Soon I was seated in Kirill's Chrysler sedan, cruising along First Avenue in the deepening dusk. The lamp posts along the streets were coming to life, spreading pale artificial light over the lines of impatient cars and crowded sidewalks. The traffic crept slowly, inching from intersection to intersection amid honking and the squealing of brakes. Since his wife was out of town, visiting a friend in New Jersey, Kirill said he was in no hurry.

"I suppose you have a frozen dinner waiting for you in the fridge," I said.

"Certainly not. I do not care for a machine-made meal. My wife prepared fresh dishes and stored them in containers. Irina is a good wife, in many ways."

"I take it you approve of married life," I ventured.

"Yes, I do, of course. It is good. But it is not so good for sex." I looked at him in shock, not trusting the words had come out of his mouth. This was way beyond his usual reserve, his usual tone of almost prudish propriety. "Irina is a fine woman, but she talks, talks. While we have sex she is describing to me the dress her mother sent her and the materials for another one." His soft laugh spread through the car.

"Maybe she wasn't in the mood that night," I offered gingerly.

"Her mood in bed is never changing."

I couldn't believe he was telling me this. Maybe he was lonely—one night by himself and he was feeling deprived. It struck me that he didn't know what it meant to be a loner. Russians lived packed in small apartments, I'd heard, with sometimes more than one family.

Our two existences must be very different. I knew little about the communist way of life. Our ally during World War II, the Soviet Union was currently locked with the United States in a cold war battling fiercely differing ideologies. Now I was stung with curiosity to know how the Russians lived, day by day. I determined to quiz Kirill at every opportunity.

The Chrysler drew up to the curb a half block from my apartment. The street light on the sidewalk threw yellow shadows across the inside of the car. Kirill switched off the engine. As I was describing the series on Russia I had been reading in *Life* magazine, Kirill turned to look out the window. After scanning the sidewalks, he lowered his eyes and leaned back against the car seat.

We seldom talked about politics. Once I asked him how he could explain the Korean War. Since the North Koreans had invaded the south, how could Russia claim that the North Koreans were only on the defensive and that the capitalist countries were the aggressors?

"How can you say that?" he exclaimed. "The North Koreans want peace! The South Koreans are the aggressors. They invaded the north. I have seen documents to prove it." His reply shocked me. I felt my blood rising. Did he really believe this or was it a deliberate lie? Now, sitting under the shadows of a remote Manhattan street, I was spurred to ask the question that had been hovering in my mind for some time.

"Are all Russians communists? Are *you* a communist?"

"Yes, of course," he said, "I am a member of the party. It is what everyone seeks. Only then will you get the best education and be assured of a good career. Many citizens do not make membership."

"What makes you believe in it?"

"It is the best system for every person to get their entire needs met and to live in equality."

"But to rob people of religion—the churches are needed to support the needy and downtrodden."

"Communism eliminates the downtrodden!" He turned his head towards me and I could feel his eyes penetrating the semi-darkness. "When communism is fully established there will be no more wars, no more mass destruction. Everyone will be taken care of. There will be enough resources for all, distributed evenly. Poverty and slavery will disappear. People will live harmoniously because all their needs will be filled." The earnestness in his voice sliced through the words. There was no doubt of his sincerity.

His words resonated. It was true that with all its prosperity and technology our society had not eliminated suffering. Individual unhappiness, although often clothed in material plenty, was as prevalent in economically developed countries as the poorer ones.

"But communists are always starting wars, attempting to expand and rule."

"Under pure worldwide communism there is no need to overrun other countries, it would be senseless," he went on. "Everyone will have work, based on their ability, and all work is valued. Men and women will have education and medicine and vacations and whatever they need."

Something in this picture was lacking. It sounded appealing, but I couldn't visualize such a society. It was too pat, too perfect, too— inhuman.

This time it was unmistakable. Kirill was scanning the sidewalks again as if looking for a missing person. The sounds of a distant siren and buses revving their engines filtered along the street. My eyes followed a tall man in a black topcoat, who turned and walked briskly up the steps to the front entrance of a brownstone and disappeared inside. What was Kirill looking for? Did he expect his wife to come strolling by and see us? Did he fear being seen with a girl in the car? Did he know people in the neighborhood who might spot us? Was he being followed?

The conversation continued for some time, with me probing and Kirill describing the pitfalls of capitalism, which would fall of its own weakness.

"How will you prevent your rulers from becoming entrenched and using power for their own ends?" I asked.

"When it is no longer needed the state will dissolve. The communities and the farming cooperatives will be run locally—all in the hands of the people in true equality." It was clear that he bought into this dream with every fiber of his being. I didn't blame him. In fact, I almost loved him for it. But there must be holes in the utopia he was describing.

"Isn't the idea a little naïve?" I countered. "It's a wonderful prospect, but it presupposes that humans are mature and unselfish. On the contrary, they are self-seeking. I'm afraid that human nature will ruin your dream."

"Man is not evil!" he insisted.

"No, but he is weak, he will always want what he can't have. The state can't eliminate all needs. What about the dissenters, the people who don't fit in?"

"They will be taken care of in a mental institution," he declared confidently, "with compassion."

A picture formed in my mind of a society made up of the mediocre, the average determined by a common denominator. Deviation would be squelched, creative effort stifled. It reeked of dullness, repetition, routine. Yet, maybe it was better to be anchored by the security of routine and predictability and to give up the highs and lows of life struggle. Maybe peace would be an improvement over heavy waves of suffering.

Would one be willing to give up the highs to avoid the lows? To give up the spice for the secure and the bland?

I wouldn't want this life, I thought. Life is to be lived. Without sorrow, joy is meaningless. I could not accept his utopia. I could not give up the artistic in favor of machines and industry and math. Kirill lived for the future, built on a new society—a dream that his country was in the process of fulfilling. I felt a bond with him despite the ocean that separated us. We both lived in societies bombarded by propaganda prompting us to hate each other, yet felt the same craving for a better world.

We had been talking for almost two hours, way beyond dinner time. I hadn't noticed being hungry. There were only a few people trailing along the sidewalk. It was time to go. Again Kirill's head turned aside as he nervously scanned the streets. Clearly, he was afraid of being seen with me. He was such a prude. I had to smile at his traditional, sensible, even timid nature. And here he was promoting the most extreme, radical ideas I'd ever heard.

His next act knocked me out of my seat. At my closing question, "When is this golden age to come about?" Kirill drew a pencil from the visor, leaned over, and marked the notebook lying on my lap. I peered down and saw **50-100.**

"In fifty to a hundred years," he assured me. I stared at the black numbers, then turned my head slowly to look into his face. He believed every word. He believed those numbers. He had to. They were part of the dream. We sat in silence for a while.

"Kirill," I said, "I understand Russia better. And," reaching for the door handle, "I can only say that I think every regime has its truth and that people should be loyal to their own country, since it is *theirs*." Getting out and shutting the door, I looked inside and could see his face outlined in the light. He returned my smile. I had the strong impression that we had in some measure merged, even though it was clear that we were at opposite poles of the universe.

Kirill's manner towards me continued to be both friendly and reserved. He was, after all, a married Russian with a prescribed future in the party, guided by his Soviet superiors. It was common knowledge in the United Nations halls that the Russians posted there doubled as spies. Representatives were carefully selected and coached to present an attractive, positive, impression of the Russian citizen and, inevitably, seek classified information.

F.B.I Archives, Washington,D.C.

In May, 1960, an FBI document signed by J. Edgar Hoover was sent to the White House. It recorded the attempts of Kirill Sirgeevich Doronkin, identified as a film editor at the UN's Radio and Visual Division in the Department of Public Information, to obtain secret photos and maps, including aerial photographs of Chicago, Illinois, from an American counterspy. Doronkin was first identified in November, 1958. Doronkin's part in the plot was aborted and he was declared persona non grata at the U.N. and sent back to Moscow on March 11, 1959. He was not arrested by U.S. authorities because he was a minor player in an ongoing espionage plot being tracked by the F.B.I.

Chapter 5　　　*Visitors*

B y November 1957, I had moved into Margo's one bedroom brownstone apartment on West 84th Street. Being located in the hub of New York brought a continual stream of visitors. The prospect of visiting New York and catching the Broadway shows drew people to our doorstep. Pals from Los Angeles, Minneapolis, and other parts kept popping up, on their way to farther shores, treating themselves to a big city fling, or testing the waters for jobs.

My parents were the first to visit our modest quarters on the first floor. No sparkling décor here, but we didn't care. We had good jobs and activities were popping. When the FBI began nosing around in Minneapolis for information about my background, a routine check required for all United Nations employees, word spread that I'd been made assistant film editor at the U.N. and that Margo and I were on hot career paths in the Big City. I assured people I held a lowly position.

I began receiving invitations from my parents' eastern friends. Bob Brown, an old family friend from West Virginia, wrote Mother for my address. The Hanson's, Mother wrote, wanted me to visit their beach house on Long Island for the weekend. The Purcell's were now living on Park Avenue, and Mother suggested I call Hazel for lunch. Del Fitzsimmons planned to visit her daughter in Manhattan, would I phone her at the Waldorf and invite them to lunch at the United Nations? "We will be in town on the sixteenth," wrote Mother. "Why don't you drive with us to Holmes and Alice Douglas's farm? It's only sixty miles up the Hudson. If you can't make it, Alice wants you up for the weekend." My parents' annual trip to Florida was coming up; could I join them for a couple of weeks in Fort Lauderdale? We could drive down to see Mrs. Sutton in Delray Beach.

The mail brought an engraved invitation: Granddad Fought's eightieth birthday gala would be held in Wheeling and was to include dinner at the Wheeling Country Club for one hundred guests, followed by an afternoon at the horse races. Please come.

I was not interested in any of this.

The pull and tug of family involvement only toughened the resolution to break off old ties and stick to my grand design. I wanted to forge my own space that would nourish my writing aspirations and reflect the values I had come to espouse. Each pull back into the old values and assumptions seemed to block this advance. My vision was focused in a different direction.

My parents made frequent trips to Manhattan. So did Margo's mother and mine, close golf and bridge friends in Minneapolis. Margo and I often joined them in doing the town—shopping at Lord and Taylor, dining at a gourmet restaurant followed by one of the popular Broadway plays on Forty-Second Street. One time, Mother and Mrs. Holt, also known as Big Margo, caught the train with two women friends and enjoyed a bridge marathon in the lounge car as they sped east across the countryside. After Margo and I got off work, we jeweled up and taxied to Keen's Chop House for dinner. "Didn't we have fun?" Mother wrote afterwards. "Big Margo and I liked staying in the apartment with you and Margo, but next time you'd better find these two old ladies a hotel down the street. I so enjoyed Ethel Merman, but that Eugene O'Neil play gave me the heebie-jeebies."

Now that we were working girls on-a-budget, we looked forward to the arrival of our mothers for a frolicking weekend of fine dining, theater, and shopping. Conflicts from the past became buried in the excitement of the city and the stretch into the more expensive levels of entertainment.

Between these excursions, we were meeting other young New York residents. Margo joined a pool of co-workers at her research job with

Compton Advertising, vigorous young singles out for action. Every week another party was held, and each yielded more invitations for the week following. Margo never missed; I acquired a tolerance for scotch. We met guys for bridge or occasional treks to Clarks for martinis, but no serious relationships developed. I'd thrown off the restrictive moral codes I had been brought up with and during college years had been relieved of my virginity, but these dates remained platonic. I was not used to formal dating and took the intellectual approach when approaching males. The path so far had been a dead end.

†

An inch of December snow had fallen on the Manhattan streets when my USC friend Abdul Alquirashi arrived in town on his way to a European tour with his friend Abdullah. I hadn't seen Abdul since leaving Los Angeles a year and a half earlier. Seated in the delegates' dining room on a bright sunny afternoon, we finished our almond chicken salad and popovers and gazed at each other across the white tablecloth. There was so much to tell we didn't know where to begin.

"I can't believe you've acquired a car," I said.

"I can't believe you are taking ballet lessons," he said.

He had the same gentle, patient face I remembered from strolling the wings of the USC campus together and scooting along the Santa Monica freeway in a borrowed car. I had forgotten how handsome he was. Under the glow of his wide smile, I recalled how well we always got along, how he put up with my arguing and opinionated ramblings—nothing seemed to bother him. He only laughed and said he thought I was sweet.

"I'm making plans," I informed him. "New York isn't the end of the road. There are enticing lands to explore, continents to transverse, civilizations to experience. I won't be matching negatives forever, perched on a stool looking for hours into glaring light that scorches my eyes." My ideas were vague—where would the next lap take me?

"I think there is no stopping you," said Abdul in a low tone. He leaned forward and laid a hand on the white tablecloth. "Judy, I admit I have thought of settling down, of giving up my roaming ways." Slowly he picked up the silver spoon by his plate and started rubbing it with his fingers, as if he were polishing a precious jewel. "Aren't you tired of drifting as a single person, from state to state, from the East Coast to the West Coast?"

I didn't know what to say. I had to admit that settling into an ordered life in Manhattan had provided a certain sense of stability. But something told me it wouldn't last. There were still drives, uncertainties in me that needed to be explored. "I want to go to France!" I leaned forward and smiled into his inquiring face. It was a sincere face, warm and familiar. His brow relaxed and he smiled back.

"Why France?"

"France has been a dream ever since I spent a week in Paris in the summer of 1954 after leaving the student tour. I vowed to return. I adore the ancient culture, the musical French language in which young people discuss philosophy and the politics of freedom, the French Enlightenment thinkers who stressed reason and the power of the individual. France is exciting, different, I would fit in." I didn't mention the handsome young Frenchman from the Parisian café, Jean Paul, who had fueled my aspirations with his lengthy letters.

The dining room was emptying; it had become quieter. Three waiters in stiff white shirts stood by a panel of royal blue curtains. Abdul's presence wafted over me like a warm familiar breeze. He had been a good friend in Los Angeles, we knew each other so well—at least he knew me as well as anyone could during those years, when I was too intent on projecting who I was to allow a glimpse of real authenticity. I didn't mind that he was quiet. I loved his gentle humor. But his passivity had no excitement in it, his acceptance was too easy. There was no way I could respond to him except as a warm and faithful friend.

That night Margo and I served Abdul and his friend Abdullah a bubbling pot roast—very American—at the apartment. Both boys were tiring of campus life in Los Angeles, and after four years, Abdul was looking forward to completing his degree in economics and securing employment, possibly in Manhattan. Meanwhile, he and Abdullah were headed for a European vacation.

As Margo spooned out servings of basil-soaked carrots and tender chunks of beef, Abdullah told of the internship he had recently completed at the Manhattan offices of Aramco, the Arabian American Oil Company.

As soon as Abdullah launched into the story, Abdul began to laugh with uncharacteristic abandon.

Abdullah had been assigned to evaluate the company's global accounts. With an oil giant of this size, it proved no small task. Abdullah worked into the night and finally presented his completed financial report to his supervisor. According to Abdullah's system of financial accounting, Aramco stood to lose ten million dollars within the next two years. The bosses at Aramco were not amused.

At this point Abdul could not contain his himself. "If left up to Abdullah," he snickered, "Aramco would be dead in the ocean. Just seeing the company's collapse printed on paper was a shock to them. He would have been fired—if he had ever been hired."

"They would have given me another chance," retorted Abdullah, laughing himself. "I have top grades in my graduate classes."

"They are very much congratulating themselves that your internship is over."

The boys took great delight in this episode.

"It was structured as a learning experience," remarked Margo, after she had finished chuckling. "Surely one mistake won't negate the rest of your work."

"I think their idea was to get Abdullah out the door as fast as possible. And if possible out of the city." Abdul was not about to let him forget it.

"You will be telling this story for years," said Abdullah amiably to his friend. "As for me, I have told it enough times to make me happy, thank you so much."

After dinner we sat around the crescent-shaped coffee table in the living room cradling mugs of Costa Rican coffee. The boys wanted to know about life in the American Middle West. Margo described the fifty-below temperatures recorded at Bemidji, the summer lake cabins where people took spend weekends in the north woods, and the Pillsbury flour mill, one of the first industries developed in the 1880s along the banks of the Mississippi River.

"Minnesotans are friendly and polite," she continued, "but can be quite intolerant. Jews are excluded from the wealthy clubs. Anything foreign is suspect, isolated as we are in the middle of the country from other cultures. People tend not to trust differences of any kind."

Abdulaziz Alquirashi

I stared at my feet uncomfortably, although I couldn't contradict her. I had tossed these values out, along with others from my background. Abdul and Abdullah, reminded that race was a barrier that would, in some locales, at some levels, hold them apart from mainstream Americana, did not respond.

"That's not true for me," I told Abdul as we stood at the front door. "I know. I'll write you from Europe," he said.

✝

By February of 1958, after three weeks of dismal snow and fog had dimmed the streets and coated people's lungs, I felt the weight of depression dragging my steps. Now settled with a good job, something was missing. The novelty had evaporated, and with nothing more to look forward to I seemed to have reached a dead end. What that missing something was I didn't know, but the feeling of malaise persisted. It was time for something new.

Journal Entry

Ode
   Time heaves along the keenly laid streets of Manhattan, it trails me to and from work as I run errands, keep appointments, slows the sheets of snow landing on rooftops of a thousand New York brownstones to the first floor apartment where I live, dusting the bare floors where I sit with the *Times* and read facts and facts and force a smile. It's *The Wasteland:* here is not water but only rock, rock and no water and the tears are absent.

Later

Nothing is working. I stay cramped up in the apartment, lacking the energy to move. I have no interest in meeting anyone, doing anything. It is best to be away from all the superficial annoyances that I can't abide. My little world is not sufficient. The structure that has built up around me is a waste.
   The inability to sustain a liking for anything, the inclination to fragment all encounters, is gaining. This isn't just a mood.
   I don't write. There is no time. To write while holding this job I would have to stay up all night. Maybe I should quit—

69

work six months, write six months. There must be a way to
fulfill this urge, to enter the zone of my dream.

I am sick of the trivial work at the U.N., the same drudge
every day, the under-light glare blinding me. I am only biding
my time.

Gertrude Stein is an ass. So full of herself.

But what do I care?

Letter to Barbara

I hope you are happy back in Decatur. Thanks for the
pictures and the earrings.

I'm leaving the United Nations. My work has become
routine and I am learning nothing new. Soon I will have saved
the thousand dollars I need to live for a year in France. I called
the steamship company yesterday and ships leave New York
for France every week. The fare is $180 one way third class
from NYC to Le Havre.

I have the address of a wonderful little pension in Paris for
$40 a month, including two meals a day. You've said you'd like
to come with me. It would be such fun to pal around again. I
am definitely going!

Letter to Dad

Yes, go ahead and bank my dividend check for me, I don't
need it at present.

It looks like I will be leaving the U.N. in March. The work
has become routine. I can't explain further, except that I want
to get on to something that really means something to me.

Much Love,

Letter to Jean Paul

My good friend, forgive the long delay. I have been busy
preparing for the future and now it is here. I am coming to
Paris! Hopefully you will have recovered from the culture shock
of resuming civilian life and learned how to be a cute, flirty

70

Parisian once again. I am sure your Jesuit upbringing has provided the stamina to withstand anything the army had to dole out. Tell me you are happy again.

We will have much to talk about. Until I learn French, we may have to sketch on the table between us. At least we will be able to gesture and exchange potent, meaningful glances.

See you soon.

Unless I decide to go to Spain instead.

Part 2
France at Last

Chapter 1　　Paris

My room on the third floor of the Pension Dessarts contained a single bed, a plain black-framed oval mirror, a fake fireplace with a distressed wood mantle, and a porcelain wash basin on a wooden stand with two shelves underneath. A large armoire with loop handles stood against one wall.

I couldn't believe I was in Paris, that I had, at age 24, finally managed to abandon my native land and embark on a life-altering experience. Setting down my suitcase, I walked over to the tall French windows and pulled open the shutters. In front of me, like a postcard from the past charged to life, I viewed a panorama of sloping mansard roofs lined with identical narrow windows, slices of buildings with brick facades, and irregular rooftops interspersed with tall rectangular chimneys. I stared for some minutes at the wrought iron railings and arched stone doorways along the brick-lined street below. Then, giddy with excitement, I descended the narrow stairway to lunch.

When I took my seat, Madame Dessarts wrote my name on a bottle of *vin ordinaire* and placed it on the shelf with those of the other residents. I squeezed in at the long table with several other youths from England, Sweden, Austria, among other countries. Many were students at the Sorbonne. The only other North American was a lanky six-foot-three boy from Canada who delivered pneumatic telegrams part-time while waiting for his girlfriend to return from selling encyclopedias in northern Spain.

Everyone inquired about my plans. They appeared baffled when I said I had come to Paris for a year to learn French. A whole year just to learn a language? They'd learned basic conversational English in *l'école secondiare*. Seen from their eyes, my goal looked pretty thin. I explained my intention to travel and explore other cultures, seek out different lifestyles. I was hungry to learn. I swallowed a humble feeling that in sight of these modest, hard-working students, my quest sounded a bit frivolous.

My first day! After paying a few francs to shower at the neighborhood bath house down the block, I ambled through the Latin Quarter, following the Boulevard St. Germain, along Rue Bonaparte to the St. Suplice Church. Whiffs of fresh baked bread streamed from shops displaying rows of crisp baguettes in the windows. At the Shakespeare and Company bookstore, hangout of Stein and Hemmingway, I perused the ceiling-high stacks of old classics and sucked in the smoky atmosphere of the old beat generation writers. Then, destination-less, I meandered past narrow alleyways, centuries-old brick buildings with carved facades, and cobblestone courtyards gated with iron-grill doors. The Boulevard St. Michel quayside bookstalls displayed thousands of secondhand volumes, reprints, engravings, dusty paperbacks, magazines, and prints. Descending wide concrete steps leading to the Seine, I settled on a bench and watched the river barges and houseboats go by, chased by foraging seagulls. Across the dark water a row of flush horse chestnut trees shadowed a pair of kissing lovers. I breathed in the faint odors of musty oil and crayfish.

Every molecule in my body felt alive. The unique, unfamiliar aspect of everything around me cried for attention and I was passionate to see all, experience all, devour all.

Mornings after breakfast at the pension, I strolled to the Café de Flore, seated myself at a sidewalk table with a *café au lait* and with a dictionary attempted to decipher *Le Monde*. The tables were full of people chatting softly or reading newspapers clamped between two sticks provided by the café. In Paris a girl sitting alone at a table was taken for granted (unlike at home), and no one paid attention to me. I'd never felt so at ease. My mind reeled with ambition: I would absorb, I would learn, I would write.

Passport Photo
Author, 1955

One morning I audited a lecture at the Sorbonne. It was thrilling to be surrounded by the nasal tones of the French language, with shades of Sartre, de Beauvoir, Nathalie Sarraute, Gide, Malraux, Rousseau, Voltaire, Diderot, and all the greats echoing between the walls. This great hall of learning was exactly where I wanted to be. The enormity of the lecture hall was overwhelming. I sat at on the top row of tier after tier of narrow seats, gazing down at the professor, a miniscule figure sanding at the dais below.

I couldn't understand a word the professor said. He speed-talked into the microphone, and his words drifted over my head in muffled notes. The fact that I had participated in conversational French classes in school and could hold my own conversing about a walk in the park faded into insignificance. Abandoning thoughts of enrolling, I signed up for classes at the Alliance Française, a more modest undertaking, and set about learning the French language with other foreigners.

No problem. I had landed in Paris with a wait-and-see confidence that the sweeping current of events would carry me, in my full readiness, where I needed to go.

I spent my first week in Paris with Ward Anderson, a shipmate I'd gotten to know on the steamship Ryndam during the seven-day ocean voyage from New York to Le Havre. We sat together on the train as it whizzed across the French countryside, exhilarated to be in France experiencing a foreign land. When we arrived at the Gare Saint-Lazare in Paris, I phoned the Pension Dessarts to inquire about obtaining a room. Madame Dessarts answered: yes, I could come right over.

Ward was flabbergasted—with no reservations! He was either impressed with my improvisational finesse and luck or horrified at my lax approach. Taking the *pension* number, he set off for his hotel, which he'd booked three months before.

Ward's off-beat good looks grew on me. He had a low brow, a small, set mouth, and dark hair with a rogue strand that fell down over his forehead. Unassuming and reserved, his dark eyes reflected a serious nature and quick intelligence. He was a fund of knowledge. Our endless discussions meandered off on secondary tracks but somehow always arrived back to the original question, now seen in a different light.

His passion was politics, especially the evolution of the political experiment taking place in the Soviet Union. He planned to tour Europe while waiting for his visa to be approved by the Russian authorities in Moscow, where he was headed on assignment for a New York newspaper.

He had allotted a week for Paris. Together we visited the Louvre, the Rodin Museum, and the catacombs, explored the metro system, and dined on *sole meunière* and Russian borscht. But mostly we wandered the streets, past_endless fountains, monuments, kiosks, street carts, *pissoirs,* columns plastered with theater advertisements, and corner newsstands selling *tabac*. For lunch we selected juicy oranges, a melon, and stalks of fresh carrots from sidewalk vegetable wagons and consumed them, along with freshly baked baguettes and hunks of gruyere cheese, on a park bench. Late one afternoon we tramped across Paris and climbed up a steep staircase to the alleyways of Montmartre and beheld the copulas of the *Sacré-Coeur* backlighted with bright impressionist colors of yellow, crimson and orange dipping across the sky.

"I'll write," he promised the last night as we stood at the door of my pension. Ward possessed one of the most conservative natures I'd ever known, yet his mind held far-reaching liberal ideas and convictions. Nothing escaped his direct, kind gaze or daunted his penetrating intelligence. I decided here was someone I wanted in my life.

†

I phoned Jean Paul, the young Frenchman I'd met during the European tour with Margo and the Golden Bears. Jean Paul personified my craze for everything French. As I waited in the downstairs hall for him to arrive, my stomach was tight, my breath shallow. We'd only spent a few hours together during the July 14 festivities; I held only a vague recollection of what he looked like. Over the months we had exchanged lengthy letters exploring our ideas, our cultures and our souls. What would he be like? What would he think of me? How would we interact? Would he be the same cocky, sensitive boy I had met in Paris in 1954, smiling at me with a mixture of flirtation and guarded curiosity?

His dark figure emerged from of the shadow of the building, looking like the French actor Alain Delon in his brown corduroy jacket and tan slip-on shoes. His eyes caught me instantly as he entered the front door, smiling broadly. We shook hands. All at once the suspense gave way to excitement. I couldn't stop grinning. I understood only a few of his words, spoken in rapid Parisian-accented French, as he led the way to a café next to the Select Hotel in the *Place de la Sorbonne*. It was the same café where we'd first met four years previously.

He selected a sidewalk table and leaned back casually in a cane-backed chair.

We looked at each other.

"So. You are here," he said, his face tilted slightly, regarding me with a coy directness that hinted of repressed emotion.

I pulled out a Gauloises cigarette. As I blew a line of smoke across the table, elation lifted in my chest. It felt like I had reached a destination—this was exactly where I wanted to be. "Yes, finally I am here. To whom will you write letters now?" I asked, speaking English slowly.

"Ah, my friend, what need I have to write letters? Now we will understand each other so much better," he replied in French, laughing. "But now that you are here, you will soon learn French, *n'est pas?*"

"I will learn," I promised. I took a long drag of my Gauloise and flicked the burning end in the glass ashtray. Now anything was possible.

Since we both struggled to speak the other's language, we agreed to each speak our own language and enunciate slowly and deliberately. Not ideal for in-depth discussions, but it worked. Jean Paul wanted to know about my ocean voyage, my activities since arriving in Paris.

After listening carefully, he leaned forward. "All right, my American friend Judy (jeu-dee), we have so much to discuss. Where to begin?" He pulled out a package of Gauloises, lifted a cigarette, crumbled the packet in his fist, and struck a match with a sweep of his fingers.

"I want to know about you, Jean Paul, your life, how you spend your days, what you think, and how you view life in Paris. *Votre vie, vos jours, la vie Parisiane.*" Merely speaking the French words produced a thrill. I repeated them, letting the vibrations linger in my mouth.

"I will tell you what you want to know," he replied, smiling. He looked at me warmly, with a touch of insolence in the tilt of his head. I'd never been faced with a young man so attractive, so assured, so full of quick charm, so alluring.

"I already know your mind, Jean Paul, from your letters full of many ideas on so many topics."

"No, letters are one-dimensional. We need to be face-to-face, as we are. To explore the intangible, the real. Then we might, if we follow the stars faithfully, learn to know each other." He fastened me with his dark, dancing eyes. "We have so much to talk about. I want to tell you, I have read and reread Gide, the divine Gide so perfectly humanistic, so delicate, so subtle, so impregnated with Greek culture that certainly the courage will come to me one day to understand his language so harmonious, nuanced, and strong, in order to better savor his style. Among the moderns I place him at the head of the best stylists of the French language. He fashions 'the pure being' and posits that to attain beauty without reason...one must be a genius, a fool, or a child."

The sound of his mellow voice, carried with an accent that threw a glow of intrigue over each word, penetrated through me and I listened, transfixed.

By the time the sky had darkened and the lights of the café lit up the crowded tables, we had discussed the fate of Emmitt Tiller, the unsettled state of the French political system, and the raging Algerian War.

I had the feeling we understood each other perfectly. Or maybe it was just the flush of being together, of hearing his ideas now carried on the waves of his actual voice.

I studied him. "Am I what you expected?"

He set down his coffee cup and looked up. "Exactly. You are the same young dreamer I met in Paris, the searching philosopher of your letters." Then he looked at me with an inscrutable smile. "And you—how do you see me?"

"Oh, you haven't changed at all. You have just as many opinions on every topic as ever. It will take years to uncover them all." I wasn't about to reveal how drawn I was to his person and every ounce of French enchantment that was packed into his dark good looks. I tended to be drawn to handsome philosopher types beyond my level of attractiveness, nothing else would do, an expectation contrary to the happy progression of reality. Robbed of confidence due to this discrepancy, I shrunk into a passive mode, not daring to show feelings that would frighten the target of my interest. I became advanced in the art of cool.

Jean Paul was now my good friend. I would wait and see.

From then on, we met regularly at *Les Deux Magots* or the *Select*. Often Jean Paul brought his friend Alain, who worked with him at *Manufacture Française de Tapis et Couvertures*, a carpet store in Paris. A stocky fellow with straight brown bangs, Alain consistently wore the same green leather jacket with a gold eagle stitched on the breast pocket.

When other of their friends joined us, it became a challenge to keep up in French. I had no time to figure out word endings—if I wanted to say something it must fit into the flow of jumbled conversation, forget correct grammar. Listening required sustained concentration. After attempts to participate in some lengthy political or philosophical topic, I would return to the pension mentally exhausted.

Jean Paul Bourquin on left, Paris

Sometimes, alone or with a couple of his friends, we dined at inexpensive Left Bank restaurants on soup, then entrée and vegetable, then salad, followed by cheese and fruit, with leisurely intervals to replenish our wine glasses and further the discussion, a significant aspect of the meal. We ripped into Richard Nixon, the French National Assembly, and America's obsession with everything big. Jean Paul, although he hadn't attended a university, was a product of the strict French education system, and could converse on any topic. He was fond of quoting the satirical *Canard Enchaîné*.

Once I brought a German boy from the pension to dinner, a well-spoken fellow full of ideas. The reception by the others was decidedly cool. I couldn't figure it out. He was only twenty, too young to be linked to Hitler's regime, I thought. But World War II was only thirteen years in the past—and my country hadn't been occupied.

Journal Entry

I love Paris. This is my city. The French appreciate creativity and tolerate individual differences. Art abounds: museums, statues in the parks, sculpture gardens, drama clubs, mime studios, art galleries, film showings, and literature groups are everywhere.

The average person's monthly salary equals the weekly salary of an American. Most people live in tiny rooms with poor lighting, walk up five flights of stairs, and count their change carefully. Students can get a meal for twenty cents and theatre tickets at half price. Most don't possess a car. Motor scooters are common, but far more people get around by bicycle.

The knowledge level of the French citizen is amazing. Every person I meet, from the concierge to the taxi driver, has opinions on the mayoral election and the raising of pigs or any topic under the sun.

I had planned to do a lot of writing in Paris. No time. It is too hard to write and live at the same time. I can't do both. Everyone wants to know me; an American girl on her own in the streets of Paris in winter is not common. Some come here to learn the French culture, but briefly. They come and go. I remain.

One Sunday afternoon I persuaded Jean Paul to accompany me to the *Café de la Paix*, the famous tourist spot on the Champs Elysées. He was dubious, the fast-paced tourist market was not to his taste, but he agreed. We walked across an ancient stone bridge over the Seine, past the fashion boutiques with whiffs of exotic perfume drifting across the sidewalk. The tables were jammed. I ordered my favorite *lait grenadine* (milk laced with cherry syrup) and Jean Paul a black coffee. Sitting on the sidewalk under a fringed canopy, we watched the string of Americans passing in and out between the tables.

"I never come here," Jean Paul remarked, looking around at the bustling commotion, very different from the laid-back atmosphere of the left-bank *Café de Flore*. The crowd was older, well-fed, dressed in Bermuda shorts and bright linen tops or wrinkle-proof dresses. Couples could be spotted consulting colorful brochures; many carried long-lens cameras draped around their necks.

"I thought it would be fun to see another side of Paris. We could be tourists taking in the tourists." I tried to think of something interesting to say about the exclusive shops filled with handbags, perfume, and *haute couture* lining the boulevards, but nothing came to mind.

A commotion several tables away turned everyone's head in that direction.

"It is out of the question!" a male voice was shouting. "It's highway robbery! Your menu misrepresented the price. We did not have a full meal. And you charge more than the hotel did for dinner last night." An American in a plaid shirt and a bobbing Adam's apple was standing by a corner table, waving a tab at the waiter.

The waiter's face was impassive as he held out the menu. "Here is the price," he began in an even voice.

"I don't want to see that! It isn't even in English!" He stood glaring around the terrace, blinded by anger, oblivious to the stares of the other patrons. He demanded to see the manager. In a minute two men in black jackets approached the table, more words in muffled English and French. Then the outraged customer again: "Never mind, too much bother, I'm going to pay, but you can bet your bottom dollar, I'll never be back here again."

With that the man threw a traveler's check on the table and stood shifting from foot to foot waiting for the change. Then he stalked out, wife in tow. The other customers turned back to their coffees and *petit fours*.

Some time later, four Americans filed in, cameras flopping against their bellies, and crowded around the table next to us. They were laughing and talking over each other, their words clearly decipherable.

"Can you beat that? The bar at the Crillon doesn't open until five. And I thought these French knew how to serve up the good life."

"I didn't tip the tour bus driver. He was so slow, I kept telling him 'let's get the show on the road' but he pretended not to understand. He didn't fool me. These French don't know which side their bread is buttered on." The rapid talk continued, the loud voices soaring over the tables. Heads turned, then turned away.

After their order had been taken, one of the men raised his arm. "Boy," he yelled at the waiter who was disappearing into the interior of the café. "Over here." The waiter came up. "Don't forget we want lots of ice. And bring us napkins and extra sugar. We're in a hurry."

"All Americans are not like that," I began, and then reflected. I'd heard this behavior described by others; it seemed to be all too common. As we stood up to leave, a couple brushed by us, and we heard the man whisper to his companion "I can't wait to get home to a good hamburger."

I was glad to get out of the trajectory of the quick pleasure-seeking heavy-spending travelers from the land of plenty and back to my side of the river where the café toilets with a single hole in the cement floor without a basin or toilet paper didn't seem bad at all.

With spring approaching, my parents' friends began visiting Paris in droves. Maude Johnston wrote that she was coming with her friend Harriet and wanted me to accompany them to the Lido. Martha Sutton would be in Paris next month and hoped to meet me for dinner at the Ritz Hotel. The Clarks would be passing through and would arrange something.

I welcomed the chance to dine at upscale hotels—a break from my modest fare—but groaned at the idea of the Lido, an obvious tourist trap. But I always agreed. Now that the confines of Minnesota lay impotent in the far distance, I enjoyed outings with people from home and describing the modest pension where I lived and the endless treasures of Paris. My hosts listened attentively—ah, the student bohemian life, where else but Paris? The young will have their day!

I missed Maude Johnston's call. By May I had left for Spain.

†

People brushed past each other to get into the crowded train, tugging bundles and suitcases bound with cord. I squeezed inside a third-class car with seven other passengers lined up in two benches facing each other. As the train headed south, gaining speed, the rhythmic vibrating of the rails coaxed everyone into a relaxed state of indifference.

Prior to leaving Paris, two letters had arrived for me at the pension, one from Ward Anderson inviting me to tour Greece and Yugoslavia with him by motorcycle while he waited for his visa to be approved by Moscow. The other was from Roz Pence whom I'd met on the Ryndam. During the voyage we had played canasta and lounged on the upper deck, along with several young people from our meal table. "Come to Madrid," she wrote, "We'll do the town and soak in the sun until we melt." That was it: the sun. The thought of the sun drew me up sharply. The chill of Paris had settled in my bones and I longed to feel the heat of the short sun rays, to melt in the arms of southern radiance. I wrote Roz to expect me.

I must have fallen into a doze, which may have lasted ten minutes or an hour, when the train came to a noisy halt. A conductor stepped into the car and informed us there would be an unexpected two-hour wait for the next departure for Spain. The French rail authority had issued a cease-travel notice so the French police could conduct a search for an escaped drug trafficker thought to be hiding in one of the train cars. Everyone was to get off.

Entering the train station, I spied two male passengers from my car standing idly under a directional sign. They recognized me from the train car, and seeing their encouraging smiles, I walked over. Since it was time for a meal, we decided to dine together at the station restaurant. One of the men was a thin, young Spaniard in his late twenties, with a long angular face, thin arched eyebrows, and a starched white collar open at the throat. Exceedingly polite, he pushed in my chair and waited for our companion to seat himself. Then he spread his napkin carefully across his trousers and picked up his fork with slow elegance. When he discovered I was traveling alone, he immediately offered to get my francs changed at a good rate and be of whatever assistance he could.

The other man was a French curate, twenty years older than the Spaniard, dressed in a wide black cape that disguised his ample midsection. He immediately ordered a carafe of wine. He was the garrulous type, and we were soon chatting merrily around the table.

The Spaniard indicated that he was a lover of women and told us he was broke since he had spent all his money on nightclubs and gallivanting in Paris. At this the curate lowered his fork and looked up.

"The faithful mind is not deterred from its spiritual path," he intoned pointedly.

"Those to whom evil never beckons are praised for their purity," replied our Spanish companion, biting into a thick crust of bread. The curate ignored this. He was returning to his monastery in Lisbon, having spent all his money on gifts for the children he taught—due to his continual generosity they thought him rich, a fact which both surprised and perturbed him. Another frustration that plagued him was how he kept falling from his Vespa while driving along country roads. After each of the first five crashes, the people who ran out to pick him up gave him wine, of which innumerable glasses were necessary to get him back on his feet. Then he crashed for the sixth time and smashed his hand, which he was at the moment nursing behind his cloak. Finally he sold the Vespa, in fact just that morning. He was still in mourning, whether for the lost Vespa or the cessation of the wine palliatives I wasn't sure.

We ordered pork roast and a bottle of wine for dinner, and the curate found the latter so tasty that he ordered another bottle and poured a glass for the gentleman sitting at the table behind us, with whom he had struck up an acquaintance. Having consumed more wine than I would have thought possible to retain sobriety, the curate enlivened the table with his free-flowing anecdotes. Occasionally he removed the cigar from his mouth and repeated the same story in another way.

He paused between anecdotes and passed Havana cigars to the men he spied from our car seated nearby. At last, pushing out his chair, he leaned back and expounded on the glitches of the French rail system, the vagaries of Spanish culture, and the heavy devotional duties of the monastery.

After dinner the curate left to continue to Madrid in first class, for some unknown reason, having directed my care to the Spanish fellow, who announced that he would perform his duties diligently. The Spaniard and I re-boarded the train and he squeezed in next to me. I opened my book while he sat looking out the window at the darkened sky. We were too full and drowsy to say much. But actual sleep, cramped in a cold car with seven other people and no place to put your head, was out of the question.

My Spanish protector reached his destination and disembarked during the night, having failed to identify any of his duties.

I left my Madrid hotel with quick steps, hastening to keep a rendezvous with Roz and Carmen at the American Café. The three of us had spent long evenings at the railing of the Ryndam exchanging information on our various travel plans to see foreign places and experience the European way of life. I was anxious to see them again.

We were embarked on a future of adventurous exploration, dependent only on our own resources and serendipity. Roz Pence had quit her job in San Francisco and, like me, anticipated the unfolding of events. Carmen Cicero, a budding artist who taught oil painting at a New York high school, had a fixed time limit and could cruise through the western world only until the opening of his Manhattan art show in October.

I was giddy at the prospect of reuniting with fellow travelers who seemed like old friends and of speaking English once more, relaxed, able to express my personality through the articulate use of words.

When I entered the café, Roz and Carmen were already seated. They beckoned to me from across the crowded tables and we greeted each other like shipwrecked sailors reunited on a distant island. "What have you been doing?" flew around the table. Roz, looking sleek and poised in her black shell blouse, crossed her long legs gracefully under the chair and explained that she was comfortably settled in *una pension*, had found a job, and was learning Spanish, with help from her new boyfriend, Jorge.

"Is this Jorge permanent?" I asked.

The word was not in her vocabulary. "I prefer to move with the flow, to catch every opportunity."

Carmen was also making plans as he went along. He aimed to visit the top museums and experience cultures that spawned the masterpieces of the art world. Upon his return to Brooklyn in the fall he was scheduled to study painting with the abstract expressionist Robert Motherwell.

We ordered wine and the conversation veered to a discussion of Spanish mentality. "So far, I find Spaniards in general to be warm, friendly, and generous," I said. "But often the men act arrogant, constantly leering and strutting about. They seem to think they are god's gift to women."

Roz whirled her head around. "You are very critical. You wait, my dear girl, you will change your mind, I guarantee it." She laughed her Auntie Mame laugh and ran a hand through her loose dark hair.

I had liked Roz's straightforward manner right from the start. Almost six feet tall, holding herself erect, with head back and long sculpted arms curving along her side, she looked statuesque, even sophisticated. But her brown eyes indicated a soft side behind the air of command and she listened respectfully, chiming in with her fun-loving laugh. I was sure her flamboyant mind masked a soft heart, but knew instinctively not to mess with her.

Carmen was slight, with the agile movements of a gymnast. He chortled. "What about the Americans you've met over here?" he asked, leaning back in his chair. "How do you two find them?" He pulled up the sleeves of his red sweater, took a sip of his drink, and held it up in the light to study the color.

"They like to exert their authority, and they often miss the ancient treasures and cultures that whiz by right under their noses," I said firmly.

"The tourists," said Roz, "come for a good time and leave, dropping tons of money along the way. They visit the museums while they're here and go home richer for it. What's wrong with that?"

I couldn't let that pass. "Americans throw their money around and have no concept of where they've been or the civilizations they've been with. They are blind to the poverty of the Spanish people under General Franco and the huge discrepancy between the wealthy enclosed in gated houses and the masses living in squalor. They gain no understanding of the Spanish way of life. They just want to be amused in comfort."

"How could they understand a culture in three weeks?" Roz asked. "Their spending provides a living for many Spaniards."

"Of course, you're right," I said. "But I wish Americans would show a little sensitivity, a little understanding that foreigners are not like them and quit complaining because they're different."

"Americans aren't used to foreigners. They don't get it," put in Carmen. He was grinning, his slender body scrunched in his chair. It was clear that he was a cutup, expressed in the clownish way he gestured and his exaggerated facial expressions. Ever ready for a laugh, Carmen had no trouble having a good time.

"How come you're not fluent in Spanish?" I asked. "With a name like Carmen, you must have learned it in the cradle."

"My silly girl," he exclaimed, "I was born and brought up in Brooklyn. What do you want from me?" He straightened up suddenly. "My parents didn't speak Spanish at home. They wanted to be *Americans*."

Roz left to meet her boyfriend, but not before she had directed Carmen and me to an out-of-the-way flamenco club, where we spent the rest of the evening swaying rhythmically to feverish Spanish music.

The next day I helped Carmen move out of his dump of a hotel and into mine. Later that night, after hours of sampling Spanish pasta and roaming the Prado Museum, which Carmen claimed was worth the entire trip to Europe, we came home to find the hotel doors locked. We shouted to be let in, following the specific instructions of the concierge, who had warned us that the doors were locked religiously at midnight and that he was hard of hearing. We screeched out "Open Door" over and over, bellowing loud refrains of *Bridge on the River Kwai* between shouts. Finally the concierge showed up in a frayed shirtwaist and slippers, grumbling in staccato Spanish, and looked at us with dagger eyes. We discovered that the correct signal to be admitted was hand clapping, not shouting. Luckily we couldn't understand a word of the concierge's frenetic reprimands.

Late one afternoon Carmen, Roz, her Spanish boyfriend Jorge, and I sat over a small table at Jimmy's bar, the smoke from our cigarettes drifting over our heads. Carmen told us that Jimmy's was a popular place to find Pernod, a derivative of absinthe, which was banned in France because of its addictive psychedelic qualities. In Spain it was legal.

We stared down at the small glasses set in front of us. The colorless liqueur looked plain and uninteresting, but its potency—eighty proof—and odd licorice flavor suggested daring and intrigue. We filled our glasses to the top with water from the carafe and watched the liquid turn milky. I didn't like the first sip, but was eager to partake of a drink with such a dangerous reputation.

Carmen reached into his knapsack and pulled out two soft cover books with uncut edges: *The Tropic of Cancer* and *Tobacco Road*. These treasures, which Carmen and I had purchased that morning at a Spanish-English bookstore, were unavailable in the United States. Roz explained to Jorge that we would have to smuggle the books back to America, since novels by Henry Miller and Erskine Caldwell were banned entry. Too raunchy.

"Raunchy?" repeated Jorge in fractured English. "What is that word?"

"The book contains graphically described sex," he was told.

"Books with sex are forbidden in America?" Jorge looked incredulous. "What is this reject of sex? Those crazy Americans. They very naive."

"It's the Puritan ethic," explained Carmen. "Sexual references are not allowed in music either—the song *Slipping Around* was banned in Boston." With this he sang a few bars:

Seems we always have to slip around, to be together, dear.
Slippin' around, afraid we might be found.
I know I can't forget you, and I've gotta have you near
But we just have to slip around and live in constant fear.

"Those are the bad lines?" asked Jorge.

"That's it," replied Carmen.

"And," I added, "In American movies, even married couples must sleep in single beds; a double bed can't be shown."

Jorge was shaking his head. "No slipping around—that bad. Too bad. Americans see sex into everything. They must have problem."

Chapter 2   Southern Exposure

I went to Málaga for the sun. I went as far south as land would take me. Southern Spain was intoxicating. Walking from my villa into town, the white and green adobe houses with black iron balconies gave way to stone archways leading to hidden patios. In the high sun, fountains banked with bluebells sparkled and bordering them pearl white carnations and vibrant red pomegranates exploded with rich color. Towards evening, I climbed the Roman and Moorish hilltop ruins and wandered among the remains of thousand-year-old baths, stomping over walls and cooking pits crumbled among the cypress. Later I returned to my room at the Villa Pedrito and was served dinner in an upstairs dining room at ten o'clock sharp. I was the only patron.

One afternoon I returned to find a message from Conchita. Did I want to see a bullfight? Conchita, her fiancé, and I had shared a coach on the train from Madrid and, on finding I'd made no reservation, they insisted on settling me at the Villa Pedrito, a family home with two rental rooms set back on a hill. Since then I'd dined often at Conchita's parents' home, where I met her endless stream of relatives and accompanied them on drives to the country for picnic lunches and leisurely walks along the seaside. We communicated in French, since I only spoke shopping Spanish and they spoke no English.

It was a bright afternoon and the trees were shimmering with sunlight when Conchita, her fiancé, a cousin, and I boarded a trolley and bounced alongside the woods to downtown Málaga. A woman sat across from us nursing her baby and conversing idly with her companion, a sight one would not witness in the United States. But here there was no such propriety; the Mediterranean people, even with their strict religious taboos, accepted breast feeding as a natural function without shame. There was something comforting about this. I smiled at the nursing woman and, seeming to understand, she smiled back.

My friends assured me that a Spanish bullfight involved skill and artistry, was more disciplined than ballet and more dramatic than opera. The scene in the bullring turned out to be a ritualized display of macho bravado. I gripped my hands tightly together. The sight of the bull, heaving and panting, feet splayed under him, getting shakier as the steel-bladed assault of the toreador continued, was painful to watch. Slowly his power was reduced to a bleeding, weakened mass of blood and muscle. Head hung low, the bull never gave up, fighting for his life, continuing to charge as *banderillas*, one after the other, were plunged into his shoulders. The toreador, tall, proud, costumed in dramatic red and black and radiating testosterone, strutted like a peacock, waving his red cape and treating each pass of the bull's horns as a victory of his prowess. There was no real contest. The attacker ran some risk of getting gored in which case he would leave the ring most likely wounded. The bull would leave the ring dead.

Afterward, we watched a parade, where school children in uniforms sang and carried crucifixes, musicians played Spanish rhythms, and images of the Christ child hung from banners. Religious signs were everywhere in Spain: altars by the roadside, crucifixes hanging in windows, and beads clutched in children's hands. Yet the brutality of past church inquisitions and the cruelty of the bull ring—how could these be reconciled to the compassion and caring life of religious teachings? It was beyond understanding.

One evening at dusk I was leaning against a fence railing, gazing over the sea to the horizon where bands of crimson and gold were slipping down the sky. An expanse of blue stretched endlessly in front me, and my thoughts drifted idly out across the rippling surface.

A man emerged from the solitary shack that stood a short way down the beach. I'd seen him down there before, a shadowy figure leaning over the woodpile or disappearing behind a burlap flap. Now he trudged up to the fence and stood a short distance away looking out over the blue-green water. Glancing over, I noticed his nicely-shaped profile and how he held his head in a stubborn, almost defiant way. After standing immobile for some time, he moved over to where I stood.

"I see you like to come and look at the sea," he said in a soft voice. Then he resumed looking towards the horizon. Evidently that was all he was going to say. I judged him to be American and near my age. Something about the set of his shoulders was unapproachable. I waited.

"I've seen you here before. What are you doing down here alone?" he asked, still without looking at me.

"I do a lot alone. It looks like you could say the same."

"I live in that shack on my own because I need to write and it fits my budget." He refused to reveal anything about his writing, claiming that what he gave away in speech was lost to his pen. I felt inexplicably timid, unable to find anything meaningful to say.

"What do you think of Spain?" he asked after another long silence.

"I love it here. It's not at all like France, although I love it too. France is intellectual and sophisticated, whereas Spain is warm and emotional. You might say France is the mind, Spain is the living body."

"Do you want to walk on the beach?" He started off without waiting for an answer. Catching up with him, I learned that he was a part-time journalist, was working on a novel, and his name was Robert. We strolled for a while, watching two transport boats weaving along the water. Then he turned and left without bothering to say good-bye.

A few days later as I sat on a bench by the Málaga beach munching oranges, Robert meandered by. He was on his way to a nearby bar and could I use a drink? When I agreed he threw me a half-smile. So he had a social side after all! The interior of the bar was dark, and it took a few minutes for my sun-soaked eyes to make out the row of men in overalls and T-shirts seated at the long black laminate counter, leaning over their drinks. Several nodded in Robert's direction.

"I come here on barren afternoons when I'm unable to write. There's good draft beer and no Americans," he said as we settled at the far end of the bar.

"What's your problem with Americans?" I asked.

"The tourists live in a materialistic world. I don't want to be bothered." He ordered us a round of beer without asking my preference.

"Beer would be good," I said, intending sarcasm, but Robert only smiled. "I'm an American," I said. "How do you know I'm not materialistic?"

"Because you're on your own, you mingle with your Spaniard friends, and you talk about writing. I would guess you're different." He sounded sure of himself, as if his judgment could not be incorrect. "And you're interested in what makes things tick. You're interested in politics."

He launched into a portrayal of the Spanish *officiales*. "Franco's corrupt regime controls all the wealth," he said heatedly. "The top layer of society is flushed with riches while millions of people languish in poverty with barely enough to live on, unable to find jobs. Franco reigns with an iron fist. His Falange party is in full control. The legislature is a sham. You must understand, there is no democracy in Spain."

"What about the rule of law?"

"The law is in the hands of Franco's 'boys,' the guys with the patent-leather Napoleon hats." I had seen these guards in the main squares, where the populace, I noticed, gave them a wide berth. "They kidnap, imprison, torture, and murder, all with impunity."

"Then why is Franco so popular?" I asked.

"It's all engineered. Franco relies on the church, the soldiers, and elaborate parades to keep the populace compliant." A man sitting nearby lifted his head and cried "Franco must go!" The men at the bar looked around cautiously, as if afraid that one of the "boys" might be lurking in the shadows.

After two hours of rambling discussion, we left the bar. As we walked home, Robert confessed that after a year on the beach he'd run out of steam and was having trouble writing. I sympathized. I hadn't even started to write yet. I hadn't been able to summon the initiative. And for once, strangely, here in the depths of sun-soaked Spain, where each day unfolded on its own terms and carried me with it, it didn't seem to matter.

The rays of sun curled around the window panes of my room as if begging entry and light poured into my room with a rare brightness. At last! The hot days of summer had arrived. I bobbed up in bed with excitement and padded over to the window. The summer sun shone in full force, blanching the sky, heating the buildings, firing the stones in the gardens, burning into every crevice. It was almost ten, and I had long missed breakfast.

I dressed quickly, grabbed my black coat with the oversized buttons to use as a mat, and climbed the back stairs of the villa to the rooftop. It was deserted. The sun beat down intensely on the tarred surface. Although crusted with plaster and paint stains, the floor had been swept clean and beautified with several tall potted geraniums and a row of chipped orange and red pots. From a dilapidated chicken cage at the far end I heard loud clucking and scratching noises.

Spreading out my black coat alongside the wall, I scooted down and opened my journal.

Journal Entry on Roof

Womanhood is appreciated in this country. It is good to be a woman. Men dote on them and make them feel they are pretty and that to be a woman is the most desirable thing in the world. No matter what, I am a woman and Spanish men make me feel proud of it. Men radiate pleasure at their own maleness. It is good to be a man.

I pass my hands along my breasts and they feel soft.

The real sun is here in Málaga. It brightens the colors and the mind too.

Projects in order of priority: Read up on Spain; study list of French vocab words; exercise (swim, long walks); write letters to parents, Margo, Joan, Barbara, and Brandon; lose four pounds.

93

I sank down and lay face up to the sky. Within minutes I felt my limbs relaxing, cradling into the fabric of the coat, my body glowing with warmth. A feeling of delicious contentment seeped over me. Moving was impossible.

A voice broke through the silence.

"Hey, Judy! Is that you?" My eyes blinked open slowly. A form, framed into shadow by the sun's rays, loomed over me. "I've been looking all over for you! What on earth are you doing here on the roof lying among the chickens? Couldn't you even find a chair?" Through the glare I saw the dim shape of an open mouth, heard the laugh. Trying to pull my wits together, I sat up crookedly, supported by one arm. It was Dolores Gonzalez, an American friend of Roz's from San Francisco. She was living in Málaga with her Spanish grandmother. The week before I'd been to their house for sangrias.

"Dolores. Hi. Just—getting some sun." Dolores leaned against the wall, shaking her head.

"You're crazy." Her indulgent laughter cleared my mind a little. "I came to invite you to dinner tonight. Afterwards there's a concert on the hill and we're all going. Grandmother would like you to come. You can invite Conchita and her boyfriend."

"Sounds good." I sat up and leaned against my knees. "Hey, do you know anything about a young fellow who lives in one of those run-down huts on the beach? An American," I asked.

"Why yes, Robert, the mysterious American writer. How do you know about him?"

"I ran across him on the beach the other day."

"He keeps to himself and doesn't let anyone get near him. They say he's writing a novel. All the girls around here would adore meeting him. They think he's too fascinating for words. Did you talk to him?"

"For a while. He seemed nice, maybe a bit touchy."

Dolores looked at me. "I can't believe you just walked over and met him," she went on. "He avoids people. He doesn't like Americans. He doesn't like tourists. I don't think he likes anybody."

"He must have been in a good mood," I said. "Come down with me and meet him. Maybe he's not as elusive as you make out."

The gong sounded—Señora Pedrito was serving my lunch.

I stepped off the trolley, a canvas tote bag draped over one shoulder, surrounded by the scent of mimosas and ripe rose blossoms. People padded leisurely along the sidewalk, wearing thin-strapped tops and carrying wicker baskets stuffed with bottles and towels. A few blocks away, pressed by the full force of summer, the sand gave off a rising blanket of heat. Reaching the beach entrance, I stood for a moment next to a clump of rocks and green bushes. Above the water, a white spread of wings flickered, soared, and glided over a cloud of glimmering tree tops.

I slipped off my sandals and tiptoed gingerly onto the hot grains of sand. Quick-stepping to a secluded spot, I spread out a beach towel, lay down on my back and let the sea air sink deep into my lungs. The warmth of the rays pressed against my stomach, moved up my body and curled around my face. Here was the sun I craved, pouring down its virile energy. I waited for the fireball overhead to penetrate my frozen bones, until finally I felt my limbs loosen and relax into total capitulation.

A few feet away a young couple spread out a blue checkered blanket. The girl, wearing a lime green bikini, removed a brimmed straw hat and stretched beside her companion. The boy wore swim briefs that clung to his narrow body. Oblivious of my presence, they spread lotion on each other's bodies with long languid strokes, then settled on their backs, bodies touching.

The next time I looked over the two were lying on their sides, faces inches apart, gazing into each other's eyes. As the minutes passed they lay still, not saying a word, faint smiles on their faces. I stared. It was too strange. How did they endure such stark proximity? The ease of their manners, the sensual nonchalance with which they enjoyed each other's presence, devoid of self-consciousness, reminded me of how much I lacked, of how little I knew of such intimacies. I was struck by a heavy bolt of sadness.

Since my hippie years at college, I had shied from male involvement, fearful of being imprisoned in the conventional role of domestic constraint. Along with this, I found myself overcome with timidity whenever an appealing man closed in. Friendship I could handle with ease and spirit; let romantic implications take over and all confidence evaporated.

The couple stirred, remained quiet. I didn't mind their proximity close to me. One can be alone with people around. I didn't so much want to be alone as undisturbed, left to pour myself into these hours, finally submerged in ripe heat. I had the feeling that I was nearing a crossroad, that some unusual event or transformation was imminent, that this was what I had come to the very end of the continent for.

I turned over, cradling my cheek in the curve of the beach towel. The sand under the towel throbbed hot against my body, and the sun continued to caress my skin and penetrate my flesh. I imagined if I lay still enough it would reach through my limbs and inner circuits until it reached the small mass lodged in a hidden recess, a nodule that had been waiting there all my life.

Hours passed, or minutes. I pulled myself up. The sea was steel blue and perfect. The young couple had gone, the crowd had dispersed, only a few figures were wading a ways down the beach. Across the expanse of the sea, the horizon dipped into a vast space that held the mysteries of the universe.

I closed my eyes and all thought vanished. Stillness covered the beach and quieted the flat leaves of the Canary palms; the scent of roses hung still in the air. Even the children romping by the sidewalk seemed to be moving in slow motion, gestures prolonged. Everything, tamed under the sun, was reduced to quiet compliance.

I don't stir. The sun ceases its arc in the sky. Time ceases to exist. A tremendous sense of freedom surges through me. I luxuriate in the pleasure of not having to move. I taste the weeds and fish brine and catch the reflections of pink clam shells. The raw smell of dirt, the sharp click-clack of the heels on the sidewalk, the purple swirl of the bougainvillea vines, all become vivid. I lie in a state resembling wholeness.

Of course, I knew this was an overheated imagination, due to my somnolent state and the sun.

As I walked home, thoughts seeped in. Having thrown over tradition, I would have to create an entirely new world, carve a place for myself. How long could I remain passive and pliable? How long could I drift? Where was I to start?

That morning Señora Pedrito had inquired about my length of stay. I had to decide. It was time to return to Paris. Yet something was holding me here, some soft beat was pulling me to the earth. The striving to accomplish that had charged me up north had dissolved in the hot grains of sand. This was where I had to be. Nothing else mattered.

By the next day my ambition had revived. When Roz's letter arrived entreating me to visit her in Majorca, I immediately determined to do just that. Three days later I boarded a bus that wound up the Costa Blanca along the Andalusian coastline under a soft citrine sky. The bright German girl sitting next to me invited me to her in her one-room cottage, situated outside Moraira on a mountain high above the ocean, where we pulled water from a well and read by candlelight. I stayed two days, then resumed the bus ride to Barcelona and reached Palma in time for a midnight snack in the hotel lounge.

When I phoned Roz the next day, she was tied up—something always going on—but we arranged to meet that evening at Mam's Bar. When I spied her seated elegantly on the bar stool, I rushed over in excitement. What had she been doing, what schemes had she dug up? With Roz there was no telling what would happen next. She had a way of ferreting out opportunities. Just the past week she'd uncovered a house for rent in Palma, with a kitchen, bedroom, and a patio, for a few pesos—a steal. She snapped it up for three months.

"A house! You're serious about living here?"

"Certainly. I absolutely adore it here. The climate is unbelievable, the food to die for, the colors exciting, the sun always shining, there's the Spanish music, the bar scene. The house is a block from the beach in a lively location full of young people and an easy taxi ride to town. There are jobs. Do you want another sherry or are you ready to switch to something more interesting?"

"I'll switch, you betcha! I was served complimentary sherry yesterday on the ferry from Barcelona, can you imagine?"

"Yes. The tourists prefer it to coffee." We ordered gin drinks. "Now tell me about Dolores." She listened, her long fingers wrapped gracefully around the cocktail glass, as I described the dinners and outings in Málaga with Dolores, her grandmother, and Conchita and her gang. When I inquired about Jorge, she informed me that he was still in the picture, but only as part of the background. I teased her about having a beau in every port, half-wishing I could say the same.

The bar was jammed with students, tourists, and business types stopping off after work, standing two or three abreast at the counter. After a while, with some bustling and knocking of elbows, the people on the bar stools next to us left and a group of American sailors in uniform swept in to take their place. They plunked down, smiling broadly, darted glances at Roz and me, and looked around for the bartender. One in particular spoke loudly and spanked his hand on the bar. "Hey, how about a drink?" He stood taller, larger than the others, wearing a waist-length pea jacket, his coarse hair shaved close around a pair of protruding ears.

The bartender moved up, a girl with dark cropped hair and short neck, wearing a long-sleeved black t-shirt. Her first words revealed her as an American.

"Coming up, sailor. What would you like?" Her no-nonsense manner did not put him off.

"Bourbon. Straight up," he barked. The rest of the gang called out orders, while the one in the pea jacket began ranting in a fierce voice that sounded across the room.

"This isn't his first bar stop of the day," remarked Roz, sending him a sharp look. But we had other things to talk about. Roz was looking for work—anything, cocktail hostess, receptionist, tour guide. Her ability to converse in Spanish opened possibilities. She might even decide to live in Majorca permanently. I admired her assertiveness in creating a life to her specifications. She struck out with confidence, took command, and would not be deterred from her purpose. She made things happen, whereas I drifted with the wind, waited to see what would develop, anticipating that things would work out in my favor.

The sailors had by now consumed several drinks and were guffawing loudly. One was trying to tell a joke but kept getting interrupted. The female bartender had been joined behind the counter by a second short-haired woman, also American. When the sailor in the pea jacket began arguing heatedly and waving an arm, one of the bartenders urged him to sit down, but he wouldn't hear of it. He was going to stand. Don't tell him what to do!

"Americans expect everything in Europe to be just like it is at home," I was saying to Roz. "They throw a fit if ice isn't served. They dole out 100

98

pesetas rather than walk up a flight of stairs. They spend a fortune in Michelin restaurants and complain that the food's too different."

The loud sailor had caught most of this and now he turned a hefty figure in our direction.

"What's this? You two girls are American. Listen to you bashing your own country! Don't you know how lucky you are to be American?" His voice boomed and the other sailors stopped talking. Roz and I looked at him.

"Hey, G.I. Joe," tossed back Roz evenly, "not every American is perfect. Simmer down. We have a right to our opinion." She turned back to me. "Keep your voice down," she whispered. Someone leaned toward the sailor and he jerked away.

I resumed, cautiously. "Too many American tourists use Europe for pure enjoyment. They have no interest in understanding the culture. They treat non-Americans as servants."

Roz nodded agreement. "I don't mess with them," she said.

"No wonder Americans are disliked," I went on. "They expect pristine conditions and appreciate a country only if it's luxed up to their standards. They come over here because it's the thing to do; everyone's coming to Europe."

The loud sailor had caught snippets of this through the ruckus and this time he walked closer.

"You girls don't know what you're talking about." His face had a red tinge. "You're anti-American! You should be driven out of town." He stood hovering over us.

"We've already been driven out of town. That's why we're here." Roz picked up her glass coolly. I snickered.

"Don't get smart with me!" yelled the sailor.

One of the female bartenders moved closer. "Watch it sailor. Leave those girls alone." Her voice was low and deliberate.

"Don't tell me what to do! Hey, I need another bourbon. Here, fill my glass."

"These two gals own the bar," Roz whispered in my ear. "You wait and see. He won't get his drink. What they say goes."

"Are you going to get my bourbon?"

"You've had enough. Come back tomorrow and we'll serve you." At this the sailor pushed over the counter and thrust his heavy shoulders towards the two women.

"I know what you are! You think I can't tell?" he shouted. "You're just a couple of dykes. You're not fooling anybody. You can't tell me when I get a drink!" He stood steady for a few minutes, buoyed by his anger, then tipped against one of the other sailors.

"You'll have to leave," said the bartender in an even voice. "Look out for your friend," she said to the sailors, who were now standing. The entire bar had quieted, expectant.

"Come on Hank," one of the sailors urged. "Let's not have a brawl. Come on, let's get out of here."

"Not on your life! These two dames can't rule me." Two of the sailors took his arm and guided him toward the door.

"They'll call the cops. Come on, let's get a drink somewhere else." We watched as they led him across the room, still protesting, and out the door.

When I turned back to the counter I found the seat next to me occupied by a rather scruffy but friendly looking young man. He had been watching and now he spoke.

"Everything okay? I hear everything. That sailor was wrong." Even sitting on the stool, I could tell he was tall, with a square tanned face, wide nose, and full sensuous mouth. He laid one rough hand on his denim shorts and studied me earnestly. I took him for European but couldn't place the accent.

"Yes. No harm done." The bartenders were passing back and forth behind the bar as if nothing had occurred. "I was complaining about Americans and he proved my point." My new companion smiled and swiveled on the stool to face me, placing his hand on the counter as he did so, a working hand, big and rough. I looked into his face. "Are you a carpenter?"

"No." A big smile. "An artist."

I laughed. With his broad chest and heavy features delicacy was not one of his obvious qualities. But then looks were no gauge.

"Of course. How could I not have known?" I said. "It's in your eyes." He fixed his blue eyes on me and I detected unexpected movement in them. I soon learned he'd been living on the neighboring island of Ibiza for some months. It was his habit to catch the boat to Palma once a week to retrieve his mail, see friends, and visit galleries, usually staying for a day or two at the Residencia Martel. He introduced himself as Frans Pannekoeken from Amsterdam.

After leaving the bar, Frans steered Roz and I to his favorite restaurant where we dined on paella, and then Frans walked me back to my hotel. He would be returning to Ibiza the next day but wanted to come see me in the morning before he left. I agreed, looking into the blue eyes that matched the soft robin's-egg blue of his shirt.

The next day I awoke refreshed. After slipping on a skirt and blouse, I made the bed and lay propped up on two huge down pillows, nibbling from a bag of *panecillos* and sipping a bottle of *eau minerale*. A brilliant Mediterranean light poured in from the ceiling-high French doors and spread over the room, which contained only a double bed, nightstand and low bureau.

As I was wiping the crumbs from my mouth, there came a knock on the door. When I opened it Frans stepped in, smiling, his tall frame almost filling the doorway. With a brief smile, he went over and gazed out the window at the scattering of tile rooftops one story below. A shaft of sunlight cut a jagged pattern across the floor, and crept slowly along to the far wall.

"I like it here. Now maybe we talk together, the two of us," he suggested, turning. I had resumed my seat on the bed.

"You'll have to sit on the bed," I said. "It's the only place. Care for an orange?" He nodded and lowered himself onto the other side of the bed.

"And now, Judy." He leaned over on his elbow, studying my face as if expecting to find clues to my character, "Tell me about you and what are your dreams?" Uneasy under this scrutiny, I nonetheless undertook to relate my fascination with Paris, my attempts at serious writing, and the inspiration that had propelled me all this way.

Frans listened intently. "You have many opinions and that is good," he said, smiling. He himself lived amid a pool of artists, rebels, and misfits congregated on Ibiza, all scraping a living or stretching their savings in order to live experimentally and create art.

"Like you I write, some, but mostly I draw," he told me. "I am poor." With that he leaned back into the pillows and stretched his legs on the bed, ankles crossed. "I also make pottery and sell to small shops."

"Do you feel passionate about what you do?"

"Yes, very much. I show you my work if you come visit me in my little house." His Dutch accent gave a lilt to his words.

Frans accepted a *panecillo* and bit into the sweet bread while I picked out something from my favorite poetry book. Leaning side-by-side against the pillows, we took turns reading Dylan Thomas poems aloud.

Do not go gentle into that good night.
Curse bless me now with your fierce tears, I pray.
Rage, rage against the dying of the light.

Frans insisted I read a poem of my own. Since I was not used to sharing my work, I hesitated to my poems aloud. But he was full of admiration. "Good, Very good. You have soul." I imagined that to his foreign ear my English words sounded cleverer than they were.

Next we read poems by Gerard Manley Hopkins and Yeats. I cut orange slices with a pocket knife and we ate them in silence, focused on the taste of the rich, sweet nectar, wiping our mouths and licking the juice running over our fingers. A shaft of sunlight cut a jagged pattern across the floor, and crept slowly along to the far wall. When a fly bounced and clamored against the screen to get in, we looked at each other and chuckled.

"You are quiet. I like that." The mattress dipped as Frans drew up his arms and leaned over, looking into my face. "I like your eyes," he said with a serious air. "I wish I could reach them. I wish to find what you keep hidden." I didn't know what to respond to this. I couldn't look at him. A nervous quiver reached down my spine and froze into my legs. "I like to see more of your eyes..." He paused. Suddenly all attention in the room was aimed at my person, even the sun's rays focused directly on me.

"You are shy, no?" His voice was low, almost touching.

"No—yes. Just a little—nervous," I said in a meek voice. The closeness of him hovering next to me on the bed, blunted all thought. A grip of tension clasped my throat and my palms felt damp against my bare arms. I was caught between a strong attraction, wanting to move close into the physical presence that beat warm and alive next to me, and a compelling drive to back off, to still my racing heart, to save myself. I looked at my watch. He had been there three hours—I couldn't believe it.

With a resurgence of energy, Frans stood up. The spell was broken. "Come for walk. I show you around."

"I'm afraid I can't. I'm moving to Roz's place this afternoon." We stood by the door, Franz hovering above me, his head tilted so that I could look into his blue eyes. He smiled. I smiled back, feeling easier.

"I depressed too much," he said without warning, in a low voice. I didn't answer, but fastened my eyes on his face. "But now you here, I feel better."

With a gesture so gradual I was barely aware of it, he slipped a hand around my waist, stepped towards me until we almost touched, and pressed his mouth on mine. The kiss was brief, but the soft feel of his lips remained as he drew himself up. He paused a second, then I heard the door close. The scent of his breath lingered after him, and I smiled.

Later that evening, venturing down to Mam's bar with Roz, I found a letter waiting.

Letter from Frans

Dear Judy,

I left you not long ago and you are in my thoughts and in my blood. Everywhere I look I see your face. How could that happen so soon? I believe it is love at first sight. I worry because I hope you are not mad about the kiss. I could not help it and I'm sorry if you object. I want you to know it was not idle and was based on love.

I plan to make an ink drawing of you and will send it to you. If you will come to Ibiza I will give it to you and some ceramic things I plan to make special. I would much love to see you. Since you arrive I am no longer depressed. I know I drink and smoke too much. I will do better. I will show you my boat. I paint picture of it in oil.

I leave at 5 o'clock. Maybe you will get this in time and come to the boat and see me off. I really hope you will.

Love from your friend,
Frans

I didn't make it to see him off at the boat or visit him in Ibiza. I mailed him a letter expressing a desire for his company and inviting him to come visit me in Paris. A week later I left for France.

Chapter 3   End of the Road

When I arrived with my suitcase at the pension on the Rue Honoré Chevalier, Madame Dessarts greeted me like a long-lost daughter. "Ah, *ma petite*! Dinner is almost ready. See to your things. I will set a place for you." The rectangular dinner table hummed with stories of my travels, and afterwards I slipped onto the back of a Swedish boy's motor scooter and spent the evening at a crowded café drinking beer with seven or eight students from the pension. It was near ten when we returned, but I couldn't resist calling Jean Paul on the hall telephone. In the whole of my five weeks in Spain I hadn't given my friend a thought, but now I felt my chest tightening.

"So you are back," he said, picking up the phone on the first ring. I half-expected a reprimand for my long silence, but he simply requested a rendezvous. When I arrived at the *Deux Magots* I was in for a surprise. Jean Paul had planned a weekend in Normandy.

We started off early one Saturday morning in a borrowed Fiat, Jean Paul seated tall and intent behind the wheel and Alain in the back seat, wearing the green leather jacket he never seemed to take off. I had become fond of Alain, of his amiable expression and easy smile. He was loyal and uncomplicated, someone who could be relied on. Not, I thought, a bit like the mercurial Jean Paul.

We arrived at the hotel in Mortrée in time to stash the suitcases in our separate rooms and stroll around the grounds before lunch, accompanied by the scent of damp country earth and newly cropped hay.

At noon we found a two-story inn, owned and run by a short French couple who lived upstairs. The small room held eight tables, set under a low ceiling of rough sycamore beams. After we had sampled the house wine and finished bowls of dark consommé with marrow balls, Alain talked of his recent engagement.

"Yes, I admit it. I'm in love and want to settle down with Anne Marie. It's time to enrich my life," he explained. He had given a great deal of thought to this leap into matrimony with the loss of freedom and added responsibilities it entailed. He claimed that freedom no longer offered the promised rewards of his younger days.

"What do you think, Jean Paul?" Alain said, turning to his friend. "You're getting on like the rest of us. Are you ever going to consider such a step?" I recalled long passages in Jean Paul's letters where he deplored the pitfalls of the marriage pact and the vulgarity of the merely physical. His ideal couple walked side-by-side, not face-to-face, he'd written, with the same goal, complementing each other in mutual independence.

I countered that expression of the individual excluded such bonds, and that to a free spirit any restriction was unthinkable. Now my feelings were sending contradictory messages. I felt a stab of hesitation and waited to hear what Jean Paul had to say.

Jean Paul tore off a crust from a baguette and dipped it into his rabbit stew with black sauce, while Madame refilled the wine glasses. "Oh—well—I don't know," he said finally. He looked thoughtfully down at his fingernails. A slip of dark hair fell over his forehead, and he brushed it back with a slender hand. "I seem to be the only one not married anymore. All my friends have succumbed."

Confronted with a future that seemed to have backed up to look him in the eye, a hesitant, almost pained look passed over his face.

I took a deep swallow from my wine glass and remained silent. I couldn't wait to see where this was going.

"So what do you want for yourself, my friend?" Alain asked again. Jean Paul wiped his fingers with his napkin and leaned back in his chair as if stalling for time.

"Yes, tell us, how do you see yourself fitting into the structure on which the stability of society is based?" I asked facetiously, then stopped, afraid he might think I took a personal interest. "Although you certainly don't have to decide right this minute."

With this Jean Paul flashed a grin and reached for a slice of Pont-l'Évêque. "I'm not going to do anything right now except finish my wine and these wild strawberries. And then we will shake Madame's hand and go visit the Chateau d'O and save further talk until later." He reached for his jacket and as his head turned I thought I noticed a residue of doubt hovering on his face.

Rue Honoré Chevalier, Paris, 1958

With summer in full bloom, the streets of Paris swarmed with the aroma of baked cinnamon and the fresh odor of wet pavement. Women vendors in black capes tended carts bursting with baskets of purple violets. One morning shortly after the Mortrée trip, I sat on the terrace of the *Café des Fleurs* enjoying the warm touch of fresh air. A pack of letters I'd fetched from the American Express rested on the table in front of me, along with a brioche, a *café au lait* and a copy the *International Herald Tribune.*

I picked up the first letter.

Post card from Carmen in Europe

[Picture on front of the pope with his arms raised in blessing]

Judy (the Paris beauty),

I picked up this card just for you. Tack it over your bed.

I'm having a ball! Majorca was great (saw Roz). Rome also great (they're my people). Are you still shaking hands with people without taking your hand out of your coat pocket?

Sold two paintings since I saw you (one to the Whitney Museum)...also saw one of my paintings in a show here in Rome...what a surprise.

Did you learn to love America yet? I sing the Star Spangled Banner *every morning.*

I will be hitting Paris soon. Drop me a card care of American Express.

Letter from Dolores in Málaga

We miss you. My grandmother is making a jacket out of the black coat you left behind—the one you were wrapped up in on the roof when you were sleeping with the chickens, ha, ha.

Thank you so much for the gifts. I hope you liked the scarf. Conchita has found a job as au pair—*she probably has told you all about it. No one sees your friend Robert. Since you brought us to meet him he has never come to visit. Did you see Roz?*

Letter from Frans in Mallorca

When you didn't come to the boat, I was afraid I never see you again. It makes me feel sentimental saying goodbye. Even if your stay was short, I will never forget the accord between us. I still believe in a dream we had together.

I am glad we talked on phone.

About ten days ago I was in Palma and I went to Roz's and thought I would find you there. You had left, but I had the feeling that there was still something of you sitting beside me on the terrace. No, I promise not to get as you say complicated. But I imagined you were thinking about me.

Since I met someone who I could be very fond of I am happy. However both of us went in other directions, to different lives. Maybe you forget me already but I do not, because I think that it was good that we met.

I hope your life is going good for you. If you don't like Paris and would like to come here you better. However you said you had to be in Paris.

Love,

Letter from Dad

I have deposited your latest dividend check in your account. The amount has increased. You are making money.

Mother says you are getting her an evening bag in Paris. Am enclosing a check for $100 so you can get one for yourself.

Your last letter arrived from Málaga. You sure do get around.

One afternoon I returned from the *Alliance* to find Carmen, my artist friend from Madrid, seated in an office chair, trying to get Madame Dessarts to understand his accented Spanish.

"*Esta muy bien aqui*," he kept repeating.

Madame Dessarts shoved a *Paris Match* across the desk and threw up her hands. "*Ne comprehends pas!*" She turned at my entrance. "I don't understand. It's bad enough to have to put up with your terrible French," she cried in French, "But at least I can talk to you! This fellow won't quit!"

"Quit badgering her," I said to Carmen, laughing. "*Au revoir*, Madame." I took his arm. "Come on, there's a lot to do."

When we stepped outside I noticed he was wearing a long-sleeved burgundy sweatshirt hanging over black jeans. "Why are you wearing a sweatshirt that hangs past your butt in the middle of this heat?" I asked, knowing he would have a ready answer.

"To hide my tempting body," he retorted, "to announce myself as a bohemian American, and because no one else is wearing one like it."

"You don't have to wear anything special to look like a bohemian American," I said.

"Don't be ridiculous. I have an artist's soul to project. Did you ever see a true artist in a business suit? You see, I really do want to stand apart and that isn't easy here where everything is tolerated—which often amounts to being ignored."

"All right, if a dark sweatshirt spells *artiste* to you. Anyway it looks cute. You just might want to snip off the sleeves and get with the poverty part."

He wore the burgundy sweatshirt the entire four days we spent together.

First the art museums. After several hours at the Musée National d'Art Moderne, we located an exhibit called *De L'Impressionnisme à Nos Jours*. We admired several paintings side-by-side, then drifted off to follow different attractions. I later found him examining Claude Manet's "Le Déjeuner sur l'Herbe." The gigantic size of this painting was staggering. The creamy body of the main subject dominated the canvas. The woman was stretched out, naked and exposed, on a blanket amid the leafy flowering of the woods, while two men sat beside her, covered tip to toe with dark suits, felt hats and beards, looking like kings of the jungle. A second woman covered only with a shimmering white scarf was reflected between the trees in the background.

Carmen declared the work a masterpiece. To me the incongruity of the white glistening female form, set stark against the dark, enclosed background, demeaned the female and exemplified the arrogance of men who reduced her significance to one of pure male pleasure—all justified in the name of art. Masterpiece or not, I judged it appalling.

"But if the men were naked too, then it would be all right?"

"Yes, as long as they were equally exposed. Or the women dressed and not rendered as vulnerable prey."

"But the women are enjoying it."

"You don't know that they are!"

"You don't know that they aren't!"

"Yes I do. Look at their faces."

"Their faces look happy."

"You know nothing about women. Let's go to dinner."

Before Carmen left for Le Havre, we giggled over our experiences in Madrid, combed the Luxembourg Gardens, and slipped into a theater showing *La Notte Bianche*, a dark love story reeking with atmosphere starring Maria Schell. Carmen understood the Italian while I read the French subtitles. Afterwards we treated ourselves to dinner at a four-star restaurant, for which occasion Carmen put on a handsome black jacket and tucked in his burgundy sweat shirt.

†

The streets of Paris in the spring and early summer of 1958 were in an uproar. *Révolution* was on everyone's lips. I received a letter from home: What's happening? Get back here. My return letter explained that there was no sense of panic, that public demonstration was a part of French existence, not to worry. Life went on as usual and tourists still swarmed in. As one French newspaper put it: "The bicycles are still flowing along the streets to work and the Americans are still in the swank bars paying 650 francs a shot."

The Paris protests began in the Latin Quarter. The student demonstrators swarming the steps of the Sorbonne complained of high tuition, lack of jobs, low salaries, and the confines and triviality of bourgeois life. They distrusted authority, criticized capitalism, and demanded the right to speak openly.

Another grievance was the escalation of the war in Algeria. Rumors spread that De Gaulle supported self-determination for the Arabs, a stand the French settlers in Algeria found unsupportable. In order to defend their property and privileges, these French immigrants had taken up arms and were seizing government buildings.

In Paris, thousands of Algerian nationalist supporters marched from the Place de la Republic to the Place Denfert-Rochereau carrying flags, singing the *Internationale*, and breaking store windows. The local unions joined in demanding labor rights. Signs posted on buildings read: POWER TO THE WORKERS, POMPIDOU (prime minister) RESIGN, and ADIEU DE

GAULLE. Police brigades with machine-guns were lined up along the streets of Paris, filling police wagons with protest groups dragged from factories, cafés, and various corners of the city.

Conversations in the cafes and bistros swirled at each new outbreak. Jean Paul, Alain, and I smoked Gauloises at the *L'Echelle de Jacob*. Jean Paul railed against the French occupation of Algeria, which he considered another pillage of a poor country by the elite of a powerful nation.

"When I was stationed in Algeria, the imbecile army killed innocents by the thousands," he said heatedly. "Take for example the bombardment of Sakiet Sidi Youssef in Tunisia by the French air force. The journalists warned that this atrocity would cause the downfall of French power in Algiers and drive the Algerian nationalistic leaders into Soviet arms." He leaned forward and rested his elbows on the table, gesturing with his hands. "I remember the day I travelled to Oran for my tour of duty," he went on. "Oran, like Sakiet Sidi Youssef, is rich with natural resources and luxurious countryside. Our army unit had been traveling by bus for hours. Seated next to me was a young French boy, married, he told us. The country along the way was calm, the air was sweet, and I was feeling heady with its beauty. Suddenly along the roadside we saw an Arab woman carrying a child on her back, hastening towards a distant house as if in flight. The young boy next to me touched my arm and said, pointing to the figure, 'That would make a beautiful target, no?'

"This is what 20 centuries of Christian civilization has produced." We all nodded in silent agreement.

The view of the Algerian war, as well as other foreign events, exposed in the French journals, differed widely from the accounts in the American newspapers. It never ceased to amaze me how vastly the version of events as seen from American and European eyes could diverge. When I returned to the States I found accounts far removed from those reported in the Paris newspapers. Even the facts differed, seen through altered glasses. It was hard to tell where truth lay.

Alain spoke up. "It's not just the Algerian protestors—the communists and the unions are joining them. They're all being repressed by the government." He picked up the newspaper on his lap and dropped it on the table. "The Parisian *gendarmes* are described here as peaceful—merely a warning presence to keep the angry crowds in check. We all know that is false." Several students at the next table turned and voiced agreement. They had participated in the barricading of the Sorbonne and seen the police assault the crowds with tear gas and grenades.

The next day the headlines read: POMPIDOU RESIGNS. DE GAULLE ACCEPTS PRESIDENT RENÉ COTY'S REQUEST TO FORM NEW GOVERNMENT. Many of the protesters, including the communists, had decided to opt for the restoration of order under a strong leader and supported handing De Gaulle emergency powers for six months.

The germ of the Fifth Republic, destined to be established under De Gaulle's guidance, was being formed in front of my eyes.

†

A three-page letter arrived from Cat Morris in Holland. I had rarely seen Cat since our co-ed days at the University of Colorado. She'd been living abroad for almost two years and was working at The Hague at a secretarial job arranged through her father's connections. Now, before heading back to the States, she planned to tour France, Spain, Italy, and Switzerland, beginning with a few days in Paris. She couldn't wait to see me. Most amazing of all, she was arriving in a brand new MG she'd purchased on behalf of her father and was transporting back with her on the ship. She assured me that nothing this fabulous had ever happened to her. She would pick me up at the pension. It would be great!

Although we hadn't been close, I was anxious to see her. The prospect of reuniting with someone from home, a popular classmate from high school and dorm mate during my year at the University of Colorado, filled me with anticipation. I'd turned down an earlier invitation to visit her in Holland for the same reason I'd resisted finding a job in Paris: It would put me in an environment with other Americans, something I had vowed to avoid at all costs. I had to admit to feeling a pang of envy when she described the spacious apartment in Brussels overlooking the sea that she shared with a girl from the agency where she worked. But I avoided seeking work where I would speak only English.

There had been opportunities. Cat referred me to the U.S. Air Force Office in Paris where she had applied for secretarial work on arrival. Jeanine Hammel, my supervisor at the United Nations, suggested I look up Benoit Levy, the well-known filmmaker, who would surely find me

113

something. Ward Anderson urged me to apply for a paid guide position with the Minnesota Pavilion at the 1958 Brussels Fair, something Dad offered to help with through his connections.

I couldn't bring myself to pursue these leads. My unshakable goal was to immerse myself in French culture so that I could learn French and not get trapped in an insulated American environment.

Following a last minute telegram BE THERE TOMORROW MORNING AT PENSION STOP MUCH LOVE CAT, Cat arrived. During the next few days she maneuvered the bright yellow MG through the clogged streets of Paris, and we drove to the Bois de Boulogne for lunch, visited museums, ate at my favorite restaurants, strolled the Latin Quarter, and lingered in the lawns of the Luxembourg Gardens, stopping in the warm summer sunshine to enjoy the white marble sculptures and fountains. We watched as children prodded rented sailboats through the pool with long wooden sticks, women in slim cotton dresses pushed perambulators, and lunchtime loafers strolled arm-in-arm down alleys of sycamore and horse chestnut trees.

As we lounged on green metal chairs, talking nonstop and watching men playing *boules* on the lawn, Cat pulled out a clipping from the Minneapolis *Star* her mother had sent. Printed in the article was a photo of me taken the previous winter standing on the deck of the Ryndam, on my way to France "to study French and the French culture." They got that right.

Les Tuileries, Paris, the Fifties

Cat's visit left me with an uplifting afterglow. It felt good to be with a companion from home, adrift in a new world of excitement and promise, speaking my own tongue. I did not invite Jean Paul to join us; he adored meeting Americans, but since neither spoke the others' language, I kept Cat to myself. There was life beyond Jean Paul!

Lately I had noticed a strange barrier arising between Jean Paul and me. It had been seven months since I'd arrived in Paris. We'd seen the sights and covered every topic. The novelty was beginning to fade and our meetings lacked the luster of the early days. After all this time, I knew practically nothing about his family or him on a personal level. When I asked about his Christmas tradition, he said only that he hated Christmas. He stayed clear of his family and lived at home, he assured me, only because he couldn't afford to live on his own. For the rest, he remained mute. I didn't complain, content to enjoy the stimulation of his company and French society we shared.

I cancelled two of our meetings in a row, seeking to break the pall of despondency I was beginning to feel. Then one day I received a letter from him. Why a letter, when we saw each other often? He seemed to be searching for answers. I couldn't even make out the question.

Mon Amie,

It is sad that even though you are in Paris I must write to you to make myself understood. I am absolutely persuaded that frankness is the most important thing.

I told you yesterday of the strange (abnormal) importance you have for me—a little like the dream of Verlaine: "I often have the strange and penetrating dream of an unknown woman whom I love and who loves me and who is never quite the same each time nor quite different and who loves and understands me."

You are at the same time someone very near and very far. I feared a little to know you. Our encounter four years ago was so brief I scarcely remember your face. Stupidly, I feared that you would be pretty or ugly. I feared to see you living, the manifestation of you in daily life. I feared your warmth. You were my friend uniquely through your letters, on paper, which proved that our two nationalities were not a handicap. Now I accept the belief that I will be closer to you by embracing you. I accept attaching myself to you. I accept the price of the dream and disillusion because I don't want to let escape the possibility of hope.

But if this delicious flirt will terminate in a failure, you must warn me so that you can remain a friend. I want to respect your ideas as an American. I only want to give you what I am sure of—and it is you Judy who will decide our relations. They will be only what you want them to be.

It seems to me that the search for new sensations is a sterile one. I love liberty, mine and others. To rid oneself of moral rules is proof of liberty, of independence only if one has a conscience and is in charge of his acts. All the rest is debauchery, libertinage, and laxity.

*But I believe that to live one must be engaged, risk
something, lose in order to gain. There is not great joy without
knowing sadness.*

*Finally Judy, beyond the confidence that I have in you, I
would like to find hope—the sentiment of a follow-up and a
future.*

I await with impatience your advice.

I stared at the letter. It threw me into a whirl of confusion. What did all this mean? I didn't doubt Jean Paul's honesty. I believed he meant what he said. But what was he saying? He was disillusioned—at this thought my heart grew weak. On the other hand, he would comply with my wishes as to the nature of our relationship to make me happy. He would accept attaching himself to me as long as the attachment bore fruit, about which he seemed to have grave doubts. But he was willing to take a risk and would stick to the friendship even if he had to pay a price.

What price? My friendship—what was that? I was a passing leaf, fluttering in the wind, connected to nothing. I had no job, no situation, no future. What had I to offer him past friendly entertainment? Clearly, with his striking good looks and the way his friends looked up to him, he could do better than me. He liked people to be simple, warm, and easygoing. This didn't describe me. On my side, his aloofness kept me at a distance. It was hard to put all this together.

An unlikely thought struck me—that he thought of me as a rich American out to amuse herself with a French lover. But surely he knew me better than that. The idea was ludicrous.

He hinted that he was prepared to take the relationship further. With caution! But how could we entertain a future when he hadn't even kissed me or shown the slightest inclination to do so?

In none of this did he sound enamored.

My confidence dropped to zero. I felt inadequate, powerless, afraid of losing everything. I needed assurance. Searching between the lines of the letter, I found only emptiness.

Jean Paul and I agreed to talk. As I approached the *Méphisto* the sky overhead was empty and bleak and the air unusually brittle for late October. I located a table in the back of the café, and soon Jean Paul appeared, looking deliberate and tense. Flashing his crooked smile, he dug into his coat pocket for cigarettes and turned to signal the waiter to bring a coffee.

I looked at him, strangled by an apprehension that made it hard to think. I rummaged in my purse among the spiral notebook, leather wallet, glasses case, and pack of Gauloises without knowing what I was looking for. The waiter returned with our coffee. Jean Paul picked up his cup, took a long draft, and brushed a stray strand of dark hair from his forehead.

"All right, let's talk," he said. "What you said on the phone yesterday was correct. My attitude towards you has been strange lately—discordant—dissonant—improvised." His uplifted hands emphasized each word. "I *do* act differently every time we are together. I don't want to confuse you, so I will try to be frank and say exactly what I can in direct terms.

"I want there to be full honesty between us. I don't want you to be uncomfortable or shocked. What I want to say is that you are the judge. It is up to you to dictate to me my future attitude, as you would like it to be." He had been leaning towards me. Now he sat back in his chair and raised his dark eyes up to mine. "It is for you to decide."

At these words, my feeling of foreboding intensified. His tone of polite respect hung in front of me like a rappelling wall over which I had to climb to see what was on the other side. He was willing to give me whatever I wanted, but presented no measure of his own. But it was the measure I needed!

I looked down at the table. "I—don't know what to say," I stammered. "What I want is—to—to be clear," I said meekly.

Jean Paul folded his hands together. "I will try to explain. There are two concerns. The first is that we do not have adequate communication. We do not speak the same language. I do not know what my words mean to your American mind. Our thoughts fly by each other and do not meet."

My French was still flawed and I had no defense there.

"Secondly, I desire above all to conserve your friendship. It has been indispensable to me over the years, especially those solitary months in Algeria. As you know, I like you very much. I want to respect your wishes as an American and as a woman." We both watched as the waiter refilled our cups.

What to answer? Nothing he said reached me where I wanted to be reached. He held the upper hand, since he was courageously spelling out his thoughts and I was sitting mute, stuck in a paralysis of indecision. I didn't dare reveal how much I depended on him and longed to be in his presence.

I forced myself to say something. "Jean Paul, you know I want to be your friend, am your friend." I stared at my hands lying awkwardly on the table. Finally I looked up and saw him regarding me carefully. I went on, trying to shake the cloud of fear that was closing in. "I shouldn't have teased you about being conceited, and I want you to know I like you anyway."

What was it I liked about him? That he looked good and that I would die for his smile or his touch? That his mind was far-ranging and penetrating? That his cocky confidence was laced pockets of insecurity? Was it the fleeting hesitation at the corners of his mouth, the look of impish daring that lit his face when I teased him, and the dark eyes that at times looked straight into mine, promising and withholding?

"Jean Paul...what I want is...Jean Paul..." I couldn't stop repeating his name. I faltered, came to a halt. "Jean Paul, you'll have to do the talking. I can't."

He sat thoughtfully for some minutes. "I wish you would let me look into your eyes," he said finally. "You are so close to me and yet I feel you are galaxies away. I can't reach you. You must tell me what to do."

I couldn't direct myself, let alone him. I was floundering in a river of raging undercurrents.

"You ask me to do the talking," he went on. "All right, I will do so. I don't conduct myself like a so-called typical Frenchman whose dearest desire is to sleep with every woman he encounters. For me that is happily not the case. I detest such gratuitous and continuous license. My great concern is to not shock you. I do not want to let myself enter into a frivolous adventure by which I will lose a friend."

"We are agreed," I cried. "I also value our friendship. We will continue to be friends." A thought pressed its way to the surface. "If only we were—closer." There, I'd said something—and felt like I was plunging into a bottomless crater.

Jean Paul picked up the spoon and stirred his coffee. Finally he smiled ruefully. "It is up to you. Tell me if I can be with you as a boy with a girl whom he admires and likes. With the single end of 'living' in the proper sense of breathing better. Please tell me this clearly."

I couldn't figure out what was required of me. My hands were clammy and the match shook as I lifted it to the Gauloises dangling between my two fingers. I had the sinking feeling we had reached a dead-end.

"Why do we meet?" My voice barely carried across the table.

"My good friend, the *letters*. I can't forget the letters—they kept me alive in Algeria—how we understood each other—you came all this way." He looked confused and worried and my heart almost went out to him for the loss of his old *copain*. I still hadn't found the words he was looking for, the guidance he sought. We were each hoping the other would come up with the magic words to catapult us over the impasse.

Exhausted, I said I had to go. We parted for the first time without setting a future *rendezvous*. As I left the *Méphisto* it started to rain, and I watched the blurred outline of Jean Paul's figure retreating along the sidewalk and disappear in a wet mist between the grey buildings.

I decided to move to a hotel. To be alone. The irony of this did not escape me. Here I was living on my own, and I abandoned my single room at the pension, where I was perfectly happy, in order to be by myself.

It was time to take stock. It was more than despondency over Jean Paul. I had to start writing. My dreams, coalescing these past years while I was occupied with school, family, jobs and apartments and I don't know what all, were not bearing fruit. Here I was cradled in the creative capital of the world, endless discovery at my fingertips, and still I was creating nothing.

Since my arrival I'd met with foreign experiences that drew me along in a rush of expectation, meeting other souls, absorbing centuries of ancient treasure and avant-garde ideas. A banquet was continually spreading out at my feet. Visitors drifted in from all sides, fellow adventurers ricocheting into the city of light.

I needed to get serious. My hotel room on the Boulevard St. Michel looked out over the bookstalls and *tabacs* of the West Bank. I seated myself at the small desk near the window, surrounded by the portable Royal typewriter, an iron-clad writing schedule typed on bond paper, a dictionary, a thesaurus, sharpened pencils, and legal pad. The scene was set. All I had to do was get to work. The pivotal question: Where to begin?

I'd heard it many times: Write about what you know. My first thought—something from those transformational high school years. I changed Margo's name to Cathe and picked up a pad. Nothing. Closing my eyes, I tried to project back in time, to visualize actual scenes: nothing. Finally I grabbed a pencil and tried making up a story á la Kafka, but my account of life as an accounting clerk, being cruelly misinterpreted by my shadowy co-workers and walking home alone every night in my raincoat to the squalor of a one-room flat did not have the ring of greatness. I switched to poetry and managed to produce a few poems. Massive missives to meandering mates practicing attention alerting alliteration. Nothing but nonsense.

As I sat at the desk watching pedestrians crisscross the teeming square, each intent on an immediate errand, I recalled the words of Henry James when he fled to Venice in an attempt to write. "Too much going on out there," he said as he looked out the window at the centuries of civilization stretching before him, "I should have gone to Liverpool."

I became filled with doubt. What purpose did writing serve, other than to blast a statement to the world—here I am and I count? A story had to be *significant*. I was crushed with a feeling of inadequacy. What could I write that wasn't obvious to everyone in sight and hadn't been said a thousand times before?

Every five minutes I ran downstairs to the *tabac* for cigarettes or took refuge at the corner bistro, where I ordered a ham and cheese sandwich and a *lait grenadine* at the bar. One rainy afternoon I met Monika, a fun-loving French girl my age who stood a few feet away sipping a steaming hot chocolate. We took to spending evenings together, along with her many friends, at a nearby bar across from the hat shop where she worked. When three weeks later I packed up to return to the pension, she invited me home to her family's apartment in Levallois for a week. I accepted immediately. My mother sent a note thanking her family for their hospitality.

During my stay at the hotel I didn't see Jean Paul. He didn't know where I was, part of my desire to create space between us. Let him worry for a change!

I discovered that Scott Molina, a fellow cinema student from USC, was living in Paris. One afternoon a letter in my box at the American Express office from Chester informed me of his address. Someone from home! Under it a second letter, this from Scott himself, stating he had heard from Chester and inviting me to dinner with him and his wife.

An American friend, living in Paris, attending the Sorbonne, who spoke fluent French—what luck! Scott Molina had been a familiar figure at the USC Cinema Department, where I'd often glimpsed his tall, lanky figure as he swung past with the easy stride of an athlete. Scott and his wife Vicky were living in Paris while Scott undertook a film study program at the Sorbonne. I immediately determined to include Jean Paul. These were people who spoke his language and would appreciate his searing French ideology.

He sounded surprised when I phoned, but quickly accepted the invitation. We had not met since our last meeting at the *Méphisto*. Neither of us referred to it. I did not offer an explanation of my recent absence beyond a succinct "I've been away." Best let him wonder. His voice was noncommittal. I sensed that since he had taken the initiative to clarify our relationship, it was up to me to draw it to an eventual conclusion.

The following Saturday evening, Scott and Vicky met us at the door and greeted Jean Paul in fluent French. They showed us the apartment, quite a find since well-furnished lodgings were almost impossible to obtain in the district. A low couch stood against one wall, with a large print of Alfred Sisley hanging above it. Bookcases and maps of Europe covered the walls. Beyond the living room was the kitchen, entered through a dark hickory door frame. Jean Paul looked around approvingly.

We seated ourselves in the living room around a low coffee table, where Vicky served us goblets of red wine. Scott described the thesis on the films of Jean Renoir he was completing under a Fulbright scholarship. Jean Paul found it hard to believe that an academic scholarship would finance the study of a single filmmaker, albeit famous, for a full year in a foreign country, expenses paid, including rent for a roomy apartment conveniently located near the Sorbonne.

"Of course, it is a very good opportunity," Jean Paul admitted. "So tell me please, when you return to the United States will you be provided with a job?"

"No, there is no guarantee of that."

"Then how will you go about finding work that applies what you learn?"

"I may not be able to apply it directly. The opportunity for me to create the kind of impressionistic films Renoir produced is not at all likely." Scott smiled widely and took a swallow of wine. "But for this one year in Paris I am able to throw all my energies into something I feel passionate about. I will never get such a chance again."

"And," Vicky put in, "I get a chance to attend French language classes at the Alliance Française and read voraciously about French and English history. It's a year I wouldn't miss."

Then it was my turn. "And you, Judy?" asked Scott. "What brought you to Paris?" Everyone regarded me expectantly

"I'm learning French." I predicted their thoughts: a year to learn a language? Really? Isn't that something you do in conjunction with something else? But no, they understood at once. A year off to travel, explore and learn bold-faced about the rest of the world before adulthood closed in. Go for it!

Jean Paul looked dubious. I couldn't blame him. There was a lot lacking in my command of the French language, which the easy give-and-take between Jean Paul and Scott made clear. Under the fluency of Scott's conversation Jean Paul opened up, relaxed his careful selection of words and began to flow with the ideas that moved effortlessly between them.

"I don't have the natural flair for languages Scott does," Vicky confided to me, smoothing the wrinkles in her blue cable-knit sweater. She flashed me a confidential smile, "Besides, he loves to do all the talking."

"I don't seem to have a flair for it myself," I answered. "And I don't do enough reading. Sometimes I think I could use more structure in my life."

Vicky leaned forward as if these words had struck a chord. "Sometimes, after four years in the rigid bounds of academia, one needs to let go and just absorb--it's a different kind of learning." I threw her a grateful look as she got up and went into the kitchen to fetch the hors d'oeuvres.

The next morning I received an express letter from Jean Paul.

My Friend,

I don't want to let a day pass without telling you that thanks to you I have passed a remarkably good evening. I still have so many questions! Learn French quickly please!

Finally I know that there is at least one sympathetic American and I regret fiercely that he will not be staying in Paris more than a few days. I would have had so much pleasure in seeing him again. If it were only possible...I leave it to you....

I hardly have a reason to write to you. And if you are inconvenienced by this letter you can treat me like an idiot. But today—for god knows what reason—I have felt my blood a little richer, a little more rapid than usual. And for that alone I want to thank you.

This evening, for several instants, you and I understood each other, spoke a language clear and precise. It is this mysterious Judy that I have been in such haste to know and whom I have (oh folly) had so many times had in front of me, she whose letters I have waited for. I don't know what I should do with you or for you. I have a troubled presentiment, an instinct more certain than reason, to keep you.

I hope that soon we can see each other much more often. Don't forget that you can telephone me if necessary or simply if you want to. I remember now that next Saturday and Sunday I have to work at Nicole's, but if I can see you I will call. All this is a waste of time!

If you could only tell me what I don't know!

I kiss your hand.

P.S. If your friend leaves Paris and I don't see him again please shake his hand for me. He is truly very fine.

I poured over his letter repeatedly, trying to piece together the turns his thoughts took and how I fit into the obscure picture he evoked. As usual, I was unable to decipher the meaning.

Standing on the bank, I stared down at the River Seine moving freely, opaquely beneath columns of ancient architecture and the swaying of timeworn Linden trees. Along the walls a nest of fishing boats silent, oblivious, swayed to the rhythm of the water. The sky towered overhead, a grey-blue monotone. On the boulevard, the muted sound of snarling traffic seemed far away, a distant echo of civilization.

Trying to make sense of my relationship with Jean Paul was proving impossible. He usually took the lead, initiating our meetings. He needed someone to take charge, to take him in hand, to say don't mess with me and set up standards. And here I was too full of insecurity to command a flea. Besides, I had been in Paris too long, was going nowhere. I had arrived bearing dreams and endless possibilities. But my path had run its course and I felt it sinking into the riverbed below.

The one truth I felt in my bones: I didn't tempt him. I was not beautiful or petite or commanding. He wanted to be bowled over. With me he was not bowled over. Maybe his Jesuit background or a lack of sexual experience caused the squeamishness I sensed in him. Sinking onto a wooden bench, I pulled out my faithful leather-bound journal. I would express my thoughts, would follow the lines to their conclusions where often insight lay. But when finished I saw only a few words. It was all I had.

Journal Entry on the Banks of the Seine

Jean Paul and I have assessed our relationship with the frankness and honesty we're always talking about.
But it is too late.

†

125

A trip to Provence in southern France was a must. Getting there was a disaster. The train trip to Arles, normally a six-and-a-half-hour ride, consumed two maddening, accident-fraught days and several frustrating train rides. First a mistaken detour to a town called *Alès,* which poorly pronounced sounded like *Arles,* via Avignon, Sète, and Nimes. Then back to Avignon again to start over, before at last arriving at Arles—a 500 mile trip—at 3:00 a. m. Luckily, the charm of Arles riddled with French history and the sunny beach restored me to sanity. For a week I explored the Mediterranean hills.

On my return, I seized the letters piled up at the American Express and hurried to the pension, packet hot in my hand. Drawing from a trunk the stack of letters accumulated since coming to Paris, I stretched out on the bed, propped against the headboard, lit up a cigarette, and plunged in.

One was from Margo, sent months ago. She wrote that Joan showed up at her apartment and they enjoyed a nice visit. She thought they would be good friends. Brandon Stewart, the good-looking filmmaker from the USC Cinema Department, had arrived in New York City armed with Margo's phone number and taken her to dinner. Margo was dating a new guy and considering a return to the church, she had even begun attending mass. She confessed that she wasn't passionately in love, but that Roger respected her and accepted her new approach to romance: No sex before marriage. She was getting serious.

Joan wrote that she was living out on Long Island and had enrolled in a nursing aide program. She had been getting together with Margo and had dined with Margo and Brandon in a Lebanese restaurant.

Brandon's letter repeated the aforementioned news and provided a lengthy rundown of our mutual friends. He had been a popular fixture in the Cinema Department, considered one of the rare talents. When he had reported for army duty in New York, he looked me up, and since then we had carried on a steady correspondence. His letters were breathlessly long, filled with intricate and perceptive thoughts, cleverly written, and maddeningly impersonal.

I set about composing a response to Brandon, an informative, stimulating, true letter he couldn't resist. The letter praised the French philosophers Voltaire, Montesquieu, Sartre, and Rousseau and the literary beak-through of the expatriate Beat Generation writer like F.

Scott Fitzgerald, Ernest Hemingway, Ezra Pound, and Sherwood Anderson. I described a book I had just read by Jack Kerouac called *On the Road* and the drug-crazed life of the Columbia University dropouts William Burroughs, Alan Ginsberg, and Jack Kerouac, who were uprooting literature, family, morals, throwing out *everything*. I commented how, following the code of the Eisenhower Doctrine, the U.S. marines had recently landed on the beaches of Lebanon to repulse communist influence throughout the world. The letter closed with:

> *So now we are heading into the sixties and where do we go from here? Rejection of all I have ever known has driven me thus far, and nothing has emerged—communism, capitalism, fascism, dictatorship, religion—that seems to bring harmony to the chaotic world.*

Abdul wrote he missed me. I laughed at his description of driving down Santa Monica Boulevard in his second-hand Oldsmobile convertible with an Iranian girl. He hastened to emphasize that I was his best friend and could not be replaced. He was enraptured with his recent visit to New York, when Margo and her new cute blonde roommate showed him around Greenwich Village and treated him to an evening at Aldo's restaurant.

Letter from my parents: Don't travel alone! Letter from a German boy from USC: he would be in New York the following May. Letter from Chester with long tales of his scriptwriting experiences in the jungles of Venezuela.

I opened Margo's latest letter. When was I returning? She sincerely believed that I belonged at home, where I was loved, and that my meanderings and scattered, blown-in-the-wind leaps from one thing to the next were leading nowhere. She was convinced my restlessness resided within and couldn't be alleviated by roaming the world or hopping from job to job.

I lay on the bed a long time, staring at the bare wall beyond the lamp. A sprinkling of lights gleamed outside the window. My palms were warm,

Part 3
Western Venture

Chapter 1   California Revisited

The phone rang in Mary Stockemer's apartment. Mary's voice floated down the hall. Putting down my book, I got off the bed and strode along the familiar oak flooring, past Mary's painting of the Madonna standing on a barren hilltop, shoulders braced against the wind, and into the kitchen where I had eaten so many meals. It seemed decades since I'd lived with Mary as a student at the University of Southern California, a bare three years ago. Little had changed.

I picked up the receiver. The minute she spoke I recognized the voice of Allison Kranz. I'd met Allison during my senior year at USC at an on-campus show of her water color paintings. Besides an interest in the creative arts, we shared a passionate desire to travel and had talked of sharing an apartment in New York City after she completed her graduate degree in fine arts.

"Judy! You're back in town! How wonderful. I got your message. I want to get together. But first I must tell you the latest. It involves you." Her grandmother, she explained, had died and the beach house where she'd lived for forty years in Santa Monica was standing idle. It was small but full of old-time charm, a few steps from the beach. Would I be interested in spending the summer with her there until the will was probated? Her parents wanted the house occupied.

"What do you think? It would cost very little and we would make our own meals and have our own bedrooms. I can paint and you can write, we'll get on famously."

The proposal couldn't have appealed to me more. "Not a bad idea," I agreed. "Given that I'm as free as a bird right now."

The stretch I'd lived in Florida with Barbara and Reba had uncovered sharp incompatibilities between us, and Tampa proved to be a dead-end town shadowed by Mafia types. Although I found a job with the local TV station splicing serials—*Sea Hunt* with Lloyd Bridges was my favorite— the work soon became routine, then unbearably dull. After four months, I gave up and caught a Greyhound bus to Los Angeles.

My former roommate, Mary, welcomed me warmly to the apartment on Adams Boulevard. Her roommate was gone for the summer, and to my great luck, the third occupant had recently graduated and returned to San Diego. I moved back into my old room.

I wasn't sure of my next move. Dad's checks allowed me time to get my career on track and maybe in Los Angeles, the film capital of the western film industry, I could find a niche in film work. Mary was continually occupied with painting classes under Sister Corita and her job as art teacher in a Catholic secondary school. Without a car I often found myself alone in the apartment left to my own devices.

Allison's invitation was just the ticket. A summer on the beach, where I could write in the supportive company of a fellow artist and investigate employment in Los Angeles. I was exhilarated—here was a place where things happened.

I was invited to Allison's parents' large home in Pacific Palisades. Over dinner we discussed the allure of France, the challenges of travel abroad, and the French underground movement that smuggled Jews out of Germany during the Second World War. Mrs. Kranz raved about the

Chaim Soutine exhibit she'd seen on her recent visit to the New York Metropolitan Museum of Art and his brilliant expressionist paintings.

Allison and I smiled at each other over the chocolate pie. The house by the ocean needed tenants and Allison's parents' gave their willing support. We would do it!

By the end of the month I had settled with my two suitcases, typewriter, and clothes iron in Grandma's beach house at 124 Frazer Avenue in Santa Monica. The house was set in a tight row of beach houses dating from the turn of the century. The quiet street was modest and unassuming. Pots of pots of red geraniums lined the front stoops. It was a short walk to the local grocery and Henshey's department store downtown. In the opposite direction, across the sandy beach and to the south, the Ocean Park Pier extended a pathway to the ocean.

Allison and I converted the two small bedrooms—one off the living room, one in back behind the kitchen—to sleeping studios. We removed the white lace table streamers, doilies, and China shepherd boys and set up easels and writing desks. Allison hung her charcoal drawings and oils in the living room, and I set a book of Henri Cartier-Bresson black-and-white photographs on the coffee table. We stuffed books on every shelf. The blonde wood tables, the couch upholstered with bulbous purple flowers, and the ivory lace curtains we kept—the taste of earlier times had its own charm.

Allison was bursting with ideas. It was her first venture away from home, and she formed a hundred projects. We decorated the house with a rich Tiffany lamp with woven pull strings and several carved bronze pots uncovered at neighborhood estate sales. When Allison's car wasn't parked in front of the house she was most likely attending classes at the University, visiting her parents, or off somewhere with her boyfriend Jack. When she was home we often worked silently in our own sections of the house, she at her easel, me propped in an armchair by the window with a legal pad and pencil.

Beach house in Santa Monica, California
(4th house on left)

At last Allison was experiencing the independence she craved. She bobbed around the house, upbeat and chatty. When pushed, however, she showed a will of steel and fought to the bone to guard her newly acquired autonomy. Returning from bouts with her boyfriend, she flung herself on the couch and in a quavering voice confided her determination not to be pressured. Jack was angling for marriage, but she was resisting. Visions of the free life, of a year on her own in NYC, were pulling at her very soul. She was determined to keep her options open.

†

I lay stretched in a canvas chair, peering at the purple bougainvillea vines spread across the latticed patio walls. The sun's rays were timid, hinting of coolness, whipped by the ocean breeze a half a block away, unlike the Spanish fireball in Málaga.

As I closed my eyes, thoughts of Jean Paul rose in my mind. He had filled my dreams during the Atlantic crossing to New York and through the clouds to Tampa. I had left Paris without a word, which had left me with an uneasy feeling of guilt, along with a tinge of triumph. I imagined that disappearing without a word would color me with an aura of mystery, would lend me the upper hand—let him worry, let him suffer. Then maybe he'd miss me. Oh, the foibles of youth! I finally wrote to him explaining my travels in vague terms and assuring him that Paris hadn't seen the last of me. His reply was polite, nonchalant. I sensed his image already disappearing behind the smoke from my cigarette that drifted up past the bougainvillea vines.

Soon after Allison and I settled in, Abdul, just finishing his studies at USC, picked me up at the beach house. We drove to Malibu in his yellow convertible and dined at a seafood lounge perched on a mountain of rocks tumbling down to the beach. I could talk of nothing but Paris.

"The French are suburb conversationalists; they track world events; they appreciate the nuances of good food and wine; they attend to the smallest details of décor with artistic flair; they indulge in pleasure without guilt; they know how to balance—am I boring you with all this?"

"Not at all! Nothing you say is boring." Abdul poked a fork gingerly into his lobster tail. "I am planning a trip to France myself in the fall with Suhail. I agree with you in everything."

"You always do."

"I love to hear all your travels. All the time you bounce around like a rubber ball, I can't keep up. I applaud you. But I wish you did not disappear so often."

"There are plenty of pretty girls in California. Haven't you found one to tempt you yet?"

"No one like you. Do not worry, I know you hate to feel pressure. You have said you fear marriage and to be in love and I feel the same. I am also cautious, and so we can be friends, yes, that is good? And I'm going to teach you one or two simple words in Arabic. You must start to learn." I smiled and told him I would learn Hello, Which Way to the Airport, and Please Don't Kiss me. As we drove back to the beach house I added Don't Mind if I Do.

Before leaving for a summer vacation in New York, Abdul called. "Who knows where we'll meet again?"

"Who am I going to discuss Mideast politics with?" I complained.

"Me! I'll keep in touch." And he was gone.

Allison and I drew up invitation lists for a housewarming party. I had four names on my list, Allison had sixty-six. The sight of my paltry list made me feel bereft, but I reflected that it didn't really matter. I was used to only one or two close friends at a time, so actually four was a lot. The four consisted of my USC pal Joel Horowitz, who had moved to nearby Manhattan Beach; a fellow film student Brandon, who would be in town on a three-week furlough from Fort Bliss army base near El Paso; my former roommate, Mary Stockemer; and my traveling playmate from Spain, Roz Pence, who now lived in Santa Monica.

I don't recall much about the party. I spent most of the evening shooting rolls of Tri-X film with the Leica I'd purchased in Germany, anxiously keeping an eye pealed for Brandon. Since he started writing, I doted on his letters, flattered that he sought me out. It was only when the clock struck one and most of the guests had left that I finally saw him. I'd about given up—his plane was due in that same evening—when I heard footsteps descending the basement stairs and emerging onto the patio and there he was.

"Just made it," he said and lowered himself in the chair next to me. "I drove straight from the airport." The night was warm, and a soft July moon beamed sparkles of light over the pink patio tiles and purple bougainvillea flowers covering the walls.

"Did you see Joel on the stairs?" I inquired. "He just left."

"I must have missed him. There are only four people upstairs. Why are you sitting here alone?" Brandon's low voice melted against my face.

"The party's over, that's why. But the best part is the downtime afterwards, and you're here for that." Brandon smiled, glanced down and swirled the copper liquid in his glass. The creak of isolated footsteps, distant strains from the Ocean Park amusement park, and the moan of the ocean beyond the housetops sounded in the summer night air.

Brandon hadn't changed. I gazed at the head of dark hair, the deep brown eyes, the sweet curve of the full mouth, and the casual way he reclined in his chair, one hand in his pocket. It was easy to see why the girls at school had been fascinated by him. We sat in the shadows, illuminated only by the thin light from the upstairs kitchen window, the low moon, and the flickering rays escaping from the nearby streets.

After routine inquiries about the plane trip and the unfortunate delays, I tried to think of what to say. For some reason I had become tongue-tied. I searched for a topic.

"Brandon, give me your take on the Vietnam War. You wrote that you worked on the Nike missile system in the army. Explain to me how the missiles will be used."

Brandon rubbed his hand along the back of his head. "Well, these are ground-to-air weapons, as you know. Each is 40 feet long and costs about a hundred grand. Soldiers from the NATO countries are stationed in Texas for a year to learn how to deploy the missiles. It's a pity these foreign soldiers have to learn at Bliss because they get a distorted view of our country's sense of justice—they see 35 thousand Mexicans cross over from Juarez every day to work in El Paso at starvation wages and return to one of Mexico's largest cities with dimes in their pockets."

I nodded in sympathy. As he talked, I watched the way the light played around his mouth and thought I detected a haunted look hovering in his eyes. But I couldn't be sure, about this or about anything. It was too hard to counter the daunting effect of his glaring good looks. I could discern only the strains of carnival music from the amusement park in the distance, the pulse of life gently pushing into the hushed, tentative little patio.

Santa Monica Pier

The next day was warm, the sky a sheer cloudless blue. Brandon parked his Volkswagen in front of the house and we walked to the beachfront and strolled aimlessly along the narrow street. It was barely more than an alley, flanked on either side by two-story wooden buildings decorated with scalloped roof tiles, gold gingerbread overhangs, and intricate carved door frames. At the lower level, row after row of shops selling foreign crafts, knick-knacks, and Mexican and Chinese food. Throngs of people passed by, going in and out of doorways, and we could smell the tangy odor of Italian tomato sauce seeping from restaurant doors. Brandon sauntered easily next to me, hands in his trouser pockets, head lowered slightly.

"You up for a beer?" I asked as we left a curio shop and brushed past a couple with double-decker ice cream cones. He was. I led the way to the Venice Café, a discovery I'd made soon after my arrival. I wanted him to see this bohemian hangout. Inside, the room was dark, with a line of dim windows stretched along one side, fronted by tables. The bartender, in a black turtleneck, sat on a stool behind the counter reading a magazine. Two men across the room, their faces hidden behind scruffy beards, were leaning over a chessboard, flicking their ashes into pewter cups piled with cigarette butts. Another table was occupied by a thin man feeding sheets into a typewriter, a dry half-eaten sandwich sitting on a plate next to him.

"What do you think of this place?" I asked as we sat at a wooden table sipping beers. During our student days at the Cinema Department, Brandon had been an elusive figure hovering in the background, all work, bent over a Motorola or marching through the patio with cameras strapped to his back. After graduation he had looked me up in New York. Now here he was in real life, and I realized I knew little about him. He seemed confident, shy, somewhat rigid. I thought his well-to-do family and conventional upbringing must have buffered him from the rebellious currents gaining steam in 1959 and I set out to impress him with my daring non-conventionality.

He looked around. "This is great. I relate to all this. A counterbalance to all the restrictions I'm trying to break out of," he said earnestly, as if reading my thoughts. I swelled with pleasure. So we had this in common. Maybe that's why he was drawn to me: I was attempting to break ground, find a different path.

Secretly, I hoped to project myself as an independent rebel who knew where it was at. Someone to chart the way. In reality, I was searching, had thrown myself out there and was waiting for answers. I knew nothing. But Brandon had never strayed far from home. Maybe he was reaching outside his staid existence into the outer bounds where he believed I existed. And where I did indeed exist, for all the good it did me.

Up until now I had thought of Brandon as a casual correspondent, but his presence raised me to an alertness I hadn't felt before. I was aware of his handsome profile and the sonorous lull of his voice. Here I was sitting beside a young man who for some reason was seeking my company. And whose expectations I had to find a way to live up to.

We ordered more drafts. "I'd like to read one of your poems," he said with an imploring look. Although I was scratching out poems every morning in my room, no one had read them. I had no idea if they had worth. Besides, I was running out of things to write about—I'd exhausted all the universal wisdom I could come up with.

"I'll select something for you to read," I promised. Maybe I could find a poem that was so elusive he wouldn't notice if it were empty of real insight.

"Deal."

†

Not long after I moved into the beach house, Dad flew into town for a series of business meetings and treated Allison and me to dinner at a five-star restaurant. We undertook to provide him with the time of his life. We arranged to attend a performance of Mort Sahl, the political satirist, a luminary among the growing anti-war activists and university students in California.

"You've never seen anyone like him, Dad. His satirical comedy is all the rage. He debunks politicians and zeros in on blunders so fast you can hardly follow him."

"I don't mind zeroing in on blunders as long as they're not my own," Dad said. Relaxing with gimlets in the muted atmosphere of the restaurant, he was in a playful mood.

"Mort's performing tonight at the NoName Theatre. I know just where it is; I'll drive us," offered Allison, tossing her mane of red hair and smiling a thin-lipped, little-girl smile. Allison could charm with her serene air and puppy-friendly manner. Her moods varied from serious to animated, compliant to bossy. Her many sides were still presenting themselves as I got to know her. Now she was in her good-girl mode.

"Sounds fine," agreed Dad. "You girls take over; I'll follow your lead." I knew the show would be a stretch for Dad, but I wanted to bring him into my world, to show him the esoteric, to impress him with the latest far-out trends. With two university-type California girls on his hands, what else could he expect?

Dad seemed to be enjoying himself. He sat in the back seat of Allison's powder blue convertible, his thin ring of hair exposed to the wind, fedora hat in his lap. I turned to see his face bathed in freeway wind. "Not too blowy?" I shouted.

"No, just messing up my hairdo. I can handle it," he quipped. The thin border curving around the back of his head was all that remained of his youthful head of hair. He was self-consciousness about his baldness, but I thought he looked handsome. Photographs of him as a boy showed him looking stiff and sober, with pressed lips, as if he had just emerged from the woodshed. Quite different from the self-possession and wisdom that now characterized his expression.

Allison whipped the car neatly into the parking lot and the three of us made our way to one of the tables ringing the stage. The club was jammed with young people smoking and ordering drinks. Mort Sahl finally sauntered out in a grey pullover sweater, open-throated shirt, and flannel slacks. A crop of black curly hair surrounded a thin face that looked wound up and intelligent. He was holding a folded newspaper in one hand, the other thrust into his pocket, the picture of casual nonchalance ready to leap.

"So, folks, here we are!" And he was off on a non-stop monologue that I had to brace up to follow. Within the first two minutes he mentioned Dwight Eisenhower, Richard Nixon, Adlai Stevenson, Allen Dulles, and Curtis Lemay. He delivered his chatty barroom banter with hardly a pause. The jokes were slipped in between news reports without warning, but the audience was right there, howling appreciatively, missing nothing.

"Vice-president Nixon has been on the cover of all these magazines like *Life* and *Time* and *U.S. World* and all those, with the exception of

True, which tells you something, doesn't it?" Roars of laughter. He went on in his nasal voice without a breath. "I was in Washington recently, you know, trying to find out what's going on—well someone must know, right?—and all the bigwigs seemed to be on the other side of the globe, making the world a better place I guess—well they *do* try, right?—and you know what they say about our leaders, they wouldn't be in Washington if they didn't know what was right—and they're not there!" I heard Allison's refined laugh and glanced over at Dad, who was dutifully watching the stage and smiling.

Mort threw in some personal stories. "So there we were, a bunch of guys in an Asian country, yeah, you guessed it,"—a snippet of laugher from the audience—"Well, you know what's coming, a bunch of hearty guys and we grabbed a cab and asked the guy where's the real action and the cabbie took us to a place where they fish illegally. Well," interrupting the laughter, "you know how that goes! And Korea! Well that's where I served and the college kids didn't want to be there. We were given propaganda like 'This little coffee-can bomb will blow up a city' and 'You call it colonialism, but we call it building roads and schools.' The audience was riveted.

Billed as an iconoclast, Mort termed himself a radical, not a liberal. "The liberals," he declared, "feel unworthy of their possessions, while the conservatives feel they deserve everything they've stolen." And later: "Three vets robbed the Bank of America the other day, which is a reversal of the social order as we know it. Well, you know how that goes!"

I glanced towards Dad to see how he taking all this. His face behind the circulating smoke was sober. He didn't laugh once, not even when the audience was hooting and clapping. To young people, searching to uncover injustice and cut into the hypocrisies of the day was as normal as breathing. I didn't usually think in terms of Republican or Democrat— comedy aimed to expose cover-ups in every direction. But with Dad sitting next to me, I squirmed as Mort dammed the conservatives, slammed them into the ground, perpetrators of all wrongs.

Maybe this show wasn't such a good idea.

"Mort has his loyal fans," I noted as we walked into the warm evening air. "They certainly appreciated his political jokes."

"That they did," Dad agreed.

"I suppose," I remarked, "some of Mort's ideas are a bit extreme."

"Never mind," said Dad with studied patience. "He was clever, I'd admit that. I didn't agree with everything but, hey, that's nothing new, is it my oldest daughter?" We laughed. I was relieved at his parental tolerance.

"They say misfits, rebels, and dreamers head west and remain in California because they can't go any farther," I remarked when we were in the car. "They seek change and are exposed to extremes that thrive here—like communism." Dad and I had differed on this topic in the past. "Some of them become radicalized."

"Communism has to be contained," Dad said. "The Soviet goal is the destruction of capitalism. Is that what these young people want?"

"No, but the United States uses this threat to promote its own interests, under the guise of saving the world from communism *at any cost*. Look at Vietnam. Why are our soldiers there?" I asked. "They say it's to prevent the spread of communism, but what we're really after is to strengthen our influence in the region and maintain access to the oil."

"I don't believe that's the case. We have to protect Western interests, the first of which is to prevent the communists from taking over the Middle East and next the entire world."

"That's what they say of *us*."

We let the subject rest there, as we did after every such discussion, each harboring the faint hope that the other had learned something. Little did either of us realize in 1959 how large a part the Vietnam War would play in thrusting our country into one of America's most turbulent decades. It would be five years before Bob Dylan put the march of the sixties into words that swept the country: *The Times They Are A-Changin'*.

Chapter 2   The Almost Boyfriend

Brandon stopped by almost every day. We visited Joel at his Manhattan Beach house, drank lemonade punch on the back patio with Allison and her boyfriend, and when the temperature mounted to 90 degrees we spread ourselves out on the beach on towels and lounged away the afternoons. Brandon would arrive in dark brown swim trunks showing a bronzed torso, a long gold-and-red-striped beach towel hanging loosely around his neck, and lean jauntily against the kitchen door, a smile hovering on his mouth, looking like a Mediterranean movie star or an ad for bronzing oil. I was so struck by this apparition I couldn't move.

In fact, I was becoming generally uneasy. After months of letter writing, with discursions on every topic imaginable, we seemed to be stymied. I had the horrible thought that we'd said everything there was to say. What was to sustain us, now that the momentum of catching up on our lives had run its course? Neither of us was prone to small talk, but we'd never lacked larger issues. Somehow my mind had gone inert.

Joel and Brandon

One evening he drove me to his parents' house in Pacific Palisades for dinner. They treated me graciously, listening with interest to my background and tales of what I had been doing. Brandon sat next to me with an expression of neutrality. I came away with the impression they found me and my solid Midwest background acceptable, despite their Catholic faith and my lack of it. Brandon's older brother sat at one end of the table, throwing in spontaneous remarks with an air of brazen confidence. I learned he had a mean streak and treated Brandon with disdain. On the way home, Brandon described himself as the black sheep of the family—that sounded familiar! I hoped he would tell me about his childhood, but he resisted efforts to probe the past. His letters had been filled with insight and compassion about our mutual friends and their personal struggles, but about himself he kept a close guard.

When we returned to the beach house it was still early. I invited Brandon in. We sat on the couch, too tired for another drink, letting the quiet of the evening fall over us. Allison as usual was out with her boyfriend. I tried to think of a way to enliven the atmosphere, but could only peer nervously down at my hands, unable to fabricate a single communicable thought. Several times I'd repressed the urge to reach out and touch him, but now that he hovered so near my courage failed. How was I to handle his mesmerizing presence? Why did my confidence shrivel and pull me down with it?

Finally, prodded by the stillness of the room, I looked directly at him, and, at that, his arm slipped gently around my waist and he slid towards me, drawing me closer. In an instant his mouth was pressing on mine, insistent, and for a moment I melted into his body, dazed by the softness of his lips and the earthy scent of him. The urge to let myself fall into the warmth of his arms almost overcame the reluctance assailing the inner reaches of my mind.

Abruptly the whirring sound of a passing car drew me up and I wrenched myself from his grasp and stood up unsteadily. Slowly he stood up next to me, his face hidden in the shadows. Neither of us spoke. The next thing I knew he was gone.

I stood by the door in a swarm of confusion, listening to the hum of his BMW fading into the distance. My stomach was curled in a ball of steel. What was missing, what was needed to allow me to accept his embrace?

The night resumed its silence and I my feeling of helplessness.

Throughout the next day I pondered. Brandon always remained so distant. Why couldn't he break through and reveal who he was to me? Didn't he seek intimacy too? Maybe he just needed a companion, stranded as he was in the isolation of army life, and I was there.

It occurred to me that *I* was the one not revealing who I really was, who couldn't break beyond the surface presentation I relied on to get by. But how could I act otherwise? Who wants to hear the sordid details of my inner life, and how could I dare to expose those feelings to someone whose good opinion and attachment I sought? And who was Brandon under all his dash? Did he care about me? He had expected a sophisticated, high-brow adventurer; he wouldn't be satisfied with only me. To reveal myself was impossible.

Yet—it was all I had to offer.

Brandon called. Time was running out; in four days he would be returning to the base. "It's a hot day," he said. "Let's go to the beach." By the time we arrived, the beach was scattered with bathers spread out on oversized towels and roaming bare-footed along the lip of the shore. After a refreshing dip in the ocean, we flung ourselves down on towels beside a green- and white-striped beach umbrella. A bag of biscotti's and a cooler containing a six-pack lay in the sand between us.

"Sun sure is bright," I began as we lay with closed eyes, sun beating into our bodies. I was determined to get through to him, to break the impasse that hung like a specter between us.

"Umm." His eyes remained closed.

"I wonder if I'll find a film job this summer."

"Never can tell."

"I haven't even had a nibble. It's hopeless. The USC placement office has nothing. I have no contacts, no experience or completed projects to submit. The guys in the Cinema Department with published film credits and inside contacts are finding good jobs. They know filmmakers and instructors who will vouch for their work."

"I'll be looking for a scriptwriter job when I get out of the service. We all go through it," Brandon mumbled.

"Ah, but at least you have impressive film and playwriting awards."

"That doesn't guarantee anything." Brandon's mellow voice flowed lazily across the sand.

I took a deep breath and continued, "I'm twenty-five and I'm nowhere, of no more value than when I was back living with my parents. I thought I'd blasted through the past, moved on to something new, but maybe it was all bluster and novelty. What have I got to show for it all?" Brandon pulled a towel over his face as the sun shifted. "I have nothing. To tell the truth, I feel like such a failure. Sometimes it's hard to get out of bed in the morning." How depressing this must be to him!

Brandon lay unmoving. "I can understand that," he mumbled from under the towel. "I have all these props and I still feel like an outsider." His voice melted away.

Author at Santa Monica Beach

I sucked in a deep breath, determined to keep going, to let him know something about who I really was. "You don't know what it's like to be disliked by your family," I said. I went on to describe the unrelenting rejection by my mother and our life-long antagonism, as well as the trials of high school, the words tumbling over each other. I even described the devastating breakup with my soulmate Sylvia, the girl I had shared apartment life with at USC, an idolized union that I had swept my entire hopes and future into. I had not revealed this defeat to anyone until now or acknowledged even to myself the devastating loss that followed our rupture.

145

I stopped. It was too late to take the words back.

Brandon reached out and pried a beer from the cooler. "Ah, that's nice and cold," he sighed. I glanced at the outline of his stretched-out body and striped swim trunks from the corner of my eye. Finally he spoke. "I guess it's been hard for you. I'm sorry." He paused, as if searching for more to say.

I had to finish what I'd plunged into. "No job has satisfied me. I'm not finding work in L.A. And I go through people, they come and go—it gets lonely. I sometime feel I am drifting among the clouds with nowhere to land. Sometimes I feel lost." I felt as if I were falling off a cliff.

Brandon nodded under the towel and groped for a pair of sunglasses that were lying at his side. The bronzing oil on his arms simmered under the rays of the sun.

I pulled myself from the chair and started running down the beach. "Got to get some exercise," I shouted over my shoulder

I lay in bed that night, enclosed in the whiteness of my little room, reliving the dreadful speech I'd coughed up like a school girl. What a miscalculation! Shame mixed with panic gathered in the pit of my stomach. Brandon must have been repulsed at my sordid confessions, must think me an utter fool. Possibly he wouldn't want to see me again. What could I have been thinking?

It was Brandon's last night. Early tomorrow his parents would drive him to the airport for the return to Fort Bliss. We were alone in the beach house. Brandon was seated on the edge of the couch, arms leaning against his knees, while I sat in a slip-covered easy chair under an orange table lamp, hemming a peach-colored skirt. As I wound the needle back and forth, I glanced at his face now and then for clues, hoping to discover his thinking, but found nothing except his usual expression of gentle neutrality. A feeling of defeat enclosed me.

We had spoken little all evening as we wandered through the grounds of Pacific Ocean Park munching tacos. Now Brandon was staring at the throw rug in front of him. Suddenly he looked up and fixed his eyes on me. My fingers flickered in and out, becoming the only reality in the room. I bent my head down, concentrating on each stitch to keep myself from floating up to the ceiling.

Finally, I looked up. Brandon was standing, hands hanging at his side, gazing at the yellow-orange glow from the lamp covering my lap.

"Speak to me!" finally emerged from his lips in a hoarse cry. He looked torn, uncertain, even, for a split second I imagined, abandoned. But all that remained of me was a guarded smile as I glanced up at him. I wanted him to go. My capacity to rebound was exhausted; I needed to slip away before I drowned.

He looked at me crouched in the chair. Finally, without a word, he turned and walked out the door. Only a powdery "good-bye" floated up the steps after him and into the circle of orange light.

Chapter 3　　Friends and Stories

It was over. Like a rocket my romance with Brandon had shot off into the spheres, a sparkling star blinking in the firmament, totally out of reach. Just as well, I told myself as I sat at a bare kitchen table gazing out the window. Brandon had proved utterly impossible. Besides, the uncertainty between us was unsustainable.

"What are you so pensive about?" inquired Allison, walking into the kitchen with a blue overnight case. "You always seem to be peering out the window."

"Just daydreaming." All she knew was that Brandon and I had been seeing each other casually, just hanging out I told her. Preoccupied with her boyfriend and their network of couples, she hadn't been around much. I wouldn't have known how to explain anyway—how to express our fragmented relationship or put words to feelings I could barely sort out myself?

"Has Brandon left yet? How's that going?"

"Five days ago. Who knows? Nothing happened." I was a coward. Not for anything would I have confessed the bumbling roller-coaster of those three weeks.

To my relief the phone rang. It was Joel, inviting me to a party. "Yes, I'll go!" It would be good to mingle with the cinema crowd again, to let memories of Brandon fade away into the far-off reaches of Texas.

The following Saturday Joel and I arrived at the appointed summer house and made our way to the back patio that faced the beach. A number of students from the Cinema Department, mostly old timers who had graduated or remained working on advanced film projects, lounged in striped beach chairs spread over the sand. People emerged dripping from the ocean, bodies glistening in the sunshine, and flopped down in the sand. A long table was spread with bean and guacamole dips, and the spicy odor of tarragon chicken roasting on a barbeque spit filled the air. Joel and I stretched out on beach chairs, beers in one hand, paper cups of beer nuts in the other.

"Joel, what have you been up to?" someone asked.

"I've been scabbing in Hollywood. I'm not crazy about cutting pictures, but it helps make ends meet. I'm trying to avoid this evil business agent who is intent on smoking me out for not being in the union. I guess he's got his job, but then I have mine too."

A fellow with curly black hair spoke up from lounge chair where he reclined in his damp swim suit, legs crossed. "Jim Ivory is in Europe shooting a documentary on Indian miniatures called *The Sword and the Flute*," he told us. Comments on Jim's work in the Cinema Department circled the group: it was well-known that our fellow student with his talent, ambition, and family funds would go far.

"Kent is still hard at work on *The Exiles*," put in a boy wearing a yellow straw hat. Kent Mackenzie was gaining a reputation for his naturalistic, black-and-white approach to filmmaking. After the success of his film *Bunker Hill*, which documented the plight of the Indians when their homes were threatened by commercial development, he finally obtained funding for *The Exiles*.

This documentary depicted the destitute existence of the American Indians living in the Bunker Hill section of Los Angeles. Kent threw his savings, his house equity, and his soul into this project. A crew of USC students worked on the film unpaid, at times around the clock. Many of us helped out; I pitched in as go-fer. Little did we know that within three years *The Exiles* would be shown at festivals in Venice, Edinburgh, Mannheim, London, and San Francisco to enthusiastic reviews.

After dinner, when the red streaks of sun had slipped out of sight and darkness reduced the beach to a shadowy glow, everyone refreshed their drinks and congregated around the bonfire. At one side, his figure illuminated by the flickering fire, a tall boy with thick blond hair falling over his forehead perched on a wicker stool and described his latest film assignment. We were all familiar with the stories of Villis Lapeniek, a former cinema graduate student from Latvia who worked for Walt Disney Productions.

"I was the head gaffer," he began, "on this film about the animal behavior in the North Country." He flashed a wide smile. "The animals were collected and caged in stacks, ready for their turn in the limelight. The first shot required two raccoons. You wouldn't believe the size of these two guys. The biggest specimens I have ever beheld. So what they did," with lowered voice, "they jabbed them with wooden sticks, carved at the end into points. They'd been starved until shooting started so they'd be good and ornery. The coons hated those sticks sticking into their sides, growled and swiped at them with their sharp claws." The hand holding his drink waved in the air dramatically, reflecting arrows of light from the fire. "When the two raccoons were worked up enough to attack a lamp post, they were put in a clearing—fenced, you understand—facing each other. All it took was a single jab to the ribs and the fight began. The cameras recorded it to the end." He paused and took a gulp of scotch.

"If the take was successful they were separated with pails of water and returned to the pens. And sometimes released to the wild. I'll bet some innocent raccoon out there got a licking and never figured out why!" He laughed cynically. "Of course, sometimes during these fights one or both of the animals gets killed." Everyone was quiet and the few strands of automatic laughter died out. It was not a pretty picture.

Villis went on. "Then there were the beavers. For one scene, the director requires a shot of a beaver sliding down the falls, a daredevil fall that the beaver miraculously survives. Great drama. So the beaver is placed in a long steel tube with a cover over the lower hole and a plunger at the top hole. At the director's signal the lower cover is removed, the plunger pressed down, and the cameras roll as the beaver drops into the water. It required thirteen takes to get it right. Unfortunately two of the beavers had their backs broken by the plungers. They had to be destroyed." Some of the listeners groaned and shook their heads.

"You can't believe the outlandish things filmmakers will undertake to get their shots," Villis added. "There's no way to protest and keep your job. But they make great dinner stories." We stared at the diminishing flames until the host walked over and threw more logs on the fire. The flames surged up ferociously into the night air.

Pacific Ocean Park, Santa Monica, the Fifties

I was overjoyed that Roz Pence, my fellow gad-about in Europe in 1958, had returned to California from Majorca and taken a well-paying job as a mechanic with Douglas Aircraft in Santa Monica. Her boss at Douglas admired the diplomatic way she was able to influence her co-workers and humored her insistence on being treated on an equal basis with her male counterparts. At first he'd had reservations: this girl was too outspoken, too sure of herself, too tall. But he liked her sharp mind and lively sense of humor and invited her to his home for dinner with his wife.

The night of our house-warming party she had walked into the beach house looking tall and elegant. We sat in a corner and exchanged stories of our escapades the previous year in Spain.

"Carmen was such a card. Did you see him again?"

"He got lost in the shuffle."

"Roz, that French boyfriend of yours was a doll. Too bad he didn't speak a word of English. How did you manage?"

"We didn't talk."

"Did you ever make up your mind about Frans Pannekoeken?"

"No go; he smothered me in syrup."

"Where can we get some Pernod?"

"I'm afraid we'll have to rely on Black Russians."

"Judy, you must come to my house this weekend. I have plans."

Roz's apartment was located in the nearby hills. She took to stopping at the beach house after work and we strolled the waterfront streets, dined on Ma Po Tofu, and attended parties thrown by her young co-workers at Douglas.

Sometimes she showed up with her current boyfriend Ralph, a slight fellow with the infectious grin of a teenager and ears that arched away from his face. He clearly adored Roz. It didn't bother him in the slightest that at six feet she was two inches taller than him.

Ralph was a cut-up with a tendency to get into crazy scrapes, after which he would come running to Roz for refuge. She suffered his erratic behavior with begrudging patience. Once he showed up at three a.m. on her doorstep, staggering from a bar brawl and covered with deep cuts over both arms. He bled on her white terry cloth robe while Roz sat over him with a wash basin. She harbored a soft spot for him and couldn't resist taking him in her arms, all the while issuing a tender chaffing.

Author with new Leica M3

Roz Pence at the Beach House

One afternoon when the air was warm and scented with sweet July flowers, Roz arrived to fetch me at the beach house. Calling hello to Allison, who was working at her easel in the back room, she passed into the kitchen where I stood at the window sill arranging two blue delphiniums for a still life shot. After we had snacked on ripe mangos, I pulled the Leica over my shoulder and we ambled along the narrow road towards Pacific Ocean Park. The ocean stretched lazily at our side and in the distance the Santa Monica Mountains dominated the northern sky. Beyond the six-legged arch entrance of the amusement park, the tip of the Ferris wheel whirled, and we could hear the seals bawling, the loud splashing of the whales, and the clang of the diving bell. When we reached the end of the Ocean Park pier, we leaned on the railing and breathed in the salty odor of brine. Our desultory comments coiled in the wind.

"Dolores sends you greetings from Málaga. She is getting married," said Roz,

"Why would she want to do that?" The idea of marriage remained far from my thoughts. There was too much in the world to explore—to learn—and maybe find some answers.

"That tall boy with the green flannel shirt at the party really likes you." The waves sloshed lazily against the piles below.

"He's cute," was all I said.

"You're much too shy. I think he's intimidated by you."

I shook my head in disbelief.

"Roz, your job at Douglas pays well. Why don't you get an apartment on the ocean?" Lifting the Leica, I caught a shot of Roz, hand pressed against her violet blouse.

"Judy, Judy, Judy, you must sell your photos and make some money. There's a job that doesn't tie you down." With a screech a brown pelican landed on the far end of the railing and fluttered its wings.

"Roz, with you there's never a dull moment."

"You don't let the grass grow under your feet yourself."

As the afternoon advanced, we left Venice and strolled up the coast to Muscle Beach, where young men with bulging shoulders glistened in citrine bikini trunks. They balanced barbells, swung on high bars, and painstakingly lifted bar weights the size of pyramid blocks over their

154

heads, faces intent and sweating. They were uniformly sleek, smooth-skinned, and tanned, with golden chests and limbs. Nearby more torsos, oiled and brown, were energetically leaping on either side of a volleyball court.

Pacific Ocean Park, Santa Monica 1959

"That one has nice prats," Roz whispered. "That one has oversized biceps," I nodded, not knowing what a prat was. Some of the men, we agreed, had gone too far, were bulging with outsized arm or shoulder muscles way too large for their bodies. They evidently thought there was no such thing as too big.

We wandered off to locate whiskey sours.

†

I decided my situation would be improved significantly by a visit to a physician. Consulting the yellow pages, I set up an appointment with a Dr. Ramsey and confided my problem. I wanted a breast enhancement. Too much insecurity regarding the opposite sex revolved around the fact that I had smaller breasts than any other girl alive. This was one area of inadequacy, among the hundreds, that I could do something about. I would go for it!

Lucky men didn't have to worry about this sort of thing. There were no photos of naked men or cheesecake calendars of male torsos lining work garage walls, and consumer ads didn't flash robust penises from billboards and magazines. For me, the loom of intimacy as a boy moved in close suggested new areas of exposure. One good look in the mirror at my skinny body was enough to send me creeping into a corner.

In my family, attractiveness reigned supreme. I could never live up to the dazzling good looks of my brother Harold or my mother's gracious southern beauty. I required too much reassurance to balance the flaws of my body against the handsome boys I was invariably attracted to. Somehow the stakes had to be altered.

I needed breasts.

"Why do you want this surgery?" Dr. Ramsey asked, sitting straight behind his desk, lips pressed into a thin line.

"Because I want to feel like a woman." Because I want to be sexy! Why did he think, the boob? He was uncooperative from the first. He said my breasts were fine. Small was fine. "If you have an implant," he said, handing me a brochure picturing various-shaped samples of contorted plastic clumps that resembled warped potatoes, "over the years they will start to sag." He leaned towards me judiciously. "You will have to wear a bra for the rest of your life, day and night. If the silicone slips or gets lumpy you'll have to have it replaced. The stitches will never disappear." He paused, looking at me steadily. "And you will lose all sensitivity, as the implant mound is placed underneath the nipples. You will have no feeling in them at all." The impact of this fact was not lost on my sex-conscious mind. Horrors! "This is an expensive undertaking. I advise you to consider very carefully whether it's worth it."

Clearly Dr. Ramsey did not approve of my plan. Maybe he dismissed it as pure feminine vanity. I was in a conservative bastion and there was no out. Maybe he was right. Reluctantly I gave it up. I would have to continue to camouflage my external defects, along with my inner ones.

In early August, an envelope arrived from Brandon containing a poem by e.e. cummings and no note.

> *somewhere I have never traveled, gladly beyond*
> *any experience, your eyes have their silence:*
> *in your most frail gesture are things which enclose me,*
> *or which I cannot touch because they are too near.*
>
> *nothing which we are to perceive in this world equals*
> *the power of your intense fragility: whose texture*
> *compels me with the colour of its counties,*
> *rendering death and forever with each breathing.*

I blanched at the note of despair that sprang from these lines, directed, I perceived, toward me. Unsure how to respond I did nothing. My sense of uncertainty deepened.

Two weeks later a letter followed, a six-page epistle explaining that he hadn't known how to react to me and lamenting the mysterious turnings of the female psyche. My elusive, mercurial presence had been beyond his ability to fathom. It seems I was in a category of female irrationality that could not be approached.

I was still cringing as I recalled my outpouring of despair that last afternoon on the beach, to which Brandon had not replied. Now it seemed he considered me unreachable and difficult. Waiting two weeks to indicate calmness on my part, I wrote back huffily that I didn't think I was that complicated and acknowledged that there were indeed difficulties between us. What really miffed me was that Brandon considered my failings a barrier, had caused him to feel confused, discouraged. If I was such a mess, he could only seek to be free of the entanglement.

It was late September before I received a reply, this time repudiating his previous letter.

Dear Judy,

I have come lately to realize many things which were lying dormant in me. What was heretofore an inexplicable, disconcerting puzzle I have come to accept and it is: woman.

We are indeed, as you say, on two different planes. At the time I was with you I was laying a relationship on intellectual terms, always maintaining an emotional distance, hesitant to possess and yet wanting to possess more than I have ever had before...I did not realize that with you it was not the possession nor the taking that was necessary to maintain the relationship; rather it should have been an encompassment, infinite and tender, of your private self.

With you I was moving into an acutely sharp and painful realization of where I had been for 24 years. I cannot state all those things I felt, enough to say that my life had been one of possessing, constantly taking. I had this loneliness, this vast emptiness which had to be constantly filled, emptiness with no bottom. I stole the emotions of others and could never return them in kind. I felt that I was lonely as few ever could be and that this vast pouring of friendship and feeling of others into me was necessary food for my existence, the only sustenance that would keep this great night of aloneness from overcoming me and pitching me into a black mood of despair.

I never regarded myself in any relation to anyone save myself. Possession of material goods was a great delight to me; my parents could never give me enough, and I felt a need for a status that I felt necessary to maintain because of the image of myself as alone and unneeded, in order to keep a surface position of sameness with others.

So with this in me I came to you. At first it was easy to talk; and insatiable I wanted to flood myself with your more intimate thoughts, feelings, finally to plumb down to your most private world, to take all this and leave you nothing, leaving myself full and satisfied. I had always done this with guys and old mothers, why not here?

Everything came to a frozen stop, and I was in a kind of shocked paralysis: at that first monumental kiss, with the yellow lamp behind you and the wash of the sea softly sounding, and I had no direction, was never so awkward...

This moment brought me a feeling I had never had in bountiful measure before—a feeling of care. This feeling built up to where I was completely unable to fathom what it was that could cause this; I knew it was you, the first person I think I had ever come to regard totally as an individual without reference to myself. You and your women's world which I suddenly realized I understood little of. Time hammered at me and I had to run back again and again to find out more; I never wanted to talk to you more than during the days after that kiss: I never had less I could say. I was a mountain of conflicts, caring so much for you that I was afraid anything I would say of a revelational nature would cause you to flee crazy, innocent, guileless—me.

Judy it was not you. I was thrust into myself, without movement or progression, during those days I never wanted to leave you, so strong was this concern, this care for you. I was kept apart, so much did I fear revealing a little part of my world (for I had an image of myself which I thought you had of me and which I had, at all costs, to maintain.)....During those three weeks I slept a total of 25 hours....I was never so alone.

The letter was a response, Brandon went on, to the comment in my letter lamenting that I had never been able to see who he really was. That it had taken him a month and a half to gain perspective on all that had happened with us, and that he had come to understand me as a woman, not as a girl on the beach or a writer or the daughter of certain parents or with a certain kind of dress and way of smiling, with certain friends, having been to certain parts of the world. He assured me he that had become more aggressive and could carry on a conversation with anyone.

On rereading this letter I fear that you might get the impression of a great emotional distance, a lessening of feeling on my part, simply because I throw my feelings down in a

slapdash manner. I hope that you can understand me with a
land between us.
*   As always, Brandon*

I clutched the letter in my hands as if hoping it would come alive. I read it over and over, looking for something that wasn't there. I had caused this agony and uncertainty in him! What had I done? Next, his claim of caring stuck out like a billboard and I was swept with hope. But reading further it became clear that his feelings had not lasted. He was thrashing in a feminine pit of quicksand that he longed to be free of. With the hint at the closing that his feelings were lessening, I came crashing down. The biggest blow was the final signature "As always"—so barren, so stiff.

It was all I needed to confirm my fear that he had been driven away and all hope was lost.

The egg salad sandwich in front of me on the kitchen table, where I had settled to read the day's mail, remained untouched. I thought longingly of the typical love letter that said "I love you, I miss you, I want us to be together."

The next day a cylinder package arrived in the mail: a 30 x 24 inch poster of *Christina's World by* Andrew Wyeth. It was from Brandon. The scrawny young girl in a faded print dress seated on a bleak prairie hill with outstretched arm projected an image of misshapen hopelessness. I was shocked at the pathetic figure, obviously meant to reflect me. Damn him, I had not sunk that low! The blood rose in my chest. Furiously, I dashed off a response.

Dear Brandon,
*   I've been thinking things over and I see no way around it.*
As you put it so well on the phone the other day, it was
unsatisfactory with us. I don't know what I want. It just didn't
work and I can't see how things would be any different another
time.

Jim Ivory popped in on his way to the East and showed us his new Indian film. I'd like to see what he could do with live subjects.

Etc., etc.

It was the last letter to pass between us. A year later I heard news that Brandon had married the sister of Kent Mackenzie, the creator of the documentary *The Exiles*.

†

Roz phoned. "Let's go to Las Vegas!"

"Sounds like a possibility. What's the deal?" Roz was never out of ideas.

"Oh, I'd like to get away for the weekend. Ralph and I are on the skids, you might say."

"What happened?" When I last saw them Roz and Ralph were exhibiting their usual affectionate playfulness.

"It's just that he's such a baby! His drinking goes beyond entertaining and cute. He keeps saying he's not smart enough, and clowning is what he's best at. It's getting worse and I'm close to fed up." Pause. "Well, I'm not going to bail him out any more!"

"Maybe it's time for a break," I said.

The following Friday afternoon, a gray Buick with two secretaries from Douglas seated in front pulled up to the beach house. Roz and I climbed in the back seat, me with a tote bag stuffed with reading material and an extra sweater, Roz swinging a black patent leather purse. As we sped along I-15 across California and into the Nevada desert, the conversation never lagged. The driver chattered away, waving one hand over the wheel and periodically checking the position of her sunglasses in the rear view mirror.

Her friend slouched against the door scratching a nail file briskly along the edge of her finger. "That Mavis is never on time," she was saying. "Last time we went to a movie she dragged and we missed the first part. Then said what difference did it make, the first few minutes were just titles anyway. I like to see a movie from the beginning, don't you? I don't think I should have to wait, she should be on time. I hate it when I have to wait. It's so boring, and then you miss part of the movie."

The driver nodded enthusiastically. "Did you brush your teeth this morning?

I don't know about you, but I simply can't exist without mouthwash. Even after brushing my teeth before bed I have to have a swirl of the cinnamon flavor for my mouth to feel clean."

"So do I! And I use it after every meal. It's so refreshing," chimed in her friend. "Do you girls use Lavoris or Listerine? I like the red stuff."

For the next two hours, conversation flew between the front and back seats. I was getting weary and glanced longingly at my book. Searching continually for something to say that had not already been or didn't need to be said was exhausting. Thank heavens Roz took up the slack—I'd never seen her at a loss—and we kept up a cheery prattle for the remainder of the ride.

The girls dropped Roz and me off at the canvas-covered entrance to the Stardust, and drove on to a downtown hotel. Rising above the Stardust an oversized neon billboard flashed FRANK SINATRA AND DEAN MARTIN. Roz and I entered a dark cavernous lobby that was illuminated by recessed lights, rows of flickering slot machines, and spotlighted posters of girlie shows. We were immediately engulfed by a constant orchestration of clanking noises, popping bells, and cigarette smoke. After checking in, we went up to our twelfth- floor room to change for dinner. Thirty minutes later we descended and padded along the dark brown and red carpet, Roz svelte and towering in a black crepe dress, and me in a black toile skirt and a soft peach blouse.

"Where's the black velvet with the scooped neck we bought you?" Roz inquired, looking at me.

"That's for tomorrow night." We moved through the lounge and sat down on stools amid a row of jangling one-eyed bandits. Clouds of smoke hanging in the airless room burrowed into my eyes. Roz won $36 within twenty minutes.

"Now we can go home," I said, taking a drag of my cigarette.

"Ha, ha. You're next. Just you wait!"

We ordered filet mignon and martinis at dinner and Grand Marnier during the floor show in the adjoining bar. Two older men in business suits bought us drinks, sliding around our table to sit next to us, explaining that they knew how to enjoy life and how much more fun it would be to enjoy it together. Finally, they whisked us across town in a taxi to catch the *Lido de Paris,* and we arrived back at our room at 4:00 a.m. Our companions accompanied us to the hotel entrance and promised to see us the next day. They went off waving and singing. Roz turned to me.

"Keep looking?"

"Keep looking."

When we woke the next day it was after 2:00 p.m. "I suppose we might as well dress for dinner," Roz suggested.

"We haven't had breakfast yet."

"Well if you intend to consume all three meals we'd better hurry. I think we'll have to eat all of them at the same sitting."

"Let's take a swim first."

After a dip in the pool, Roz announced that she had set up hair appointments with Wesley at seven. He came recommended by a woman in the Douglas shipping office who drove regularly to Vegas, she claimed, just to have her hair done. She assured Roz there was no one like him.

That proved to be true. Wesley and Roz talked me into trying a dramatic new style and I watched warily in the mirror as he stretched the hair off my face and swept it up on top of my head into a firm pile that looked like a cross between a bee hive and a baked Alaska.

"Oh, you look so sophisticated, " cooed Roz.

"You like different person, so beauuutiful, so elegant, so smart," applauded Wesley, waving his hands. "You made for thees hairstyle." It *was* different. Quite severe. My face was exposed in all its angularity, thrust out naked for the world to see.

"Oh, do say you like it!" urged Roz.

"It's different. I'll have to get used to it."

Roz emerged with an upsweep piled over her forehead and long, dark strands of hair falling evenly over the front of each shoulder. She was pleased.

"You look real glamorous," she said as we descended the staircase. "Gets you away from that little girl look. You look great!"

"Always willing to try something new."

"And Judy, it will put you in a different mood. Not so outdoorsy. And fun! Pull you out of that serious streak, lighten you up. I know you like to have fun!"

After a late dinner in the lower lounge featuring the New Sebastian Jazz Band, Roz went off with a tall man in a bowler hat she'd met at the blackjack table. "He's got a taxi waiting; we're going dancing."

I continued to sit at our table with a heavy set man in a checkered seersucker business suit who had joined us earlier. He held my hand under the table. After Roz left, he brought out samples of rubber and brass doorstops and hardware and laid them on the tablecloth.

"I make a very good living," he told me, tightening his horn-rimmed glasses behind his ears. "I have a house with a swimming pool and a vacuum cleaner for each floor and a counter sink with running water in the garage. And I spend a week each year at St. Pete's in sunny 'ole Florida. Stuff is easy to peddle and I don't mind driving the roads of California and Nevada and Utah— I have a big territory." He grabbed my hand again and grinned at me expectantly. "Let's go to Cicero's for a nightcap. The evening's young." We piled into a taxi.

Finally it was late enough for me to make an escape, and I coaxed the salesman into dropping me back at the hotel. Our room was dark, Roz was still out. I fell into a heavy sleep and did not hear her come in. The next morning she declared that her date of the previous evening was a good dancer but a loser. He dished out a line a mile long and it took some maneuvering to circumvent his crude expectations. From her tone, I could tell she'd slipped through his lustful ploys with her usual skill.

"I don't stand for unwanted pressure," was all she said. "But," she went on, a look of gaiety brightening her cheeks, "he took me to a great place with a fabulous floorshow featuring the Amana Brothers. Now *they* are adorable. Get your jacket. We're going out."

After a weekend of entertainment, I returned home rejuvenated but relieved. The adventure with Roz had been a lark, different than anything I'd experienced, but I was glad to get back to the fresh ocean air and sanity.

†

The air in Santa Monica had cooled and the careless lightness of summer was replaced by an autumn crispness. School kids were lined up at Woolworth's supply counter stocking up on pencils and three-ring notebooks. After purchasing onion skin paper, a tube of white out, two rolls of Tri-X film, and three jars of salted peanuts, I left the dime store and walked back to the beach house and up the front steps.

Screwing off the lid of a peanut jar, I sat down at the desk in my room and stared at the typewriter. Allison was away for the weekend, and quietude filled the house. I was often there alone, with no car and Allison gone a great deal of the time. Sometimes while I was working she would rush in the front door, rosy and breathless, gather some oil paint tubes and brushes into a canvas bag, grab a straw hat edged with miniature pompoms, and be out the door. I could hear the hum of her boyfriend's car idling outside through the front screen.

I'd spent the past weeks contacting flimsy film job leads and following up on résumés I'd submitted to listings culled from the yellow pages. Nothing. There were no more avenues to search, no more places to try. Not even the hint of a film job had surfaced.

I intended to resurrect a writing project that had fizzled in the folds of the summer months. But the impetus had dried up. Tentatively, I struck a few keys onto the blank white page protruding from the typewriter. Looking down, I saw I had typed "the beginning the end that's all there is." I could get no further. I was going around and around, like the Ferris wheel at the amusement park, getting nowhere.

I was beginning to feel like a sponge living in Allison's house without an automobile, even though I was paying a modest rent. The golden splendor of the summer was fast disappearing into the dark severity of fall.

Besides, the beach house was up for sale.

I reviewed the months that had passed since I finished college. What did I have to show? Harold's law degree had launched him directly into the Burlington Northern Railroad offices, where he worked his way up to trial law: one job, a solid, straight line. His career had definition, purpose. Dad had made allowances for me, a girl. The goal was for me to be as happy as possible until a husband came along. Until then I was given everything that came my way and everything I thought I wanted. It had seemed easy. My parents' unfailing generosity kept me afloat,

165

allowed endless choices and freedom. But having choices that scoped the earth was daunting, too much possibility, too many paths out there and no sign posts. No laid-out gate of entry. The world of endless opportunity was too vast, looming colossal when all I wanted was a single step. It wasn't easy!

I sat all morning without writing an acceptable sentence. Then I received a letter from Margo in New York City, who had recently moved into an apartment in Chelsea with three other women and was having the time of her life. This time her words produced an echo. I made airline reservations.

It was time for a new chapter.

Part 4
The Last Round

Chapter 1   Settling In

My small room at the Barbizon Hotel for Women on East Sixty Third Street was spartan but adequate. I shared a hall bath and had access to a swimming pool in the lower level. From the window I could hear the strident squeal of traffic and rush of people in fur-topped boots hustling along the sidewalks and calling for taxis. A surge of exhilaration flushed through me—here I was in New York City, the business apex of the nation where things happened. I held an unshakable faith in the favorable unfolding of events. All I had to do was keep going. The explosive energy around me would do the rest.

The spacious lobby of the hotel was filled with Chesterfield sofas and arm chairs set in conversational groupings. Girls in black pumps tapped back and forth through the lobby at all hours, ambitious young women striving to make it in the big city. The large television room a few steps beyond the lounge was usually empty—who had time to sit and watch others live? A few girls showed up at the pool while I was doing laps, but they didn't hang around. They were too busy preparing for appointments, dates, or shows, dressed in two-piece print dresses, gloves, and heels or, for evening, black empire sheaths and pearls. Most were new in town, although a few lived at the hotel on a residential basis. Those seeking to be models informed me that Grace Kelly had occupied the Barbizon when she launched her modeling career. They also pointed out the brick apartment building down the street where a young Montgomery Cliff lived with an older woman.

The evening of my arrival I opened my address book, picked up the phone on the narrow nightstand next to my bed, and started dialing. Margo wasn't home. On my next call, Joan Aquino picked up the receiver.

"Hey. I thought maybe you'd returned to California," I said.

"Oh, that didn't pan out. Where are you staying?"

"The Barbizon Hotel for Women."

"My goodness! Just women? What's the point of that?" Joan scoffed at the house rules, especially on learning that males were not allowed above the first floor. To her the hotel was hoity and unfriendly. "I like my freedom," she declared.

"It's clean, reasonable, comfortable, and central," I said, "Not like a tourist hotel." The hotel was a perfect base while I job hunted. I would end up staying three months.

Joan and I met the next evening for dinner. The following afternoon I walked along Lexington Avenue to Bloomingdale's and purchased seamless nylons and a slim navy dress with matching jacket. Then, gripping a three-page list of publishing companies in Manhattan lifted from the yellow pages, I began trudging the sidewalks. I took elevators and climbed stairs, dropping off a neatly typed résumé and cover letter at office after office—crisp papers without letter folds. At the reception desk I asked to see the head of the editorial department. If the director wasn't available, I recorded the name and direct phone number for a callback. It became a daily routine: up at eight, breakfast, hit the sidewalks, up First Avenue, down Lexington, and so on.

Few directors would see me. The ones who led me into their office didn't offer a job but were curious about a girl who appeared unexpectedly without calling ahead. My literary background was interesting, they said, and I appeared acceptable. I offered to start at the bottom.

Barbizon Hotel for Women
NYC 1960

"Why did you leave the film field? What have you been doing for the last two years?"

I had my youth and ignorance to sustain me. And my unsubstantiated confidence. I thought I had a lot to offer. Wasn't I educated, weren't books my field, wasn't I bright and promising? I carried an assumption of entitlement (degree). I could go anywhere and do anything. I'd landed jobs before. I didn't guarantee permanence, and it wasn't requested. A girl of twenty-six wasn't expected to promise any such thing. Employees often pursued new opportunities, and the potential for dropping out for maternal reasons was not so great—girls in Manhattan tended to be serious and stuck to their careers.

169

The directors promised to phone when an appropriate position opened up.

One warm, rainy afternoon, I climbed a flight of stairs and walked up to an opaque glass door marked METRO PUBLISHING. Tiny drops from my umbrella accumulated on the floor as I checked the name. I knocked and a woman in a green dress opened the door. She looked slightly familiar.

"Weren't you here yesterday?" She peered closely at me.

"A—I don't think so. Although...." I peered inside. The office chairs didn't look familiar. "Well, I'm back," I blurted, unable to think of anything else to say.

"Mr. Jenkins wasn't here yesterday and he's not here today," the woman in green rasped. I hurriedly retraced my steps out to the rainy sidewalk. Like how stupid was that! I still wasn't sure, but the woman had remembered exactly, recalling that I had been carrying a navy handbag. How could I have gotten that mixed up? So much for Mr. Jenkins.

The rain was beating down more heavily and I quickened my steps. The fresh smell of moisture vitalized the dry space under my umbrella. It's okay if your feet get wet. Just keep going.

One more stop, the last of the day. Arriving at West 40th Street, I entered the elevator, shook the drops from my raincoat, and straightened my shoulders. The elevator stopped with a jolt and I got out. DAVID MCKAY COMPANY, PUBLISHERS was marked in bold letters on the first door down the hall. When I entered, the smartly-dressed girl behind the desk looked up and smiled. She accepted my résumé and pointed me to a seat while she dialed the phone. Several minutes later she announced that Mrs. Ryan would be with me shortly.

Ten minutes later Mrs. Ryan appeared, tall, solidly built, rotund in the middle, graying hair pulled back on the sides and long, pallid arms. Her smile was gentle, almost timid. She was, I soon learned, anything but.

"Come this way." When I was seated across the desk from her, she rested her fleshy white hands in her lap and began in a friendly, personal tone. "I usually don't see applicants without an appointment. But I'm impressed that you were out making the rounds in this downpour. Most people," she said smiling, "including me, would have stayed home on a day like this."

"I stayed home Monday. That's enough," I responded. "The rain doesn't bother me."

Mrs. Ryan looked at me kindly. "Tell me about yourself." This was the hard part, having to explain my slaphazard meanderings of the last few years. I attempted to describe my job at the United Nations as impressive, my travels in Europe as educational, and my summer in Santa Monica as an attempt to break into an iron-guarded film industry controlled by the unions. I explained that matching tiny numbers under glaring light at the United Nations had jeopardized my eyesight, and I had decided to switch fields. New York was the center of publishing. I was back to stay and forge a new career.

Mrs. Ryan straightened and laid her hands on the table. "I'll be honest with you. The job I have in mind is eighty percent proofreading," she said firmly. "What about your eyes?"

"Oh, it was the harsh light underneath the negatives that bothered me," I assured her. "Regular text reading is no problem."

"Good. Well, I'll tell you," she relaxed back in her seat, "You're in luck. You walked in here at just the right time. I hired a girl three weeks ago and she didn't work out. I had to let her go." She hesitated.

"That's a shame," I remarked, "After going through a long hiring process."

"Exactly. The fact is she had some—problems. I won't go into it, but she was overly emotional, and causing a great deal of difficulty. Do you know what I mean?"

"Absolutely. It's hard to detect those things before you get to know someone."

"How would you describe yourself in this respect?" Mrs. Ryan leaned towards me with a slightly embarrassed expression. "Do you consider yourself emotionally stable?" She waited motionless for an answer.

The question took me aback. "Yes—I'd say so. I've had several jobs—listed there on my résumé—you can check, I've never had a problem." Nothing in my scanty job history had arisen to cause such an issue, but I wasn't at all sure. I hadn't really been tested. Emotional was my middle name, if you got down to it. I was pretty sure it would never come to that; this wasn't the family cauldron in which my emotions usually erupted, this was work, this was predictable, this was sane.

171

"To tell the truth, I can't face going through the process of running an ad, interviewing applicants, and all that again so soon," Mrs. Ryan continued. "You just might be the answer. The position is assistant editor. There are several editors in the office and several associate editors under them. As an assistant you would be the third tier, doing proofreading, maybe some formatting of title pages and text, and possibly from time to time reading submitted manuscripts for initial evaluation. But it will be mostly proofreading. How does that sound?"

This small company held a feeling of closeness that I liked. David McKay was a publisher of trade books (in contrast to text books), and Vance Packard their best-known author. To work for this firm—with zero publishing experience—would be a dream.

"It sounds excellent."

"Good." After perusing my résumé one last time and asking a series of questions, Mrs. Ryan laid my papers on the desk. "Of course, I must check things out. I warn you, I can't promise anything. I'll get back to you."

I left with a big *maybe* hanging in my mind. Mrs. Ryan was down-to-earth, homey. Not the NYC cutthroat type. I would like working there. I stopped for a steaming hot chocolate, carried it the Barbizon, and wrote a few letters while sitting on the bed. Best to put the interview out of my mind and continue the job-hunting routine. Time would tell.

Four days later Mrs. Ryan called and offered me the job.

"Anyone who pounds the sidewalks in the rain has guts," she declared.

✝

In 1959 Paris was all the rage, and Americans took off in waves to explore Europe. My parents caught the travel bug, touring France, China, and Italy, as well as a month-long tour of Asia with their best friends, the Johnstons. When they stopped over in New York, I joined them to do the town. Mother would phone from the Carlyle or the Pierre. "Are you ready? We have tickets tonight. Dinner first at The Four Seasons. Get yourself gussied up."

Dad's interest in plays had perked since he became an investing partner in a Broadway production. We taxied to Forty Second Street to see *How to Succeed in Business without Really Trying* and *Flower Drum Song*. Theater-goers in New York adored the naughty, oh-we're-bad musicals like *Cabaret*, where Gwen Verdun belted out her bawdy songs, "*If my friends could see me now, they'd never believe it.*" Audiences found the naïve and childlike prostitutes pursued by sugar daddies charming. This unrealistic portrayal was not to my taste, but I had to admit that a night on the town was entertaining, despite the occasional glorification of vice.

For Dad's birthday we spirited him to dinner at Asti's in the Village, where he was serenaded by one of the opera-singing waiters. The waiter sang out an aria from *La Traviata*, followed by *Happy Birthday to Harold*, leaning over Dad's chair and throwing his deep operatic baritone to the far reaches of the restaurant. "Let's get out of here," Dad whispered to me under his breath.

When my parents weren't breezing through town, they sent newsy letters. One item came as a surprise: my brother Harold was engaged. At thirty, he had finally abandoned his stance of aloof bachelor. Until then he had doggedly avoided the trap of domesticity and its softening, emasculating effects. According to the typical male viewpoint of the day, his freedom from female dependency had collapsed, and he was being sold into responsibility and bondage; he would be tamed.

Both parents in separate letters urged me to attend the wedding, a small affair without fanfare. Not a word from Harold. I shouldn't have been surprised; we were almost strangers. After a childhood spent chaffing under his indifference and what I took as scorn for everything I did, I had no expectations. He lived in another world. I did not attend.

Big news: Dad agreed to establish a branch of Investors Diversified Services for the company in Geneva. He and mother set about moving to Europe for a year. They studied French and mother began signing her letters *vôtre mère*. To add to the excitement, my sister Susan was to accompany them and begin college life at the American School in Lucerne, judged a broadening experience for an eighteen-year-old. Mother admonished me to write every week or she would worry. Three weeks after they'd settled in their Geneva apartment I learned that mother was shopping her head off and Dad was longing for a hamburger.

Chapter 2   East 81ˢᵗ Street

One afternoon I sat at a café near the hotel enjoying my favorite lunch: cherry Jell-O topped with cottage cheese and sliced pear halves arranged on a fan of iceberg lettuce and an almond croissant. As I broke off a piece of croissant and popped it into my mouth, a flash of yellow jacket whirled by and a girl with a wide open smile, not at all New Yorkish, took the stool next to me. She ordered a coffee and grilled cheese sandwich, looking around the room appraisingly. Before long she was telling me about her family back in Santiago and her wide array of cousins and distant relatives. With heavy black hair, a thin mouth, and a slightly crooked nose, she was not beautiful, but the animated expression, sparkling dark eyes, and a smile that never left her face were magnetically attractive. By the end of lunch I had grown used to the smile and the occasional gurgles of laughter, both of which accompanied her chatter in great doses.

Gladys had come to this country from Chile. She was overjoyed to meet a girl her age from mid-America who came complete with contacts and family. Her girl Friday job at an import company brought her more than she could ever earn in Chile and enabled her to send money home.

In town only six months, she had already returned to Santiago with several suitcases full of American clothes and goods. An American girlfriend was just what she needed, she said, to improve her English.

She was easy to get along with. She was cheerful. She liked to have fun. She was looking for an apartment.

Manhattan, the Sixties

The next month we moved into a small walkup with a front window overlooking East 81st Street. People combing the sidewalks were smartly dressed in business suits and stylish dresses cut at mid-calf. A ruby and gold stained glass window decorated the front door of the brownstone building, and the stairway to the second floor was flanked by carved wrought-iron banisters. Best of all, the rent was reasonable. Apartments like this in our price range were difficult to find. We signed a year's lease. I was tense with excitement. I'd had roommates before—I could do this.

Little did I anticipate the challenges that would invade our new home before the year was over.

Soon I was happily settled into city living. I'd obtained a library card, purchased a series of tickets to off-Broadway theaters, and secured a regular dentist, optometrist, and hairstylist. My address book contained names of local friends, and my wallet held a charge-a-plate from Bloomingdales. I knew how to get to the airport by heart. I had mastered the subway lines and how to fold the *New York Times* into narrow columns to read in the hairline space between the mass of swaying bodies. I even assumed the typical half-asleep look as I stood pressed against a row of knees, clutching a leather strap, while other breathing, nostril-twitching faces hovered inches from mine. I elbowed out others angling to catch a taxi and left the driver a hefty tip to avoid getting snarled at. I became inured to the noise of brakes squealing, horns blasting, and the sounds of clashing metal. At the end of the day I slept soundly through the strangulated cries and sirens of whatever city drama was erupting outside in the night.

I learned to snap back at the corner tobacconist or breezily ignore him.

"Do you want two packs or three? Make up your mind."

"I'll take four and I'm in a hurry."

I was home.

Our living space consisted of two rooms and a bath. The front room incorporated a one-wall kitchen with a drop-down eating table. The bedroom was only large enough to accommodate twin beds, squeezed head to head along two walls, a chest, and bed stand. Mother shipped us furniture that included a black modern coffee table from my studio bedroom, and an old red, gold, and purple wool rug from the den at 57 Groveland. A few additional pieces from Sears filled the living room. The walls were freshly painted, with high ceilings, cream wainscoting, and built-in floor-to-ceiling bookcases in the front room. The suggestion of quality gleamed from the walls. Tiny it was, but we were delighted.

In such tight quarters, we soon got to know each other. Gladys wore rollers to bed. Fat, pink spools of plastic that she rolled her hair around tightly and pinned, somehow, to her scalp. They ran in rows across her head, like barrels in a winery. On these she slept, her head raised raft-like from the pillow. She claimed to sleep like a log. I should try it. No way

José! I had to admit the soft curls suited her oval face, and one night I decided to try out a few rollers myself. After lying for fifteen minutes, with sleep out of the question, I sprang up with a yowl and ripped them out.

A roommate was a plus socially. Two people were more inviting than one, had access to more connections. One of us would entertain the other's company while the one going out was getting ready in the bedroom. My friends liked Gladys. She was perky, easygoing and game. That was until the conversation turned intellectual, when she would lapse into silence or excuse herself. Debates were not in her repertoire.

Gladys at E. 81st St. Apartment

We invited our neighbors in the brownstone to a housewarming party. Since we knew few people it was a small affair, but in the cramped space the apartment seemed crowded. It was at the party that Gladys met Chester. The day before the event, Chester phoned from Brooklyn for directions, and when Gladys answered he discovered I had a new roommate. He and Gladys talked for an hour and a half.

When he arrived, he scrunched next to Gladys on the couch and held her in tight conversation. He was clearly smitten with her bubbly, full-throated way of talking and the sensual glimmer in her eyes. He confided afterwards that she was the most beautiful, sexy women he had ever known. He invited her to chamber music concerts at Washington Irving High School, to the cocktail lounge at the top of Beekman Towers, to Carnegie Hall, and to the Russian Tea Room. They usually wound up the evening at a cozy neighborhood bar in Yorkville.

Gladys was taken with Chester's gentlemanly manner and the cultural expansion she experienced under his attentions. Sometimes, returning after an evening out, they perched on the steps outside the apartment door, Gladys in Chester's lap talking endlessly, while Chester allowed himself quick kisses on her cheek. He was encouraged by her affectionate nature, her way of taking his hand as they walked, and her admiration of what she termed his American breeding.

But she put him off. She envisioned life with a successful businessman in the heart of Americana, not living with a struggling novelist in a flat in Brooklyn. She was a strict Catholic, she informed him, and her mother expected her to remain a virgin until marriage, like all the women in her family.

Chester at the Cinema Department, USC

"He treats me so well," she said. "He is likeable and we have good times. But I think he likes me too much."

"What's wrong with that? You'll get used to him. He grows on you."

"I suppose." She didn't want to give him up and didn't want to proceed in the direction he was going either.

I soon found out why.

It was clear from the first word out of her mouth that Gladys had a crush on her American boss, John. Handsome in a blond, undistinguished way, he treated her with formal indifference. As a nephew of the bank president, he enjoyed privileges and an assured ascendancy with the company. Just recently he'd been appointed manager of the loan department. He was everything she had ever wanted or dreamed of in a man. Occasionally she ran across him in the subway on the way to work and sidled up to him, allowing the shake and swell of the car to push her into his shoulder as they clutched parallel straps above their heads.

Once evening they left work late, a little after eight, and John walked with her to the subway, unexpectedly got off at her stop, and invited her to a nearby bar for a drink. I was asleep by the time they arrived at the apartment. I heard a door slam and opened one eye. Their mumbling voices from the couch seeped through the bedroom door as I drifted groggily back into oblivion. This was repeated other nights, always late in the evening after I had retired. Soon it fell into a weekly routine and I became used to the click of the front door, the shuffling, the rustling of pillows, the muted interplay of male and female voices, the silence, and then the slow and throaty sounds of pleasure, the soft moaning and eventually the stronger, sharper groans of male release.

The encounters always took place on a weeknight after work and never varied. Gladys did not speak of these intimacies—girls didn't usually share this aspect of their lives. But when she spoke of John her eyes would light up. She was flattered that he, the bachelor catch at the office, had chosen her to be his girl.

I was torn between tolerance and wariness. My discomfort grew as it became clear that John's pattern wasn't going to change: he would buy Gladys drinks at the bar, pour another from the scotch bottle she kept under the kitchen sink, and then they fell on the couch. He never called. He never took her out. He didn't introduce her to his friends. Even at work she claimed he had to behave as a disinterested superior, for the sake of appearance. She understood. She expected nothing, except maybe at some point he would overcome his reticence and inexperience and return the passion she felt for him.

"Why don't you suggest going out somewhere?" I asked. By now I was convinced she was being used and that this aloof snob would never take her seriously. I didn't dare say much; at the mention of him Gladys bubbled and lapsed into a dreamy, unreachable fog. "It's hard for him," she said. "He lives in Westchester, too far to drive in on weekends. He's shy underneath. I don't think he's dated too many women."

"But he's not treating you right," I said. I could say no more. She would not see my side. I was also concerned about Chester. Should I warn him? He would be crushed. Maybe with time Gladys would see how she was being used, and would learn to appreciate Chester's sweet nature and devotion. I kept my mouth shut.

†

I first spied Robert (Ro-BERT) at a party. He stood by the window, arms folded, listening to two men conversing in French. His broad, craggy face, prominent features, solid arms, and head of thick dark hair imparted a Latin boldness. "You're the first French-speaking person I've met in New York," I said in French as I approached. He fixed a penetrating gaze on me and began speaking with a beautiful French lilt that reminded me of Paris. I found myself clinging to his every word. He told me he'd lived in Manhattan for five years and worked at a foreign import-export company. Did he like his job? No, he was sick of soybeans and chickpeas, and especially resentful that he wasn't getting the promotion he felt he deserved. But so far he had been unable to give up the salary.

The next Saturday we drove in his old Citroen to Queens, where a group of young French people congregated every Friday night in a local bar. I was the only native English-speaking person. My expectations of fitting into a French environment, given my recent stay in France, were dashed. Gradually, as the conversation moved down the table, the group dropped the linguistic allowances they had been making for my benefit.

180

Due to the intruding voice of the French singer Charles Trenet, the noisy bar chatter, and people turning their heads away to speak, in addition to my mediocre command of the language, I couldn't follow what was being said. My spirits plummeted. I sat next to Robert, straining to follow the conversation. All I could make out were blasts of music and the scrape of pans from the kitchen. Finally I gave up.

I was disappointed that I had lived in France for a year and was unable to converse in the French language like a regular French person, without the props. In Paris I had sacrificed the company of English-speaking people who did interesting things and had interesting jobs so that I could learn French. Did I devote myself to the Greek god Jean Paul for nothing?

I continued to see Robert now and then. We made love. At first, it was blissful. I liked being held in his arms and the feeling that my body had found its natural expression and was performing its womanly function. I was tired of celibacy. It was gratifying to be attracted and have the attraction fulfilled. And I savored the idea of intimacy with a Frenchman, having spent almost a year in France without experiencing the sensuality of European manhood.

But lovemaking with Robert proved to be rote. He became impatient with kissing and knew easily how to satisfy himself. He was not used to ignorant girls like me. His amours were more sophisticated and kept him jumping with sensual ploys and temptations. His last affair had been a roller coaster of standoffs and reconciliations. There would be wild struggles of will, heated arguments followed by periods of separation and tentative relenting, ending in a powerful, passionate sexual reunion.

I was not up to this theater myself; the nuances of thrusting and parrying for deliberate advantage did not fall in my comfort zone. Although I would have liked to entice him—to feel him enamored and stalking me with unrelenting persistence into a dead-end cave where he lost himself in desire. Better than the blasé way he breezed in and out of the apartment, snapping the door behind him without a backward glance.

One weekend I badgered my companion into returning a day early from a jaunt to Washington, D.C. so I could keep a date with him. He didn't show up. After that, I determined not to take his calls. But I didn't hear from him. I recalled hints, when he'd restructured our dates, of another girl installed in the wings. Oh well, I thought, I don't like steak tartare anyway.

I was beginning to feel deprived. Here I was twenty-six years old and had never had a long-term boyfriend. My failures with men were starting to add up. Maybe it was an area, like advanced physics, that I would never grasp. How was it that I couldn't develop close, romantic relationships with men long-term? Was I doomed to connections that aspired and fizzled?

The experts claim that a relationship doesn't bond until you allow your truth to emerge. But what was that truth? My reality was still buried, unknown by anyone, including myself. No one would ever know me. And no one would ever care.

†

A wire from Granddad Fought announced his upcoming visit to New York. Now in his eighties, Granddad was living at the Windsor Hotel in Wheeling, West Virginia, nursing his gout and watching his many friends dwindle with age. He was still full of frisky banter.

Letter from Granddad Fought

> *It's lonesome here. Everyone is retired, sick, or dead. I miss the dead ones the most. I'm looking forward to meeting your roommate. She's probably beautiful. That is if she's not missing an upper lip.*
>
> *I'll be arriving on Saturday.*

Gladys was anxious to meet him. Grandad was known to be a fascinating social companion, but I had reservations. Much as he loved the ladies, and my pretty, pulsing-with-life roommate would be to his taste, I feared his well-known intolerance. His Southern blood couldn't abide Catholics, Republicans, or foreigners. Granddad was born in 1880, a mere fifteen years after the devastation of the civil war left the South bowed and humiliated. After its defeat, the South refused to change

182

culturally. Despite the crippling of its agricultural base, it guarded a gracious way of life based on formality, gallantry, and stiff standards about what was acceptable. Granddad Fought fell into this mold.

Granddad Fought (Gordon P.) 1955

Gladys was Chilean. I anticipated Granddad's blithe remarks about immigrants leeching off our country and questions regarding her past life as a maid. He was liable to inquire how her mother managed to feed eighteen children. How could I stop his mouth?

Gladys and I spent Saturday preparing a fancy dinner. The card table was set up in the middle of the living room, covered with a cornflower blue tablecloth and matching napkins. An arrangement of white roses and daffodils decorated the coffee table. Gladys prepared pitchers of iced-tea and limeade. I bought yellow-rimmed goblets at Bloomingdale's basement, rib-eye steaks for the broiler, a bag of ice cubes, and a bottle of bourbon.

Granddad showed up promptly at five, dressed in a green-and-yellow plaid vest, brown trousers, and chocolate-brown shoes with white leather strips across the toes. As he dropped his wide-brimmed hat on the hall table, I noticed his neat, scrubbed hands, nails trimmed with colorless polish.

"The taxi driver wouldn't shut up," he exclaimed as he stood on the threshold. "I told him if he kept his thoughts to himself he'd get a double tip. He never said another word."

"And did he get the double tip?"

"Yes, certainly. After I halved it for driving too slow." I knew this was merely ribbing. Granddad had always been a generous tipper. The habit accompanied his wide popularity among his contemporaries. He was putting us on.

After being introduced to Gladys, he laid his broad-brimmed straw hat on the side chair alongside his carved pecan wood cane and seated himself slowly in an arm chair. As I poured cocktails, he filled us in on his trip and the unlimited failings of his Manhattan hotel, which included cranky room service, blinds that came crashing down at the slightest pull, and no spittoon anywhere in sight. Accepting the glass of bourbon and water with a gracious sweep of his arm, he turned to Gladys. "You're a pretty thing," he said.

She blushed. "Thanks," she giggled, smiling nervously. Here we go with the insults, I thought.

I was dead wrong.

"Now my granddaughter here tells me you come from Chile. Is that right?"

"Yes."

"Santiago?"

"Yes."

"I've heard a lot about the Chilean mountains and the magnificent coastline." Granddad fell into an easy conversation, clearly comfortable in the company of two young girls. "How far is Santiago from the ocean? Chile is a rich country is it not? Are people there well off? Does your boyfriend take you to the beach? Does he behave like a gentleman? What does your mother think of your living in New York? And with a young whippersnapper from Minnesota? If Judy gives you a hard time you come to me. I know how to straighten her out."

Gladys was getting the idea and before long was laughing at everything he said. She was not at all put off. In fact, she enjoyed the fancy flights of this gregarious southern gentleman and was eager to oblige. I soon learned details about her family life in Chile I hadn't suspected.

When we sat down at the card table for dinner, Granddad lowered himself with cautious elegance.

"You girls set a lovely table," he declared. "They can't do better at my favorite club. You did all this for me?"

"Granddad," I said, "You came all the way from Wheeling, and the least we could do is provide you with a home-cooked dinner. You must get tired of hotel meals. Besides, it's not often that we get visits from my flamboyant West Virginia grandfather."

He chuckled. "This is a first. But not the last. I intend to return and take Gladys dancing. Gladys, buy yourself some dancing shoes, and don't take too long. We're going on the town and I'll teach you how to do the shimmy."

Gladys laughed. "Oh, yes, with you, Mr. Fought, I'll dance anything you like. And I'll teach you the bossa nova."

I couldn't believe how they hit it off. Granddad's acerbic wit had dimmed to a faint, almost affectionate tease. The malice lurking under his barbs was gone and he treated Gladys with kind appreciation. Had age softened him so much? Was he so close to the grave that he was cleaning up his act for a last Cyrano de Bergerac flourish of goodness?

But he was still full of salt. Now that I realized he had a big heart, I liked him that way.

A horn set up a series of honks outside the window, echoed by several blares in the distance. Granddad laid his fork next to the dessert plate and meticulously wiped his mouth, sweeping away traces of chocolate pie. "That was wonderful. Now I'm not going to say more because I don't want you two to get big heads. It doesn't do for women to get too big-headed."

"It won't do for you to get big-headed either," I said, "Or you won't be able to get your crazy hat on."

"I've got plenty of big hats for big heads, never you fear."

"I never wear hats," put in Gladys inanely, "so I don't care how big my head gets."

"Listen, you girls. I suppose you go out with boys, don't you?"

"Now Granddad, don't expect us to tell you all our secrets."

"We date guys, but no one serious," Gladys said carefully. I thought of John and the romps on the couch.

"No special love?" Granddad pursued.

"No, not yet." We both shook our heads.

"When are you gals going to get married?"

"What's the rush? We're too young," I replied.

Granddad pulled out a long-tipped cigar—do you mind?—and puffed vigorously on it while Gladys and I lit up Paul Malls. He appeared to be having the time of his life, smiling with an air of breezy benevolence, residues of his old good looks and bon vivant air reappearing from time to time. He liked being with two single girls in a Manhattan apartment, a contrast to his stale hotel room in Wheeling.

Over coffee, he related stories of his past. How he had run away from home at age thirteen to escape the ravages of his fourth stepmother and made his way to a distant town, where he got work delivering fish. There followed a series of aimless jobs: He posted advertising signs for a vaudeville company, had a stint as a log roller, sold airplanes, and clerked in a post office. Self-taught, he moved up quickly, working his way into management. At one time or another he owned an oil company, owned and published a newspaper in Pennsboro, and was a long-standing racing commissioner in Wheeling. A major force in the Democratic Party, he was eventually elected mayor of Wheeling, a position he held for two years.

Parentless, self-made, Granddad fabricated a life from his good looks, gregarious personality, stamina, street smarts, and wit. Formed by challenges of the road and the defeats and successes that carried him along, he hadn't the internal imprint to be a successful husband or father. A product of the social society that formed him and the political forces that gave him sustenance, he reflected the attitudes of his milieu.

At the end of the evening, Granddad returned to the hotel to watch Ed Sullivan, with whom he was acquainted.

"There's no one like Ed," he said as he pulled on his coat. "You'd never know it, but Ed can really dish out the sarcasm."

What a pair they must have made.

Chapter 3   On the Job

The windowless office at David McKay Publishing was just large enough to hold three heavy wooden desks and a wall-to-wall bookcase. The desks were arranged in hierarchical order: Mrs. Ryan, the supervisor, sat at the first desk near the door and facing us, Maud Tsien, the young associate editor, at the second desk, and me, the assistant editor, behind her at the third, both of us facing Mrs. Ryan.

I liked the intimate quarters, with two congenial editors working silently close by. The three of us made every effort not to infringe on each other's space and guarded a respectful quiet. Maud was an expert at non-disturbance. In her quiet way she slipped in and out of the office, avoided unnecessary comments, and spoke in undertones into the telephone.

Mrs. Ryan ordered a special desk lamp with a moveable goose neck screwed onto my desktop to illuminate the galley proofs that were the meat of my work. Proofreading wasn't difficult, but the lack of activity, bent hour after hour over long strips of white galley paper, was tiring. The hardest part of proofreading was not to get caught up in the story. Since McKay produced fiction it was easy, as my eyes ran across the line looking for errors, to slide over and get lost in the story line. I finally devised a way out of this pitfall: by scanning every other line backwards, from right to left, the meaning would be obscured. Occasionally I grasped what was going on anyway and was drawn to know more. It required discipline.

Mrs. Ryan's primary goal was to avoid trouble. She wanted the job done with no fuss or complaints or temperamental demands. Maud and I were quiet; she liked that. The daughter of a former Chinese ambassador to the United States and an Ivy League school graduate, Maud understood decorum. Her slim figure and pale pumpkin dresses with mandarin collars looked stylish, complementing her neat cropped hair and composed features. I knew right off she was someone I'd like to know, but she maintained her distance, rarely initiating conversations or sharing confidences.

Finally, assured that things were going to work out, that no problems were about to rock our tight little ship, Mrs. Ryan started to open up and confide in us. During breaks, between sips of fresh coffee, she would talk of the latest holiday with her husband or Macy's May Day Parade. Twenty years our senior, with a rounded, no-waist figure, Mrs. Ryan became a sympathetic mentor to Maude and me.

One afternoon she led us across the Hudson to David McKay's New Jersey printing plant. We were greeted by Mel, the contact who processed my marked-up galleys, and he led us into the barn-like building where the massive lithograph machinery was chugging loudly and spitting out printed papers. We watched the offset process used for McKay books, where the image was stamped onto a round cylinder plate that in turn transferred the image to a rubber roller, which was then pressed onto the paper. The term offset, Mel explained, referred to the fact that the image plate itself doesn't touch the paper. Next he led us to a letterpress printer. In this method, the raised type-set plate was stamped directly onto the paper. This process, costlier and less popular, gave the printed material an older, medieval look.

As we left, Mel presented Mrs. Ryan with a beautiful hardbound book with an elaborate imprinted cover. The three of us, fascinated by seeing how our labors were converted to the final product, discussed what we'd learned on the return train ride. Maud enlightened us on the intricacies of Chinese printing methods and we poked fun at the two puppies across the aisle trying to break out of a covered wicker picnic basket. Mrs. Ryan even joined in our giggling.

As I got to know her, Mrs. Ryan revealed an unexpected modesty, even shyness. At work we were now indulging in quiet chats, and a sense of camaraderie imbued our little office. Even when there were deadlines to meet and we worked bent over our desks at full speed with no breaks, a sense of harmony prevailed. It was a productive work environment. I had never felt so comfortable or plugged in.

Mrs. Moser stepped up to my desk occasionally to chat. A senior editor at McKay, Jean Moser was a short woman in her fifties. Her neat, permed hair gave her the look of a den mother, until a manuscript passed over her desk. Then her mouth tightened and she was all business. She had the reputation as the best senior editor in the office. "She knows everyone. She looks like a homebody, but don't be fooled," Mrs. Ryan advised us. "Jean's sharp and gets what she wants without anyone knowing it."

Mrs. Moser told me about her frequent lunches reviewing manuscripts with authors and prospective clients. She not only shaped manuscripts, her success depended on building relationships. The artistic temperament had to be treated with kid gloves, she said. Her clients were her friends. I wanted to know how one could move into such a job. She tossed me a sympathetic smile. "There's no standard path. Tracey, the girl down the hall, has a degree in Creative Writing from Vassar. She's been with McKay for four years and has demonstrated talent and dedication. There's a model to follow."

When I asked her how to determine if a book was high quality, Mrs. Moser responded readily. "The answer is, I don't know. Books aren't measurable, readers' tastes change, trends come and go. Editors have to use their own judgment. Granted, it's always a risk, but also a rare opportunity to lead the public taste by promoting something you believe in. That's the joy of publishing."

Mrs. Moser took me under her wing. She assigned me extra projects, like critiquing published French books and evaluating their suitability for translation into English. For each completed assessment, I received $25. I was overjoyed at the chance to revive my French reading—and get paid! Evenings I read French novels, then wrote up reports. Once Mrs. Moser popped her head in the door to inform me that these reports were just what she wanted. She added that my writing captured the flavor of the books as well as the needed information, and she had further projects in mind for me.

On one of these projects I got in big trouble. Mrs. Moser brought me an original manuscript titled *Twelve Dead Geese* to edit. This was an unlooked-for opportunity, and I bounced home ecstatic, manuscript under my arm. It was a farcical tale by a Hungarian author named Eugene de Thassy. The narrator, a young fellow fleeing his native Hungary penniless and alone, encountered a whirlwind of mishaps, scandals, and offbeat characters in Paris. He managed to survive through his good looks, innocence, and willingness to accommodate the sexual desires of roving women. Mrs. Moser warned me to respect the creative authority of the authors, who considered each word inviolate, and to be ready to back up every stylistic alteration I made. Writers, especially successful ones, had to be reassured, guided, and placated. She would be behind me in the wings, doing just that. As I sat at home, pouring over the manuscript in my lap, I whipped my pencil over the page to delete a description of the narrator that I judged was glaringly egotistical. He shouldn't be puffing himself up like that— can't show our hero in such a light!

Three days later, Mrs. Moser called me in and informed me my deletion was a mistake, that the author had *intended* to mock his hero's shortcomings. Evidently Eugene de Thassy was in a bit of a fit. However, Mrs. Moser hastened to assure me that she had reinstated the section and managed to pacify the author, explaining my status as a promising novice.

Never mind, she said less severely, I was learning.

More than a year passed in industrious harmony. One morning, Maud announced that she was leaving—she had taken an advanced job with Doubleday. Mrs. Ryan and I were stunned. Mrs. Ryan bit her lip, expressed her regret and left the room. She remained absent for several hours. I had learned by this time that Mrs. Ryan, who managed to run a steady ship in our office, did not respond well to stress. On the surface, she was precise and poised. Only Maud and I were privy to her behind-the-scenes scrambles when faced with the slew of demands that passed over her desk from time to time. Once or twice she appeared to crumble under the onslaught of unexpected phone calls, lost galleys, last-minute refusals, and the rush to meet a revised deadline. I kept my distance as she clutched, tottered, and then finally settled down into a problem-solving mode until everything fell back into place.

The idea of our well-balanced editorial office breaking up was not to her liking.

About this time one of the front office editors announced she was leaving for California. My ears perked up. What I would give to be her replacement! I hurried to Mrs. Moser's office. She said I could apply if I liked, but it was a long shot.

Although not unexpected, I received the rejection notice with a jolt. My attitude turned negative. It occurred to me that proofreading was becoming a drudgery. The confined office life was stale. After several weeks my application to be considered to replace the senior editor in the front office was denied. I resented this slight. It was too much.

I quit. It was a foolhardy move. Other job applicants possessed credentials that far surpassed mine. And I'd finally found a permanent job in Manhattan where I fit in and had proven suitable. Where else would I find work to equal it? Hundreds of young job seekers swarming the streets of New York would pay a prince's ransom for my job. My friends were impressed, my parents pleased, and my life had congealed around the security I now enjoyed, the foundation of my New York existence. What was I thinking?

However, in those days I ran through people and situations without giving them weight. Whatever existed didn't seem to be enough. With no pressing problems to latch onto or desires to chase, I felt something was missing. There was always a better situation up ahead, and if I didn't plunge into it I would miss the fulfillment that was there. I wanted more. I deserved more: my potential, my education, my determination, the backing of my family and the fancy of my dreams, all demanded the level of achievement to which I was entitled.

If not at David McKay, I would find it elsewhere.

The extent of my actual capabilities and weaknesses were yet to be revealed. It would be a hard lesson to learn.

Mrs. Ryan was beside herself. "You as well? What's going on here?" she cried. Mrs. Ryan decided to leave too. She started sending out résumés to contacts she had amassed over the years. By the end of the month, she had found an excellent position and all three of us had given notice. We lunched at an Italian restaurant on our last day. I never saw Mrs. Ryan again. Maud invited me to her wedding, two months later, but I didn't attend. I was—unlike Mrs. Ryan and Maud—out on the streets job hunting.

Other changes were about to occur. The disenchantment with my roommate that had been escalating was coming to a head.

Journal Entry

Gladys is obsessed with American ways. When we first moved in, she was transfixed as I lined the drawers with shelving paper. She considers my habits snobbery—like when I threw away the food left by the former tenants—but now she has started to adopt a fastidiousness of her own. Now she gets indignant when napkins are not set on the table alongside the plates.

But her resentment grows. She watches me like a hawk, her eyes following me as I take my dinner plate over to the couch and pull out the Times. *Sometimes she picks up the paper and enunciates sarcastically, "I think I'll see how my stocks are doing today." Her favorite word has become "elegance" and she says things like "I shall now retire to the blue room."*

It didn't take long to discover that she lies without blinking and will say or do anything to cover up a mistake or get what she wants. She told me she was 26, my age, but I don't think she's more than 21 or 22. When on occasion we're both seated in the living room, she rattles off elaborate stories of her wealth back in Chile, her house in the country, her car and trunks full of clothes. I have grave doubts about all this; she scrambles too carefully to send checks and bargain merchandise back to her family. I no longer pay attention to her tales.

The blaring rock music she plays constantly on the radio is bad enough. What I really can't stand is the way she copies me, following me around like a shadow. She is everywhere; she seems to inhabit all rooms of the apartment at the same time. When she hears a sound she rushes over; whenever I make a move—like pull out a drawer—she appears in a flash, pretending to have business. There is nowhere to be alone. If I shut the bedroom door she comes bounding in.

I swear she never sleeps when I am awake. I don't know how she does it. She keeps vigil like a panther stalking prey, never missing a creak or glimmer if I turn or cough. The heads of our beds meet in the corner so she is right there, yet I never hear the deep breathing of sleep next to me.

This apartment is too small!

Lately it's gotten worse. She only goes out on nights when I am at my writing class at The New School or have plans. And she never fails to appear when I have a friend over, slipping past us into the bedroom, leaving the door cracked.

I got a call from the power company that we were in arrears—Gladys's responsibility. That was last week and she still has done nothing. I expect the lights to go out any minute.

All she ever wants to talk about is John. If I don't answer from my chair she says "Oh, I'm so occupied with my paper!"

Though I could strangle her sometimes, I can't say that I dislike her. She is cheerful, good-natured, warm, fun, and has spunk. I don't really want to live alone. Never mind that she is shallow, has no interests, and that she pouts and whines.

Later

Gladys has been reading my diary. It's the last straw. After Chester's revelation I am furious. "Gladys says you hate your mother and don't get along and have all sorts of problems. She can't understand that, since she and her mother are so close. She feels sorry for you," he reports. I don't like her any more.

The promised Spanish lessons never materialized. She can't converse, she only knows how to be silly—and the art of subterfuge. I want a roommate where there's a sliver of commonality. Is that too much to ask?

Chapter 4   Change of Scene

Two inches of snow had fallen during the night. In New York two inches of snow was considered a storm—offices were closed, entrances were blocked off, until finally, stubborn and growly, plows churned up the streets as if they'd never dealt with snow before. I stepped outside to a scene of white-coated streets, dim in the grey cast of the sun. Being Sunday morning, the traffic was thinner than usual. A few pedestrians trudged along the snowy sidewalks, ignoring the red lights at the corners. I walked slowly down Fifth Avenue, peering through the windows of Tiffany's at the showcase of glittering gems. The bulging diamonds looked static in their velvet cases, without effervescence or purpose, their glow diffusing helplessly in the stale air.

Sundays were like that. Sunday was the lonely day of the week. Sundays called for family, for intimate gatherings that weren't taking place in my life. Everything stopped: work, grocery runs, maintenance chores, the evening entertainments that took up Saturdays, all evaporated on Sundays. How to fill the hours? Gazing in the store window, I glimpsed my skewed reflection in the glass, like a face caught behind an ocean porthole, searching the horizon for signs of life.

Sometimes I meandered to the Metropolitan Museum of Art or stopped at a Horn and Hardart Automat for a glazed donut and coffee. As I sat at a small laminate table, the noise of dishes scraping in the kitchen, compartment doors clicking shut, and voices droning through the room sounded in the background like echoes from another dimension. Of course, I could have stayed home and read or listened to the radio or written letters or even gone to a movie—in New York you could do anything alone and no one cared. But I didn't have the heart to sit in a comfy easy chair in my living room and fake being warm and cozy. It was *Sunday,* the day to relax and enjoy, but I wasn't relaxing and enjoying like everyone else in the universe. Rather, I was drifting like the white flakes that circled between the jagged skyscrapers before dropping, lifeless, to earth.

It was on one of those deadbeat Sundays that I picked up the phone to hear Margo's voice on the line. "What's up? Long time no see," she began, ignoring the fact that she hadn't returned my calls for weeks. In fact, I'd seen little of her since my return. She'd been preoccupied, with never a moment to spare, not at all her usual self. I couldn't imagine what had changed. Maybe she'd forgotten her roving high school friend now that she was sharing an apartment in Chelsea with Kerstin Patterson, a sorority sister from the University of Minnesota.

Margo's tone was encouraging. The Chelsea apartment was undergoing changes, the third roommate had moved out, and she and Kerstin were seeking a replacement. The rent was only $100 a month, split three ways. As soon as she discovered Gladys and I were splitting up, Margo invited me for dinner and suggested I consider moving in with them. I decided to forget the non-returned phone calls and the time she stood me up for dinner and agreed.

I moved to Chelsea the first of April. The West 17th Street apartment abutted the north end of Greenwich Village and had the same beaten-down funky look as the Village. And it was rent-controlled cheap.

Margo Holt

My first morning, Margo and I lounged at the chrome-legged breakfast table while Kerstin brewed a fresh pot of coffee at the sink. The lime green Formica counter was covered with miscellaneous jelly and peanut butter jars, a pepper grinder, a faded porcelain crock holding cooking utensils, and a toaster with pull-out sides. A metal coffee pot was perking and spitting water at the lid. The scrappy state of the small kitchen didn't bother me in the slightest. I liked the continual flush of people coming and going and the cheerful air of something always happening. And being part of a threesome with girls I knew and could relate to. I had admired Kerstin during our Delta Gamma days together at the University of Minnesota. This was going to be just the thing.

Kerstin ceased piling dishes into the sink and leaned against the counter, wiping her hands on a green towel. Her full dark hair fell in a stylish bob around her face, a distinctive face with a sharply etched nose, arched cheekbones and gracefully carved chin. Posed against the counter, she looked smart, attractive, and sure of herself. "Do you take sugar?" she asked. Then, without a pause, "I hope you liked your bed last night."

Three single beds were lined up in a row in the small bedroom, and as the newcomer I had been assigned the one in the middle. Next to the beds, on the other side of the single window, a black iron fire escape plunged to the second story below. We could crawl out on the rungs to sit, smoke, and catch a stray breeze on a hot August evening.

"No, white please. The bed was fine. I always sleep like a log."

"So," said Margo, "Are we agreed on how to manage the household?" She leaned back in her chair and studied the ashtray in front of her, one of those round bean-bags where you pushed the center plunger and the surface tray spun around, dropping the contents into the bag. Margo had tried for several years to give up smoking, without success. The thought of it prompted her to pull a Chesterfield out of the package lying on the table. "Judy, are you okay with our slap-dash arrangements? We play by ear around here."

"Absolutely. The chores, the bills, the shopping, I think we've covered everything. The rest is serendipity."

Since their standards varied substantially, Kerstin had convinced Margo that they should hire a maid a half-day a week. Beyond that, we each made our own bed, cleaned the tub after use, washed our own dishes, and were responsible for specific chores. On Saturdays we bought communal groceries and hauled them up the four flights in a shopping cart. With conflicting schedules, most of our meals were on the fly, although occasionally someone got inspired and cooked dinner for three.

Kerstin sat down, cradling her coffee mug in one palm, the other hand balancing a cigarette next to her mouth. I was to learn that it wasn't often she settled in. She was usually tied up in acting classes, auditions, or her part-time accounting job and was rarely around for long—places to go, people to see.

"So, Kerstin, what are you doing now? How do you like your acting classes?" I asked. I braced myself to listen as her thoughts dipped and crossed over each other.

Kerstin flicked her cigarette over the ashtray. "I'd really like to return to the Allenberry Playhouse in Pennsylvania, you know my last stint paid $65 a week and got me an equity card. It's hard but I've got a good chance as Timothy is putting in a plug for me. The idea is that the show will be taken on the road and the summer is not what it's about, you see. Of course I'll have to give up these classes, but Germaine is not adverse to that plan, and it looks like by June I'll have an answer. It's very exciting, not a big deal, just a small part, you understand, but Jonas has the fastest car around. It's not really his turn. By fall the whole thing will resume. That is if it all falls into place." I was not able to decipher much of this train of thought and planned to pry the details from Margo later. But I was impressed with Kerstin's dramatic appearance. With her dark hair brushed back from her forehead and cryptic expression, she looked like the film actress Alexis Smith boarding the Orient Express for the Kasbah, sophisticated and steamy.

"You remind me of Alexis Smith," I remarked.

"Oh, no," she protested, smiling.

"So what are you working on now?"

"We're rehearsing O'Neil at Herbert Berghof Studio. After each scene we pair up and improvise in our own words. John calls it 'racing to the moon.'"

Margo, who had gone to the next room, re-entered the kitchen, carrying an armload of soiled saucers and cups.

"I found these under the bed. Don't know how they got there. Can't tempt the ants!"

"The food is soldered onto those dishes like cement. It's not going to do the ants any good," Kerstin remarked, wiping her finger over a plate.

"Better let them soak for a week," said Margo.

"Better make it a month," said Kerstin.

"Why not throw them away?" I suggested. "They look like they cost ten cents apiece."

"Can't afford such luxuries," retorted Margo. "I'm on a budget."

"Good, maybe now we can pay the electric bill," said Kerstin. She snuffed out her cigarette, stood up and disappeared into the bedroom with a half-smile. In a while she emerged, pulling on a rose-colored sweater. "John and I have some rehearsing to do," she said, stuffing an orange into her purse as she passed the kitchen.

"Better take a sandwich. All you have to do is spread a piece of bread with peanut butter, it's really not that hard," Margo remarked as Kerstin reached the front door.

"Don't be smart," Kerstin shot back. With a twist of her head, she drew a tote bag over her shoulder, grabbed a ring of keys on a camel hair chain from the counter, and reached for the doorknob.

"Are you going to meet us later at the White Horse? " Margo called after her.

"Can't. Got a date later. See you guys." And she was gone.

Summer washed over our neighborhood precipitately, without warning, bringing warm asphalt nights. Margo and I wandered over to Greenwich Village, past old buildings where artists wearing headbands lived in loft studios and across crooked streets and tree-lined squares crowded with young people and university students setting about at any cost to do their own thing. Bookshops with wrought iron doors displayed carts of paperbacks, narrow stairs led down to bright open rooms displaying oil paintings, and sidewalk restaurants were packed with slim youth in leather vests and bearded men in berets. Notes from a plaintive guitar drifted from a nearby square, and caterwauls from jazz bands soared out from underground dives as we passed.

Sometimes we caught a blues singer at Charlie's Bar or the Village Gate, often accompanied by two guys from upstairs, one of whom employed Kerstin as a part-time accountant. One evening at the White Horse the four of us, accompanied by Kerstin and a male friend, spied Dylan Thomas seated at the bar clutching an enormous German stein. Glen offered to buy the next round if one of us would invite Thomas over to our table for a drink. But no one dared, and as we watched him chugging beer after beer it became obvious that the swirly-haired figure swaying on the bar stool couldn't have made it to our table if he'd wanted to.

†

Manhattan pulsed with jobs, friends, and variety. Entertainments and events materialized from all sides. Soon after moving in, I tagged along with Margo, Kerstin and the two guys they were dating to an apartment overlooking Central Park, a five-room flat furnished with modern walnut furniture, print sofas and Tiffany lamps. The dates, George and Steve, shared an apartment on the Upper West Side. George was a loquacious secondary school teacher whom Margo was attempting to shape into a promising partner. Kerstin was half in love with Steve, a good-looking Wall Street broker of Greek extraction wearing a cream seersucker jacket. Steve reached over politely to hang up my black mohair coat, eyeing it with admiration. The coat had a lush silver fox collar that clasped at the neck and continued down the front opening on both sides. Mother had picked it out, assured that it would accommodate all my fancy New York engagements. I was still waiting for an invitation from the governor's mansion. In some part of my mind, I understood that in wearing the coat I was caving to the pretensions of society that I had so hotly repudiated, that expensive clothes, meant to dazzle, were no more than gloss. But I wore it, enjoying the softness next to my face, feeling pliant and two-faced.

The young singles at Margo's workplace often threw Saturday night parties. Kerstin and I usually joined the cluster of males around the kitchen table discussing politics while Margo chatted with captivating prospects in the crowded living room. We dated some of the men, off and on. Margo and I played bridge regularly with two boys who worked at the state office of management and budget. I was entranced with everything. Margo with her energy and assertiveness made things happen, and I went along without much thought, still coasting with the gusts that blew my way.

As the months passed, the rain of parties began to slacken, the bars we frequented lost some of their luster, and Margo and I felt the forward momentum of our lives slowing to a dull hum. A pressing issue was inserting itself into our single lifestyle, becoming more and more insistent: what to do about sex. We were determined to break the sexless—or sex-limited—pattern of our lives. We had thrown out our puritan upbringing, the question was what to replace it with, how to specify what we wanted for ourselves and how to go about getting it. Having made the calculated decision that, at age twenty-seven, we wanted sex in our lives, we had to find a way to break through the old prohibitions. We wanted to be fully sexual. But how? We could reject the strictures decreeing that girls who "like it" aren't nice, that men don't respect girls who "give out," that when you give in to a male's requests you lose some precious, private part of yourself and become the underdog. We could change our attitudes, but how could we handle the rejection that accompanied giving men "what they wanted?"

We tried various approaches. In her relationship with George, Margo attempted abstinence. In remaining celibate, she appealed to his Catholic upbringing and ensured that he was not out just for sex. Eventually George not only acquiesced, but he grew to appreciate her stand. They would wait, and she would be respected. Then things took a turn. She decided she wasn't madly in love with him. But he was decent and would make a good husband, and she would forgo love for a stable family life. Unfortunately, she couldn't sustain her interest. There was no chemistry. Eventually her feelings for George faded and she broke off with him.

Kerstin fared no better with Steve. Her qualms were complicated. She liked Steve too much to risk giving herself to him entirely without a commitment—her own emotional involvement would be increased by such a step, while his would likely diminish—while she continued to assert her aversion to marriage. Steve was confused. Kerstin struggled with the conflict. Like me, she had come to Manhattan putting her career first—now she was faced with adapting her womanhood to this choice. Marriage, which would stifle serious work goals, was out. Sex with a serious partner required marriage in order to sustain respect. So the thinking went.

At last Margo devised a way out. During a Christmas office party, with the Christmas lights sparkling and the booze flowing, she deliberately made her interest in finding a sexual partner known. The man in a grey suit seated next to her had straightaway taken her down the street for a drink and broached an arrangement. His wife was mentally ill and incarcerated, he explained, and he would like nothing better than an affair with a fetching woman like herself. Margo liked him, and from then on every Friday he would take her out nightclubbing, then back to the apartment where they made out on the couch as I lay on the other side of the wall.

Although I was hit with a quick touch of envy, it was soon replaced by distrust. Once or twice the two of them returned to the apartment from a nearby bar and we sat over a nightcap in the living room. I was not impressed. This man was all nodding smiles. Once he didn't show for a date, and Margo came home alone. It seemed a shame she had to resort to this suited, wise-cracking businessman, whose wife was probably not at a mental institution but home darning his shirts. Margot countered that she considered him a good, decent guy and hinted that his attentions brought her to heights of pleasure she'd not experienced before.

Kerstin attempted the same path with a married project manager, recruited without much difficulty from Margo's office. But it didn't take. The lack of commonality put her off. I understood the attempt to resolve the problem: it involved creative compromise.

After six months Margo broke off with the businessman. The restricted routine of drinking and bedding and lack of similar interests wore on her. Evidently the arrangement didn't fill her romantic needs. He failed to show one too many times. Flowers didn't make it up. She'd had enough.

As for me, I attempted another route. I turned to Frank, the waiter at the Village bar where Margo and I occasionally hung out, with or without dates. Frank was boyish and thinly handsome, with a tall, slender figure. One night, as we sat over Manhattans listening to the sounds of a mellow jazz trio, I watched Frank as he moved through the shadows with his tray, looking like Frank Sinatra slinking to the stage. When he stopped to talk, I told him I liked the dark type, admiring his head of loose black hair.

His name was Nathan Feinberg, and he lived in Queens, but I called him Frank. He took to coming over nights he didn't work. One evening, the two of us were seated on the couch in my apartment, the strains of Sinatra crooning in the background. Frank asked to go into the bedroom; I said yes. After we kissed for a while longer he made love to me. He was tender, and it felt good to be held against him. I loved the kissing and the way it pulsed my heart and spread flames deep into my groin.

Afterward Frank sat on the edge of the bed and lit up a Chesterfield.

"Was that good?" He wanted to know. "Did you have an orgasm?"

The question took me aback. I hesitated, then some unexplained daring broke through my reserve. "Frank, I have something to tell you. Do you mind if I speak candidly?"

"No, go ahead."

"I've never had an orgasm with a man." The words dropped like cement blocks to the floor. Only in the dark, faced with a direct question, with someone non-threatening like Frank, could I have made that confession.

Frank wiggled. He stood up. "Too bad. Well, I guess you can't help it." He was quiet, not finding much else to say. He kissed me at the door, long and deep.

I never heard from him again. Evidently my confession had spooked him. He wasn't interested in assuming my problem. I kept to myself the fact that I was crushed. We had nothing in common, I reasoned. But for a while I was ashamed to look at my image in the mirror.

What was the route to a satisfying sexual relationship? I couldn't buy the theory of American writer Eleanor Perenyi that women must develop a technique to capture men, must learn the traditional play of advance and retreat, of resistance alternating craftily with surrender, ploys mastered by civilized European society. She admonished women to learn the power of flirtation and suggestion, to cross swords with their male partners in order to spur desire. It was true, she admitted, that American men can't understand this form of coquetry. They take it as another form of female aggression. But women must learn to play the game. "No longer," she wrote, "like Artemis can we flee through the forest certain of pursuit. There is an awkward pause, during which we realize that no one is following." Americans, she believed, were missing out on the best sex.

Another writer cautioned women not to reveal their happiness to a man, as it would be used against her. A man despises the ability women have to be happy with their life, she claimed. He will press to find out if you are happy and on discovering the affirmative, will tear into your life to find out what makes you so and then turn away disappointed and aloof, as he knows this will never make him happy and therefore you are a fool.

All these machinations were too high-minded; I couldn't even contend with the basics. Despite my eagerness to have sex in my life, I was held back by feelings of inadequacy, and deep reservations about the appeal of my body and lack of sexual skills. Besides, I knew nothing about forming a relationship. If I was enthralled with a boy, I became defensive, afraid he would shrink from an interest on my part, and cloaked my feelings with indifference.

Journal Entry

I want sex. Margo and Kerstin want sex. We feel deprived.
We're twenty-seven years old. We're single with no knowledge

of the future. I have no interest in marriage. Kerstin feels ambiguous, she wants marriage and she doesn't. Margo seeks marriage but doesn't know if it will happen, and what does she do in the meantime?

We don't believe the old garbage. Females are responsible for saying no to sex. Men try, women refuse. Men enjoy sex, women have babies. Men get carried away, can't control themselves. Women only want to be caressed. We understand this is hooey.

We've been turned off all our lives, programmed to denial. How to get turned on and retain our dignity? You can't count on marriage to solve the problem. We are coldly controlled until then, protecting the virginal core, the religious commandment. Then marriage and the big switch. The woman hasn't a clue. The man performs his self-loaded ritual. The woman is left behind, aloft in the beginning stages. The wolf and the lamb climb into in the marital bed expecting to transform into two doves.

At least this is what female essayists write.

†

The following spring, Kerstin moved to Ninth Street to be near the acting studio, and Margo and I were on our own. Our lives in Chelsea had settled into a predictable routine. We had exhausted the neighborhood haunts, and people entered our lives and moved on, swept up in the continual flow of Manhattan transition. Everyone seemed to be going somewhere, while we sat on the fire escape gathering dust.

The long hand of inspiration inserted itself late one Sunday morning. A shaft of light flashed under the window shade and spread a bright yellow ribbon over the couch where Margo sprawled full length, gazing at the ceiling. I sat cross-legged in the green tweed chair perusing the Sunday *Times*. Two cups of coffee sat on the coffee table, along with a circle-stained *New Yorker* and a stack of Sinatra records. Groggy from staying up late, we were content to wallow in the sun-laced room and feel the heat from the radiators rising over us.

The apartment didn't always feel so cozy. Habits unnoticed during the years of our friendship now surfaced. I found Margo's messiness and unreliability irritating. She had a tolerance for disorder and didn't let me know when she would be leaving the apartment or returning. She followed my every move, what I wore, what I was doing, what I said on the phone. As I withdrew and kept more to myself, Margo felt compelled to move in closer; in no way would she brook my distancing. As for me, Margo accused me of being self-centered, wanting things to be my own way, of being testy without saying what I wanted, and scatterbrained to a fault. There were more gripes, faded now from memory. That I had trouble adjusting to roommates was not surprising. The skills of talking things out without blame, setting up expectations, compromising, and tolerance were light years away back then.

I had to admit Margo was benefitting from counseling sessions with Dr. Allen. She claimed they were changing her life. Never had she felt so stabilized. Seeing a psychiatrist was the best thing that had ever happened to her, she said. Taking the first step had been hardest, but she was sick of being depressed. Sick and tired. Dr. Allen helped her quit smoking, regulated her erratic use of anti-depressant pills, and put her on a diet and exercise program. She began to be on time. He persuaded her to organize her life, to set deadlines, to clean up her space and put things away—in short, the basics.

I was amazed at the common-sense simplicity of the routine that pulled her, as she said, into the land of the living. I could have used therapy myself to deal with sporadic bouts of depression, but harbored a stubborn belief that I was unique and it was the rest of the world that was flawed.

On this Sunday morning, lazy and mellow in the living room, lapsing into girl talk, our differences evaporated. Last night's rambling discussions with our dates had lasted into the wee hours, the four of us seated with night caps around the kitchen table. The old high school relationship with Margo had revived, the social synchronization reestablished—the sense of play, setting each other up for humor, cutting through the other's meaning, recalling past anecdotes. We enjoyed the sense of moving on the same track.

"Something's missing," Margo announced unexpectedly from the couch, leaning on an elbow to reach for her coffee cup. "We've been living here a year and a half."

"And...?"

"And where are we headed, tell me that?" We'd already had discussions examining our lives, trying to figure out what was next in the progression towards—towards happiness. When we came to Manhattan, we were young, presentable, free. While waiting for the clock to toll an answer, we'd been having fun gathering flowers. But the petals were beginning to fade. The stagnant odor of yesterday's bouquets seeped in occasionally through the window. What followed down the line?

I got up and fetched a second cup of coffee from the kitchen. The faint odor of gasoline, wet cement, and black dust drifted in through the open window as I passed. "It's clear," I said, settling back in the chair, "something has to be done."

Margo nodded. "We can't go on like this."

I drew my legs under me. "Why don't we like it here any more? This is a perfectly adequate apartment and within our price range."

"It's grubby," she said thoughtfully. "It's old. It's in a lousy neighborhood. And I'm sick of sitting on the filthy fire escape to keep cool. I'm sick of smelling the dirt from the window and getting dusted with soot as I lie in bed at night. Don't you think?"

"Yes, the apartment is old and faded. But it's a symbol of freedom. It's *ours*. We never cared before. Why should we care now?"

"Look at it this way. Have we established promising, fulfilling careers?"

"No."

Are we satisfied with our dates?"

"No."

"Because these guys are going nowhere, have dumb jobs, do nothing. They take us out, buy us a few drinks—but that's getting old. Judy, would you marry one of them?"

"No."

"You see!"

"But I don't want to get married."

"Ever?" Long pause. What *did* I want here? "You've done your thing, traipsed around the world, lived places. Is this your last stop? Do you want to live here forever, become ensconced in the bar life of the Village, grow old in a rent-controlled walkup?"

"No, but aren't you missing a few steps?" Yet something in me resonated to her words. Exactly where was I on the success scale? The drive to write, my lifelong passion and directive, had withered on the vine, unattended and unnourished, superseded by the search for I wasn't sure what—some fundamental elixir of life. Or the futile attempt to lift happiness out of daily living. No career had developed to lift me to the clouds. I knew no writers or painters to share artistic aspirations with. What I did have was not substantial. Maybe I had reached a turning point.

"You have a point, kiddo," I admitted. "We do need to meet more promising men." With George out of the picture and me with no one special in view, a new setup was in order. Lackluster boys were wearing thin. Maybe the same old parties and dates were no longer enough.

"And," resumed Margo, "I'm sick of going to the movies to escape from the heat. We saw fifteen movies last August trying to keep cool. We need air conditioning! And a clean place without ants. We need to look good. We can't rely on our youth forever. We need to move on!" She drew her hand through her cropped hair and scooted up on the cushion. "Come on, Judy, we've got to get serious! We've got to get ourselves situated. Enough said."

I had to admire Margo's resourcefulness. She had made up her mind to be married, and I was considering it a direction, if not a goal. She was right. My wanderlust had sunk under the streets of the city, the old siren calls buried in the iron rattle of the subway trains. Sometimes, sitting on a bench alongside the peaceful flow of the East River, I'd felt a nudge of emptiness press against my chest. Yes, it was time to make a move.

Our future depended on us. and we needed to locate ourselves in a milieu where it could take off. Moving to the kitchen table, we tallied our salaries and expenses. It was within our means to move up.

We went apartment scouting.

Little did I dream that a door would be opening to a new path, or rather back to an older path that I thought I'd abandoned forever. And that I would go willingly through the door.

Chapter 5 — Gramercy Park

The Gramercy Park apartment came with a uniformed doorman and a view. It felt quite elegant to be greeted by Chad every evening with "Hello Miss Bradford," sometimes accompanied by informative comments: "The delivery man has driven round the back and will be at your apartment directly." We were used to old, faded, and atmospheric, not modern, accommodating, and bustling.

We bought some second hand furniture and mailed our new address to everyone we'd ever met. I'd been employed at Academic Press for several months doing secretarial work, but the chance for advancement was not promising. Margo was still in marketing at the same level. If our careers didn't sweep us up into the high ranks of achievement, living at 32 Gramercy Park South would.

"This is unbearable. There's no pool," I said to Margo.

"Not only that, but we have to take our garbage to the bin at the end of the hall. It's too much!"

"I can see trees out of the windows. I don't know how I'll ever adjust."

"Meanwhile, maybe we can start with getting rid of our little friends in the kitchen," Margo said. We'd seen a cockroach scurrying in and out of the kitchen drain. "Chad tells me they're almost impossible to eradicate since they crawl through the pipes from one floor to another. It only takes one dirty kitchen to infect the whole building." Faced with the disgusting black creatures that could detect a raisin a block away, we were forced to keep every surface in the kitchen constantly clean. The cockroach survived the poison treat we set out for him and finally Margo decided just to adopt him and named him Charlie.

"We don't bother him, he doesn't bother us," she said. "Just don't leave out any trace of food." Our housekeeping improved; the kitchen became spotless.

The dinner routine was a model of efficiency. Margo and I filled our plates directly from the pans on the stove and consumed our food standing sideways in the Pullman kitchen. Soon the plates were dispensed with; it was easier to transfer the frozen vegetables or canned stew directly from the hot pan on the stove into our mouths, thus paring down dish washing to two forks, a serving spoon, and a pan. When rushed, we simply opened the refrigerator door and ate directly from the storage container. Before long we began storing leftover food in the fridge without transferring it from the cooking pan to a container, using even fewer dishes. Instead of balancing the meal with primary food categories, we balanced the week, each night consuming one food class: vegetables on Monday, meat on Tuesday, salad on Wednesday, etc. The dinner hour became practically unnoticeable.

Soon after we moved in, an opportunity opened up to spend alternate weekends skiing in Vermont. A girl at work belonged to a ski club and they were one person short this season, were my roommate and I interested? Margo and I could split an $80 season lift ticket and share a single spot with a group of young avid skiers. The idea was appealing. I hadn't been on the slopes since my college days when I spent Easter Vacation skiing at Aspen, Colorado. I talked Margo into alternating weekends with me.

Every other Friday after work I joined a carpool for the four-hour drive to Mt. Snow. We occupied the top two floors of a small house just outside of town, with the guys sleeping dorm-style in the attic loft and the girls in bedrooms on the second level below. The girls did the cooking, and the guys drove everyone up the mountain every morning in time to hit the slopes when the gates opened.

The diehards took off as soon as we hit the chair lifts, and I watched them careening back and forth in the whiteness, throwing up curves of snow like alpine ballerinas. I followed the group in their descent down the mountain, bringing up the rear. Some of the slopes were too steep for me to navigate and I stood peering down the perpendicular cliff, knowing there was no way I could make the turns at the speed I would be forced into by the steep grade. I looked around for alternative routes, but there were none.

The choices were slim: go down or stay there forever.

The rest of the group had long disappeared. Finally, clutched with fear but tired of standing alone on the upper crest of the mountain, I held my breath and started down, a wild descent as I flailed and spun around the turns, barely under control. Mostly I flew down like a speeding locomotive, attempting brake turns whenever the mountain relaxed its plunge.

Finally I signed up for lessons. I had to give up the thrill of speeding in order to practice the turns, but I didn't mind. Skiing had gotten into my blood. I never missed a weekend the entire season. Margo only made the trip a few times. Speeding down mountains didn't tempt her as much as the plethora of activities taking place in the city. Animated by our move to Gramercy Park, she was busy volunteering at the John Lindsay mayoral campaign headquarters, attending parties given by our new neighbors, and persuading the bright checkout boy at the local grocers that he should develop his talents and enroll in college.

One Saturday afternoon, as I sat in the living room checking the mail I'd retrieved from the rows of metallic slots in the first-floor mail room, Margo came bounding in. "We've been invited to a party tonight. By the *cutest* boy!" She was grinning from ear to ear. How could she be so perky? She'd been getting little sleep, always out, arriving home late. Plus she was up and down all night. Every time I brought a date home, or the phone rang, or anyone came in, she would wander out to see what was up. Sometimes she even slept in her clothes, ready to leap into whatever was to happen next.

Dashing into the kitchen and returning with a cup of coffee and a plate of bismarcks, she fell on the couch, itching to tell more. "We met in the elevator. You know how everyone chats it up in the elevator. Well, that little poodle who lives upstairs got in with his owner and this boy and I started teasing about mistaking it for a dust mop, and when the dog got off—did he say good-bye?—be quiet—the boy and I were left alone. We got to talking and he rode past his floor—he's on the fourth—and accompanied me up to the seventh and right to our front door." Margo leaned over and snatched a bismarck from the coffee table. "He's a manufacturing distributor, grew up in upstate New York, and guess what—he's Irish *and* Catholic. His name is Will Heatherton." Margo watched excitedly as I took a long drag of my Pall Mall and blew a billow of smoke into the room.

"You found all that out between three floors?"

Margo uttered a bouncing laugh. "And more! We have a lot in common. Will's never met a woman from Minnesota, but claims to have a great interest in the Midwest. He has a roommate; you'd better come to the party tonight."

By the third date, Margo was declaring that she and Will had amazing rapport, great chemistry, and compatible backgrounds. She anticipated his calls, and if one failed to come she tossed her head and said she was going to date other guys. Sometimes Will showed up at our door unexpectedly. If Margo was out, I'd tell him she was on a date, without mentioning the gender. "Don't know when she'll be back. Any message?" A frown would spread over his forehead and he'd hesitate a few minutes before finally turning to go. We girls had to stick together.

With the arrival of the Christmas holidays, the city became awash in overhead arches wrapped in blinking garlands and evergreen wreaths. Christmas trees sparkled on park corners, and shoppers squeezed into revolving doors laden chin-high with colorful boxes. On the plaza at Rockefeller Center, Santa Claus-clad figures glided skillfully among skaters dressed in short fur-trimmed coats.

In our seventh-floor apartment at Gramercy Park, a Christmas party was ending. Most of the guests had left. Plates dotted with crumbling remains and olive slices littered the serving trays, and glasses stained with butterscotch-colored liquor and overstuffed ashtrays were scattered around the living room. The only light came from a small Christmas tree on a corner table strung with red and yellow bulbs and a Chinese table lamp next to the bookcase.

Margo and I, released from hostess duties, were relaxed into the couch cushions. I breathed in deeply, feeling a release of tension ease through me as four of us conversed quietly in the dim light, nursing the remains of our bourbon or scotch. Our voices had slowed, shifting to a lower register. It was that exquisite time after a party when the hype and excitement had quieted to a soft hum and those left felt freed up and special and ready to address the real issues.

Ward was seated in the high-backed chair across from me looking austere and reliable. A fellow-traveler from my European sojourn two years earlier, Ward had recently returned from a lengthy assignment in Russia for the *New York Times*.

The Saturday after his return we dined at a Russian restaurant in the East Village. Sitting across from him at a low-lit table, I had looked eagerly into his intelligent, reliable face, relishing something about him that was different, down-to-earth, unfluttered. He looked much the same as he had in the days we sailed on the Ryndam, his dark hair still lay carelessly across his forehead, and his narrow brown eyes regarded me with the usual intensity.

Despite his off-beat look hinting at some exotic extraction, he assured me that he came from solid Norwegian-Celtic stock. After growing up and attending college in Wisconsin, he had moved to Manhattan where his passion for social justice grew, along with his love of Russian culture. We shared a fierce objection to the wide civilian casualties and devastation of the Vietnam War and distrust of current American governmental policies.

After dinner we strolled along the streets to a nearby square, continuing our political discussions under the swaying branches of the overhead crabapple trees. Before the evening was over we'd rekindled our old spark of commonality and I felt certain we were friends for good.

Our meetings after that were casual, occurring when his work on the newspaper allowed him free time. He would arrive bearing the results of his latest research on the questions we'd been discussing the week before. I found his conversation continually interesting and my own as well; he had a way of asking questions that brought things out of me I didn't know I knew, prodding at just the right place to push my thoughts one step further. Our discussions burrowed into paths I hadn't followed since the

212

idea-crazed days at the University of Southern California and the proliferation of ideas that swirled around the Parisian cafes.

He encouraged my serious side, admired my writing, and supported my drive to learn about everything in sight. Most endearing was his keen sensitity to the needs of others and judicious support of the underdog and the defenseless. He had a way of giving people credit no matter how clumsy their efforts or poor their skills.

I didn't ask myself why Ward chose to date me. Next to this staid thirty-five-year-old, I was a flighty girl who squeezed in a couple of New York University literature classes on the side. I'm not sure whether he appreciated or tolerated my lighter, more mundane traits. Since he didn't bring friends around, I didn't know if others esteemed his uniqueness and intellect as much as I did. But I was hungry for mental stimulation. He wasn't the typical come-on male and no doubt cautious because of his past divorce. In the noncommittal, non-pressured terms of our friendship, he provided something special.

I would not hear from him for some time, then he would call complaining about the confining schedule of the *Times* office and invite me to Fire Island for the weekend or somewhere equally enchanting. I enjoyed these platonic excursions. Although he didn't strike a romantic cord, he was the most interesting person I knew. But I hadn't been swept off my feet. He was not a sweeper.

"Need a refill anyone?" Margot's voice brought me back to the present. She reached for a bottle of scotch on the table.

"No thanks, I'm fine," I said.

Kerstin, sitting on a leather hassock near Ward's chair, shook her head.

As Margot had resettled herself on the couch, Ward picked up the conversation. "At the *Times* we're debating whether acronyms should be spelled out at the beginning of an article," he said. "One assumes the reader has the intelligence to know their meaning."

"Oh, the reader should be given credit," Margo exclaimed. "For instance, everyone knows what NATO stands for." She had scrunched into the pillow, missing Will, who was visiting his family for the holiday, but now her interest was perked. She enjoyed conversing with Ward. Often when he came over I could hear them talking as I was getting ready in the other room. Their minds worked in similar patterns and their ideas spun on a singular track that others couldn't always follow.

Leaning against one arm of the couch, I pulled my legs under me, thinking. Let's see, NATO—North Associated Treaty Organization—I recognized the organization the term referred to, but associated wasn't the correct word. I wasn't about to show my ignorance.

"People may know what a term refers to but have forgotten the exact wording," I ventured.

"It's a waste of space to keep repeating the full title in every article," insisted Margo. "And that would be a major consideration I should think." Ward nodded agreement.

"The *Times* isn't a tabloid," put in Kerstin. "It should expect its readership to be knowledgeable." She recrossed her legs on the hassock and leaned forward, her chin raised. In one hand a pencil-long cigarette was perched between two fingers, which she waved in graceful arcs in front of her face.

"Who's your favorite French author these days?" Ward turned his head in my direction. He was cradled into the chair, drink in hand, an unfamiliar look of relaxation on his face.

"Umm, let me think. Right now I'd say Collette." I'd been reading *Chéri* and was taken with the frank bedroom intrigue between the spoiled young man-child and the older woman of the world. Just as interesting was the story of the author's life, which I proceeded to relate. "Because of her promiscuity she was termed a nymphomaniac—sex crazy," I commented. Ward unfolded his arms and laid them along the arms of the chair.

"I'm not so sure," he said gently. "The term has been misused. Women have been given that label, but there are many reasons behind the female craze for sex and they don't necessarily have to do with an uncontrollable sexual urge." The rest of us looked at him. "In fact I don't believe there's any such thing as a nymphomaniac," he continued. "A lock of dark hair had fallen over his forehead, without his taking notice. "A woman may have low resistance to pressure, or not be able to say no, due to extreme poverty or low self-esteem. Most likely, she's striving to meet an emotional need. Extreme behavior like that is based on motivation, not physical drive."

"Oh I don't know," said Kerstin, "Women are certainly not equal in their drives in that respect. Any more than men."

"Yes, certainly, but their so-called insatiable need for sex is almost always mental or emotional. There are many drives that cause uncontrolled promiscuousness—the need to feel loved, or feel depraved, many more than I can name. A girl who acts sexually irresponsible has made an intellectual decision."

"In the same way that girls who leave a sheltered home go hog wild with newfound freedom," I added. "In which case, they're protesting against restraint and, I agree with you, it's an intellectual decision." I hadn't heard this theory before, but Ward's words rang true.

Margo tilted her head coquettishly. "You're probably right," she addressed Ward. "If sex is really all about the mind, it stands to reason that those with good minds will have good sex. And since I've been told I have quite a good mind, I'm in luck. When can I start?" We laughed.

"I think Ward is on to something," said Kerstin.

Encouraged, Ward continued. "Many girls go through a period of sexual irregularity and emerge fiercely moral. In fact, most so-called nymphomaniacs are actually frigid because of their overwhelming emotional problems. They seek male partners to satisfy a drive, but they are tackling the wrong one."

My girlfriends and I never shared the details of our sex lives. They knew little of my sexual history or my views. Even conversations such as this one were unusual. It felt liberating to be discussing, for once, a significant aspect of our intimate lives, even on a theoretical level.

It was unlike Ward to be discussing sex with three girls, given his puritanical bent, but he seemed comfortable, more relaxed than I'd ever seen him, sunk into his chair, one corner of his jacket twisted under his arm. He was really quite fetching like this, I thought, loose and open, like if you hugged him he'd smile.

We talked until all the lights in the adjoining buildings had flicked off and the traffic beyond the window dimmed to an occasional drone.

†

The job at Academic Press was pure routine and I had been searching for something better. Soon after the Christmas party my job search efforts finally paid off, and I was offered a position with *Forbes* magazine as an editorial researcher. I trudged every morning to the *Forbes* offices, a twenty minute walk from 31st Avenue to 14th Street, ignoring the red lights like a native. It wasn't the editing position with a book publisher I'd wanted, but after weeks of fruitlessly chasing leads I had to take something.

My work at *Forbes* consisted of shaping columns to fit on the magazine page, cutting sections or rewording the text while maintaining the exact meaning. The writer's report was not to be touched, other than cosmetically. After a few weeks it became clear that this part of the job was rote.

But there were compensations. The office was lined with desks set sideways against the windows and the researchers, all girls, sat lined up behind each other. We were a team in a fast-paced environment, propelled by deadlines and demands, dealing with errors and elusive column sections, all under the direction of our supervisor, Ruth Myers. Mrs. Myers ruled from her office at the head of the desks and kept close tabs on the eight of us, assigning responsibilities and making sure the current issue of *Forbes* was put to bed on time with no pieces missing.

Bertie Forbes—a jokester of Scottish-Irish descent, who once penned a book titled *499 Jokes for the Price of 500*—had founded the magazine in 1917 and immediately instituted a humanistic, personal approach to the workplace. Two of his four sons now served as *Forbes* executives. I was called into Bruce Forbes's spacious presidential office for his annual meeting with staff members, where he shook my hand, asked where I was from, and wished me luck—part of the personal approach, no doubt. The other son, Malcolm, publisher and editor-in-chief, contributed articles. Well-known around town for his colorful flair and outrageous exploits, Malcolm lent a glow of celebrity to the magazine. His bid for the Republican senate seat from New Jersey failed because he was deemed too liberal.

This was not my dream job, but it paid well. As soon as I announced the new position, everyone bombarded me with congratulations, going a little overboard, I thought. My parents were full of encouragement. Dad said it was the chance of a lifetime to be in the center of the financial world, dealing with the ins and outs of major corporations, privy to the latest developments. Mother's Minneapolis friends recognized *Forbes*'s prominent place on the stands and were impressed to see my name listed at the front of the magazine: "Judy Bradford, Editorial Researcher." A telegram arrived from Ward, "My heartiest congratulations."

A banner waved in my mind's eye, a tribute poised over the Minnesota state capitol building: JUDY BRADFORD MAKES GOOD IN THE BIG CITY. Maybe the house I grew up in would be restored and a sign put on the front lawn: *Judy Bradford Lived Here.*

Margo suggested that now I could afford to have the couch recovered and provide the living room walls with decent artwork.

I didn't hear from my brother Harold. We did not correspond. As far as he was concerned, I was pampered and self-centered. He watched me move to one more location and leap to one job after another, with no end in sight. He wanted no part of it. Except for occasional acerbic exchanges between us, we passed each other with mutual indifference. My resentment surfaced surreptitiously in depreciating remarks thrown in his direction. Maybe that would wake him up. Why should I care? I had long given up longing for his attention.

My new job involved content research. Between high-pressure periods accompanying the bi-weekly publication of *Forbes* magazine, I crouched in the upstairs reference room, digging for discrepancies in the latest articles sent fresh from the writers. The facts had to be checked, the figures reliable, the references legitimate.

The writers were not always ready to accept my changes. Slowly, a startling picture emerged from their evasions and protests. It was not necessarily the truth the writers were after. Their first goal was to create a catching article. Stale news was not good enough, and fresh news could be elusive. So they devised an angle, some twist to distinguish their news piece from all the similar ones cranked out by their competitors at *Fortune, Business Week,* and *Barron's.* They sought zip and impact. To this end, facts were carefully selected and figures padded to back up their slant. For a researcher, to whom accuracy was paramount, it was a challenge to deal with writers who fumbled with the truth and resented those who dug and unbent the facts they had artfully adjusted.

One of the regular commentators began his piece with "There are forty-seven public retailers..." and went on to give a price index using a composite of twelve companies, then further on ran his sentences together in a manner that incorrectly applied his conclusion to all forty-seven companies.

Nor were the company sources always reliable. My phone call to an executive of Great Canadian Sands ran into a wall of resistance. "The Canadian government regulates the amount of oil produced by your company," I began, after the introductory comments, "Could you tell me what percentage of your oil is withheld from production by the government?" The executive hemmed and hawed, then emphatically disagreed with my original statement. When I persisted he finally gave me a figure of forty percent, which I didn't hold much confidence in.

In another phone call, Great Canadian Sands claimed to have poured more time and money into Athabasca Sands than any other company. But research of the competitors showed that Cities Service Group had made the same claim. Further digging showed the Cities Service statement to be correct.

Ruth Meyers, Sandra, one of the senior researchers, and I discussed this one afternoon after the office had emptied for the day. It was best, I was told, to make every correction according to the most reliable source, mark the galley with explicit references, and let the writer deal with the implications. It was not in our hands to make publication decisions; we were there as support. As for external sources, note any doubts and get as many confirmations as you can. We the researchers must stay out of it.

At first I was incensed. The readers want to know the truth! But then again, maybe they wouldn't even pick up the article if there weren't a draw to pull them in. Then they wouldn't know anything at all. As I thought about it, my integrity didn't feel so compromised. What we were doing was balancing the punch of the article with the lineup of the facts—but we strove for the true facts.

I almost remarked, as we made our way out of the office, "Oh well, everyone has to make a living," but thought better of it. Best to acquiesce without the flippancy.

My work week settled into a routine. At lunch hour I walked down the block for a sandwich, returned to eat at my desk and read the *New York Times*. Occasionally, I joined the other girls at a small restaurant where we ordered a martini, maybe two. After one of these wet lunches that had gone on too long, I sat back at my desk, head drooping, the galley in my hand a blur. "The international consortium had its final conference under the auspices..." I could barely make it out, my mind was drifting towards sea breezes. If I could only lie down for twenty minutes I would be fine. I made my way to the small nursing room on the floor below and lay down on the cot.

It was not long before Ruth Myers caught me up. "Judy, what are you doing here?" She stuck her head through the door, then walked in and stood by the cot, frowning in disbelief. I sat up quickly.

"I ate something that disagreed with me and came down for just a few minutes."

She followed me up the stairs, saying only, "You must take naps during regular breaks only. And for heaven's sake, let me know where you are." Then she turned and walked away with rigid little steps.

This was not the only time I got in trouble. One afternoon, just before quitting time, a match I tossed in the wastebasket started some papers on fire. One of the researchers standing nearby doused it with her water glass and within two minutes the little flames were out. Ruth Myers was horrified. How could you do such a thing? I was sorry, I said, the match wasn't extinguished, an accident. I was sure this episode, like the other, was entered on my report.

The truth was, I was affronted that so much fuss was made about these incidents. If I grabbed a fifteen-minute lie down when I needed it, my work would be the better for it. I was a conscientious employee, I worked hard. And a tiny flame, a silly accident, could happen to anyone. What was the big deal? Rules, those arbitrary norms set up to meet the majority of cases, sometimes need to be altered to the requirements of the moment. Such a big production! Wasn't I good at my job? Wasn't that what counted?

The next faux pas I committed was not so easily explained. Several times Jerry, the magazine's photographer, had stopped by my desk to chat. Although he was outgoing and personable and talked to everyone, he seemed to have taken a liking to me. One afternoon, Ruth Meyer informed me that I had been assigned to assist him on a photography shoot with the top executives of ABC Company for a feature article. When we arrived at the ABC offices, six executives were waiting, standing by the picture window, suited up in navy and gray, combed and immaculate and looking less comfortable than their usual commanding selves. While I assisted with the equipment and lighting, I noticed one of the executives fingering his ring with an uneasy expression.

"Jerry's a professional," I remarked as I passed. "Just be yourself. No need to feel self-conscious." There was no comment from the executive block, each of whom stiffened and looked straight and expressionless at the camera. I was enjoying myself. Jerry projected an easygoing, friendly manner and knew exactly when to snap the shot. With luck, I might be assigned to work with him on a regular basis.

My projected collaboration couldn't have been further from the mark. The next afternoon Jerry called me into his office and shut the door. He was not pleased. He looked at me in his usual freehanded, easygoing way, but this time there was a rigid line running along his mouth.

"You can't say things like that. You don't talk about the process when shooting people. Your remarks interfered with my shooting and colored the result. Don't ever do that again. That's all. Just so you know." His voice was streaked with fire and there was no doubt he meant what he said.

I stared at him in shock. What had I said...? I couldn't remember—something to the executives about ignoring the camera. Didn't acknowledgement dispel feelings of unease? But Jerry seemed to think my concern only made the executives more self-conscious. It was confusing. Evidently it was best to stick to neutral remarks on the wall artwork or the weather.

I couldn't get a word out. Instead of explaining that I totally understood what he meant and that it would never happen again, and I would do whatever he said and please give me another chance, I stood abjectly, bent with shame, and said nothing.

Jerry didn't contact me to work with him again.

Ruth Meyer's disgust with me soon reached new heights. The next incident was more serious. The monthly issue of *Forbes* was due out on Monday morning and the work of the editorial crew was to be completed on Friday. Ruth came in on Saturday to put together last-minute details and discovered that a lead article was missing from the prep bin, where the others were waiting to be collated and sent out. Ruth searched all corners of the office, frantically digging in every drawer and file.

Finally, after her assistant had been called to the office and the wastebaskets had been unturned, the missing piece was located.

I heard about it the minute I walked through the door Monday morning. "Judy! Into my office!"

I walked in and immediately felt the full blast of Ruth Myer's fury. "We spent the entire afternoon searching for John Smith's article for next month's issue. Guess where we found it!"

"Ah—well...."

"John Smith's piece."

"I was handling that."

"And what did you do with it?"

"Well," I could feel my beating heart shrink and sink down into my toes. This was going to be serious. "I had one question left that I didn't get to and planned to ask Dennis about it first thing this morning. You see, I wasn't quite done. I must have put it..."

"We found it in your top desk drawer."

"Oh, yes, where I would be sure to see it first thing."

Ruth Meyer could not contain her displeasure. "Do you realize the trouble you've caused? The office was frantic. Sandra came all the way in just to help us search. See that this doesn't happen again."

"Yes, I'm sorry," was all I could manage. I was drowned in guilt and fear for my own plight. It never dawned on me that anyone would show up to work on the articles on Saturday. *We didn't work on Saturdays.* But clearly I should have alerted someone. Mortified, I wanted to crawl away and disappear.

At my annual review I didn't get the anticipated raise. Ruth Meyers informed me I was not ready to move up to the next level. At least I wasn't fired. I felt thwarted and kept to myself for the most part, scrunched behind the *Times* over lunch hour. Ruth Meyer was cordial but distant; evidently I had to work my way back into her confidence.

My position at *Forbes* was fast losing its luster.

The job must be at fault. I was convinced that if guided by perceptive, encouraging superiors I was capable of high achievement. The routine tasks of the job, once mastered, became dull—I longed to be consumed with work that held significance. I don't know what it would have taken to persuade me to turn my gaze inward. To face the unrealistic expectations that I operated with and my passivity under fire.

To accurately judge the extent of my job skills. To convince me that I needed a job more than it needed me.

I resisted the temptation to quit. Up until now, many jobs had come and gone. This time I decided to stick it out at *Forbes*. For a while.

Chapter 6　　Politics and Philosophies

It occurred to me that I was the daughter of the president of IDS Mutual Funds and might as well have been the daughter of a dog catcher. If I were asked to define a mutual fund I couldn't give a proper answer. Never had we discussed business at the dinner table, Dad had not allowed his work life to intrude on his home life. He was a bastion of the financial world and I, his daughter, knew *nothing*.

I was determined to break through the wall that separated Dad's business interests from his family. The next time Dad flew into town he took me to the Cotillion Room of the Hotel Pierre. As we waited for the shrimp cocktail, Dad twirled the silver fork on the white tablecloth in quick little circles while I described the Cassone storage chest we'd acquired for the apartment. When the shrimp arrived buried in crystal cups of ice, I launched my line of questioning.

First, I asked for an update on the status of the stocks he'd given me sporadically over the years. Then I went on. "You say gold is an important financial indicator. What's its relative worth?"

"In October of 1961, the gold market topped out. It's now worth $36 an ounce," he explained.

"Could I buy gold myself?"

"No, you can't purchase a gold bar, it's illegal in the United States. But you could easily buy gold by phoning a New York City broker who can buy bars on the Toronto stock exchange. This is a poor restriction, since it brings dollars to Canada and deprives the United States of profiting from the exchange." He picked up a large shrimp, scooping it through the tangy sauce. As he explained gold prices and markets, I tried to press the information into my memory. I wanted to know everything about the stock market, even if most of it was over my head.

"Closed-end companies," he responded to my next question, "are traded on the stock exchange. Their capitalization is more fixed, and shares are not redeemable at asset value. Open-ended companies, on the other hand, are usually purchased through investment dealers. They're more recently referred to as mutual funds." And so on. He did not back out by suggesting I get myself a book on the subject. Nor did he question my ability to grasp the intricacies of the market. I wasn't sure if he was being patient and accommodating out of remorse, wanting to make up for his absence in the past, or if he actually enjoyed teaching me about his area of expertise, now that we were alone without Mother to break off any serious discussion with her fluff.

Back at the apartment, I filled a spiral notebook with thoughts from our talk. But there was nowhere to apply this information. It wasn't until Dad's death, years later, when I came into a modest inheritance, that I was faced with decisions that required an understanding of finances. I had a lot to learn.

It did not occur to Dad to train me in this field. Women were taken care of; finance was not their domain. His concern was that I settle down, find a home base, preferably through the stabilizing institution of marriage or a stable career if that failed to materialize. Dad counted on his children to carry on the successful life of health and happiness he had achieved, with material needs met, aspirations fulfilled, and able to enjoy the amenities of society. He wanted to maintain the advantages he'd lacked and worked so hard to build for us and the next generation. I had strayed from the tried-and-true path, an obvious fallout. I wasn't following the usual route into domesticity. My vagabond ways, straying from the beaten track, pained him. Nevertheless, he was anxious to back me up whatever direction I took. He attended to my every move, and I was denied nothing. Anything to keep me in the fold where I would be happy.

†

I invited Ward to accompany me on a visit to see my sister Susan at Briarcliff women's college in Briarcliff Manor, New York. As soon as Ward arrived at the apartment I knew something was up. He looked disturbed. Throwing a hello and brief smile in my direction, he walked quickly across the wool rug to the living room window and stood for a few minutes looking out over the rooftops. Then he swung around and faced me, a frown between his eyebrows and his mouth set in a rigid line.

"Have you heard the latest? The government plans to build a gigantic fallout shelter underneath the ganglia of Rockefeller Center in case of nuclear attack. Big enough to hold 200,000 people. What do you think of that?"

I hadn't given it much thought. "President Kennedy is concerned about the soviet defense missile warhead buildup in Cuba. Has it gone that far?"

"Worse. The government is urging every American to set up individual underground bomb shelters on their property. It is manufacturing them throughout the country, at a minimum cost of $1500—in Philadelphia they're going for $2800. Minneapolis is planning an elaborate bunker beneath the Federal Reserve Bank, complete with hi-fi music."

"A bit excessive, I'd say."

Ward paced to the couch, then returned to the window and stood staring out, his brown tweed jacket highlighted by the fractured rays of sun. "This is how the civil defense office advises everyone to furnish the shelters: a two-weeks' supply of food and water; an air-intake-exhaust system; chemical toilets; sandbags, for Pete's sake; periscopes to prevent people from emerging from the shelter and dying of curiosity; weapons to ward off wanderers who might try to break in to save themselves; and sleeping pills so one can doze through the ordeal. And we mustn't forget the burial suit, a polyvinyl chemically treated wrapper in case someone

225

dies while in the shelter. It doubles as a sleeping bag. Survival stores that stock such items are springing up in every city."

I had to laugh. "You've got to be kidding."

"It's incredible," he exclaimed, running one hand along his chin.

"I read that radiation spreads for over a hundred miles and lasts for weeks." I said. "How long are people expected to remain in these shelters?"

"After two weeks you can come out, provided you're protected from head to toe." He shook his head. "Invested interests are making money on this. People are buying it—they're going berserk. It's a national craze."

We were standing by the window facing each other. Ward's expression was grave as he looked at me.

"An atomic bomb would wipe out everything in its path for five to ten miles from where it hits. And that's just one bomb. They're building dream houses, not safe shelters."

"I don't suppose the government will fund these constructions," I said.

"No, each family must purchase their own. Plus the civil defense leaders plan to install one in every public building in the nation capable of serving as a shelter." We stared out the apartment window as if expecting concrete ramparts to rise from the neighboring wall and barricade us in an airless tomb. I admired Ward's insight into the follies of society, able to pierce to the bottom of any issue. I was reminded of Pete Seeger's rousing words promising freedom from injustice, a new land for you and me, words that had once raced through my blood with passion, promising a new society. Looking at Ward's figure, stolid, slightly round-shouldered, with his sharp brown eyes and warm expression, I knew the freedom song ran in his blood too, although he was far from the beatnik type I identified with. He seemed to operate above the turmoil of protest and angry fist-shaking, paving his own way with his keen intelligence and spreading the message naturally just by being who he was. I stood next to him, his jacket sleeve inches from my bare arm. I had never respected anyone so much.

I checked my watch. "Come on, let's get going. We told Susan one o'clock."

Ward headed the Volkswagen towards Westchester. The sky stretched low above us, dusted with feathery clouds. The countryside was quiet, the hills and scattered houses bathed in a cool wintry light. I had a copy of the *New York Times Magazine* on my lap and was scanning a recent article on communism by Harrison Salisbury. Since Ward had studied Russian on the GI Bill and subsequently undertaken several journalistic assignments to the Soviet Union for the *Times,* I wanted to probe him about the article. I was interested in the experiment on societal living that the Soviet Union had embarked on.

I looked over at Ward alert behind the wheel, eyes riveted on the road. "Communism offers a new social system to alleviate inequality and the privileged dominance of the wealthy," I began. As usual I had Ward's full attention. "But the Russian Revolution hasn't done away with inequity. The dictatorship is a privileged class."

"The dictatorship will collapse and disappear when the local units are strong enough to run themselves," he replied easily.

"And who will they be accountable to?"

"It's self-motivating. Remember the slogan: 'From each according to his ability to each according to his needs'? When the peasants merge into self-sufficient collectives, people will work to their capacity because they share the profits."

"Wait a minute. So those who produce little will receive just as much as the top producers."

"Yes."

"So why should they work hard?"

"The key concept here is the role of the group. The group comes first. It is the opposite of the American way, where the individual reigns supreme. In Russia the community takes precedence, individual needs are secondary. Each member is like a limb, crucial to the main body, and because all the parts are linked, they attend to each other's needs. No one is stranded or alone. It's to each individual's advantage to see that everyone gets their needs met."

This admittedly sounded attractive.

Ward brushed a lick of hair from his forehead. "You aren't judged on the amount of work you do," he went on. "Your collective conscience is developed from an early age and if you chose to shirk responsibility there must be a reason. If there is a problem, it is addressed collectively."

"That is unbelievably tolerant."

"All right, remember there is no private property, no rich and poor. With labor undertaking its own production, there will be an abundance of goods."

"And if I want cars and trips abroad and jewels?"

"You can have them. There will be more than enough to go around. Coveting disappears. Struggle for goods is eliminated."

I stared at his profile next to me, the conservative set of his mouth, the flashing eyes now warmed to the topic. A flutter stirred under my ribs, the implications of his words were mind-boggling. Maybe here was the answer to my dream of a drastic upheaval that would throw existing structures up in the air and everything would fall back to earth, reconfigured into a new order that took care of peoples' needs. "Does the collective supersede the family as well?"

Clearly Ward had thought this through. "The isolated family as a possessive unit will have no place, it will exist only as part of a greater whole." So here was a construct offering a better way to raise children as well as see to everyone's needs. I pulled up in the seat.

"And romantic love?"

"That too will become superfluous. People will form liaisons as they desire, with comrades or neighbors, and when a couple tire of each other they will take other mates if they wish."

This sounded tricky.

"I see. And what about love?"

"When love is not based on need, it isn't as heavy as in the love-crazed West. There are larger concerns. The entire community contributes to raising children, and the neuroses of the parents are diluted. With no inheritance to guard, the nuclear family becomes obsolete. No longer is the individual pitted against the family, the family against the community, the community against the nation, the nation against the world. People work together for the benefit of all."

The car began climbing the hills leading to the town of Briarcliff Manor. We were approaching Briarcliff College.

"All right, Ward. These ideas sound credible in some ways. Do you admit they are ideals yet to be achieved?"

"Yes, I believe so."

The figure of my sister Susan standing on the top step of a white portico came into view. She waved as the car rounded the circular drive

228

and rolled up to the front door of the Student Union. Over the past eight years my sister and I had seldom interacted—she was ten when I left for college. I noted her scrubbed complexion, neat brown hairstyle, the short-sleeved sweater, pleated skirt, and loafers as she guided us around the campus, the picture of a clean-cut collegiate.

She described life at a two-year woman's college. "It's a good school but the girls here are dumb," she told us. "They talk of dating and football and formal gowns. It's hard to adjust after my year at the International School in Switzerland." During her freshman year abroad, she had been exposed to standards different from those we had been brought up with. After her return in 1960, she resonated to the cause of the anti-Korean War protesters, the beating of the Freedom Riders in Missouri, and the nationwide headlines of the civil rights leaders. The next few years would see her change her short bob to long tresses reaching down her back, her oxfords for sandals, her cardigans for cotton halters, and the proprietary environment of Briarcliff for the raging politics of the Berkeley University campus.

Now that she resided in New York, I was getting to know my sister for the first time. She had developed into a bright individual with an interesting mind and far-ranging ideas. Eight years behind me, growing up she had been merely a pest in the household, reaping all the privileges extended to the youngest, attentions I coveted for myself. I ignored her—let her be the adored pet, I wanted no part of it, I was headed elsewhere. It was only in later years that I became aware, during long midnight talks, that we shared a common depravation during childhood, living under a shell of isolated protection. That she suffered from the same scars created by parental absence. And that my cruel rejection had scarred her in ways I had not imagined.

After a tour of the campus, Susan led the way to the school cafeteria, where we sat at a corner table and lamented how the burgeoning peace movement against the Vietnam War was being destroyed by the anti-communism campaign in Washington. I encouraged Susan to stay with Margo and I at the apartment when she fancied spending time in Manhattan.

As we drove back to the city, Ward marveled at the caliber of Briarcliff College. It seemed an ideal learning environment, with its high-ranking teaching staff, small, intimate classes, and regular meetings at the homes of the professors. But in these changing times, we agreed, far too insolated.

I reached over and pushed in the cigarette lighter on the dashboard. "Ward," I said. "I have another question. Under the communist system, how will homosexuals fit in?"

He turned to smile at me. "Each case is different. But the theory holds that individuals are born neutral, that is, the external object of attraction isn't built in. Society teaches us to prefer the opposite sex. A man may possess feminine traits that are not culturally acceptable for a male. He may be highly emotional, sensitive, or need to be dominated, traits our society doesn't tolerate in men. He may repudiate the male role. The same with women. There's no inborn drive towards one sex or the other. Attraction is conditioned."

"What of people born with ambiguous genitals?"

"Those are special cases and are, I grant, physically based."

"So homosexuality is a cultural choice?"

"Yes, that's the way it's regarded in communist society." The car lighter glowed a red circle as I guided it towards a fresh cigarette. Inhaling, I watched the smoke drift toward the window.

I pondered Ward's characterizations of the Soviet Union. The Marxists had created alternatives to long-standing assumptions of society. I could understand the appeal of this system. Although I longed for an alternative paradigm to the present system of society, the boldness of the Soviet experiment was staggering.

For some time I stared out the window.

"Ward, I'm not convinced that this new communist society you've been describing will create the beautiful world of happiness it promises."

He laughed. "Nor am I," he said.

"One more thing. Communism can't succeed unless the entire world embraces the system, or its enemies will destroy it. In order to maintain communism, the Soviet Union will have to conquer our country."

"They don't think they'll need to subdue us. Capitalism will fall of its own weight from its built-in flaws."

"I think I'll just have to live long enough to see how this works," I said finally.

As we sped along, I gazed at the scattered clusters of trees lining the hills and the darkening sky that was slowly pulling a gauze curtain towards the horizon. Then I turned to regard Ward sitting next to me, gripping the wheel with steady hands that never seemed to falter.

"Ward?"

"Yes?"

"I'm glad I know you." He glanced over at me and a slow smile lifted his mouth. He slipped a hand over mine for a brief instant, the brush of a butterfly skimming my skin.

"I'm glad I know you," I said again, "and I mean that."

Chapter 7   A Giant Step

February turned to March, April, and then slipped into May. Walking past Gramercy Park, I spied three yellow buds poking their heads from the forsythia branches. The arrival of spring loosened the ground and sent the odor of moist soil over the sidewalks. My blood started to move faster.

It was time for a new venture.

The next day I placed an ad in the Village Voice:

> LONG ISLAND BEACH GETAWAY. Looking for
> three single professional girls in their twenties
> to share a summer cottage in the Hamptons
> for the summer. Provide references. Call...

Since Margo preferred to stay in the city weekends to support the latest political campaign and enjoy dates with Will, I needed three roommates to support the house rental. I received quite a few responses and arranged to meet the most likely three girls at Schraft's. The first to arrive was Ginger, a tall ash blond employed in a travel agency. A collector of old furniture, she anticipated prowling the plentiful antique shops of the Hamptons. The next, Kathleen, showed up on the dot of seven and sat quietly. She was quiet, thin, and dark-haired, with a small face and uplifted mouth that showed even, white teeth when she smiled. She wanted to get out of the city weekends, away from her auditing job at a local bank. Myrna, the third one, bustled in late, apologizing as she flung her short, plump figure into the empty chair. I was almost put off by her round, droll face and deferential manner, but she tossed out such funny observations that we were all laughing and I couldn't help liking her. We spent the evening over coffee and peach sundaes, exchanging stories and background information about ourselves. The prospect of spending hot summer weekends at the edge of the ocean quickly bonded us.

The girls were anxious to sign on, and after checking references I notified them that we were a foursome. That weekend I located an ad for a small, two-story house in the village of Southampton a short mile from the beach. It had two bedrooms, a small backyard with a barbeque pit, and was within walking distance of the Southampton shops and restaurants. I phoned the contact, Mrs. Hunter.

"We're four working girls," I told her, "looking to get out of town for the weekend and enjoy the beach. We won't be having any wild parties."

"Don't worry, my dear. Mr. Hunter and I will be living behind you over the garage," she replied. "We'll see that you have all you need." Mr. Hunter ran the service station on the other side of town and would mow the grass and keep an eye on the house during the week.

The four of us inspected the house one weekend and found it clean, convenient, and perfect for our modest needs. Myrna offered to draw up a plan of kitchen duties. "I'll make sure we're never out of food. You can see by my figure that this never happens to me." And she emitted a coarse-throated laugh. Was it all right, she wanted to know, if her boyfriend visited from time to time? We all agreed that boyfriends were allowed, provided they bunked elsewhere, and that it was okay if the Hunters lived right next to us—we had nothing to hide—as long as it was clear that we could have visitors and play records.

Within two weeks all was settled—the house was ours.

233

†

Summer brought more than one surprise. The first, which concerned Margo—my turn was yet to come—I found out about as Ward and I returned one Saturday night from seeing *The Guns of Navarone* at a nearby movie theater. We ran into Margo, Will, Kerstin and her date in the downstairs lobby, returning from a party in the Village.

"There you are!" exclaimed Margo. "We're on our way up to the apartment for a nightcap." She pushed the elevator button. "I've something to say," she whispered to Ward and me. "And a bottle of scotch to say it with. Come on."

We settled in the living room, Kerstin and her date at one end of the couch, taking up very little room, while Ward dropped into the high-backed chair and I curled on the yellow arm chair opposite. Will, his brown eyes glistening, passed out drinks, then lowered himself next to Margo on the other end of the couch. She leaned against him with a bubbly laugh. A Johnny Mathis record was playing.

"We just have to tell you guys," Margo began, her face beaming, "I couldn't say anything before because it's not official." She put her drink on the table and interlaced her fingers together in front of her. "Will and I are engaged." She paused, letting everyone take in the news. "It's not for public announcement. It just happened tonight. Our parents don't even know yet. But you guys are our closest friends—we couldn't wait to tell!" She and Will grinned at each other at the sight of our surprised faces.

Then: "How long have you known? Have you met each other's parents? What's the date? Here or Minnesota? Have you considered simple co-habitation? Congratulations! Let's have a toast!"

Margo, laughing, described Will's dramatic proposal three times, each version differing from the last.

"Margo, get your facts straight. Did he kneel or hand you the ring in a bouquet of roses?"

"What do facts matter when you're in love?" Margot breathed. Like the rest of us, she was feeling the drinks.

"Did he tell you he loved you? Did he tell you he was besotted?"

"Besotted," Will groaned. "I was in love but I definitely was not besotted!"

"Well, you are now," someone ventured.

"We all are," came another.

"I am not inebriated," I remarked inanely, "But I am definitely besotted." And I burst out laughing. I wasn't sure if it was the scintillation of Margo's news or one too many drinks, but I felt I was about to break into an uncontrollable fit of merriment. "Please don't anyone say anything funny."

"Poor old Will's biting the dust. Isn't that funny enough?" remarked Kerstin's date, who was plying the usual marriage putdown, which of course was not one bit funny, but we all hooted with laughter. I held my sides.

"Give her a kiss. We want proof," someone urged. Will obliged. I glanced at Ward. This must be a bit frivolous for his taste. But he was smiling and looking relaxed, and I even heard a chortle from him when Will twisted Margo around over his back, to teach her, he said, who was boss.

"Yes, dear," Margo breathed when she had recovered, "you can be the boss, as long as I always get my way."

Will was all grins, friendly and accommodating. "I'm afraid all her dates will have to look elsewhere," I told him on Margo's account.

"They sure will!" Will said.

Margo threw back her head and laughed. "Judy can have them all."

"I don't think I can handle the volume." And so on.

The conversation meandered. Kerstin related stories of her recent acting role off-Broadway in *Night of the Iguana*. Will fetched another bottle of scotch. Someone turned over the stack of records and Johnny's voice melted over us: *I feel like I'm clinging to a cloud/I can't understand/I get misty, just holding your hand.* An atmosphere of intimacy closed around the room.

Around 3:00 a.m. the rest of the party left, a little unsteadily, leaving Ward and me alone. Margo returned with Will to his apartment downstairs. (Although they were together every minute, she and Will were abstaining until marriage in deference to their Catholic faith.) I had moved to the floor and was sitting in front of Ward's chair, leaning my back against his knee, lost in vague thought. Someone had dimmed the lights, and the edges of the room had retreated into shadow.

Ward didn't move.

"I've been meaning to tell you," I said finally, "you were right about CBS. It strictly prohibits commentary by its newscasters. Analysis is allowed, but absolutely no individual opinions. Only if you are Walter Lippmann, or Huntley and Brinkley at NBC, are you allowed to voice a personal opinion. The networks claim the newscaster's job is to give the facts and let people make up their own minds how to interpret them." The words slipped out slowly, bolstered by the scotch, and I wasn't sure they were making sense, but something needed to be said. Now I couldn't remember the point I wanted to make. Idiotically, I started to giggle.

Ward didn't speak. I felt him slip down the chair and come to rest beside me. Within the shadows, I could make out a half-smile on his face and a rough blush on his cheeks. The next record flopped down on the exchanger and the mellow tones of *I'm Glad There Is You* floated towards us.

"Whom did you hear this from?" he asked in a low voice. I was leaning back against him and could feel the soft gabardine of his jacket against my arm.

"Sandra's brother at *Forbes* works at ABC. They're all alike, he thinks—the networks I mean. They won't let their newscasters tell the real story, they're too afraid of political backlash. Let the locals do the commentary." I was feeling shaky; there was no way I could go on. Ward coughed, a soft, hesitant sound, as if he were contemplating a reply. "Ward, I'm going to get some coffee." But I didn't move and the idea went out of my head. "The newsmen, they feel it's their job to make the news meaningful to listeners, especially on complex issues," I droned on. Then, "Ward, say something."

"You are absolutely right," he mumbled. This time I could feel his breath and turned towards him. I felt his arm slip around my back, becoming tighter. I looked for something to say, then gave it up and leaned my head back, closing my eyes. I felt his mouth, searching for mine, finding it, and my arms all of a sudden were around him. His mouth was soft, sweet; it felt strange to be kissing him after all this time. My head was full of spider webs, I couldn't think.

I raised my head, breathed in the odor of his skin, pressed my mouth again on his. My eyelids wouldn't lift, my whole being was gathered in the kiss and the intimate press of his jacket and the warm feeling of his arms around me.

After he left I stood in the living room amid pockets of light and shadow, blinking at what had just transpired. I had not considered Ward romantically, but now—those kisses—I wasn't sure. There were things about him I adored, his endlessly fruitful mind, the depth of his observations, the gentle sweetness of his nature, but never had I fanaticized about sex with him. It just didn't seem to come up with us. I appreciated that he was consistently considerate and respectful and approached life with a firm uprightness. We weren't in the habit of exchanging confidences of a personal nature. We were connected by an intellectual affinity, which had carried us this far. Maybe it was enough.

Yet—having his arms around me had felt so good.

I wasn't sure. I couldn't think about it any further. Tomorrow, when the light of day entered the room, washing out the misty illusions of the night, maybe I'd find clarity. The only recourse now was sleep.

†

Margo's burst of happiness came just in time. Margo and I had been having difficulties over apartment responsibilities and individual space. Our partnership as roommates had been swaying up and down roller-coaster fashion: we resented, liked, avoided, preferred, tolerated, and needed each other. But during that crazy summer our conflicts became buried in the rush of activities that took up our lives. The wedding would take place in New York, and Margo and her mother undertook a whirlwind of preparations with local churches, agencies, and retailers. I attended lectures at NYU, rehearsed with the Methodist Church choir, and spent weekends on Long Island.

Margo being a night owl and me a morning bird, we saw each other mostly as shadows in the wings. She was busy with Will and as for me, I soon became caught in unexpected developments in Southampton that were to lead me down the aisle as well.

Chapter 8 Southampton Days

Every Friday afternoon I merged with the after-work throng at Penn Station and boarded the Long Island Railroad for the two-hour train ride to Southampton. On my first trip, I lounged in a padded armchair in the bar car and watched women in smart two-piece dresses and heels and men in fedora hats carrying briefcases get off at various stops. Ignoring the Jane Austin book on my lap, I gazed out the window as we passed clusters of residential houses and, further out, stretches of flat land leading to rolling dunes and finally glimpses of blue ocean flashing in the distance. It had been awhile since I'd traveled out of the city. I felt the thrill that always accompanied forays into fresh places and unexpected sights. Whatever was in store out on this raw island, this outpost from the norm of city living, I was ready.

My three roommates and I showed up at the Southampton house one by one as our work schedules permitted. Myrna and I shared the first bedroom at the top of the stairs. Occasionally Myrna's boyfriend drove out in his Ford jalopy, arriving at unpredictable hours, due, I was told, to his erratic assignments as a writer for some obscure magazine on male fertility. Evidently this prize boyfriend, Roman by name, was indispensable to the magazine, the pride of his family, and the answer to every girl's dream. According to Myrna, with his movie star good looks—Stewart Granger was mentioned—and his creative flair, he deserved these accolades. Why he had picked her when he could have anyone she'd never know.

My first encounter with Roman was a shock. One Friday evening I arrived around seven-thirty, anxious to begin the weekend. Hello, hello! I flew past Ginger, past a boy I'd never met standing in the hall doorway, past Kathleen, and up the stairs to dress for dinner. The three stared after me in stiff silence. As I reached the top, I heard the boy's voice from below, "Better not..." But I was already inside the bedroom. The sight of Myrna and a very heavy male lying naked and entwined on one of the single beds caught me up short. I hastily backed out the door.

"I guess you met Roman," someone said as I descended the stairs with a white face. No more was said as we all turned uncomfortably to busy ourselves with tasks in the kitchen.

The next day Roman—who had spent the night at a nearby hostel—and Myrna entered the backyard where Ginger, Kathleen, and I were reading the newspaper. I disliked him from the start, particularly the look of disdain on his face, which had been handsome once before a layer of fat dulled his features. All that remained was an attractive hairline and a head of scruffy brown hair.

I especially didn't like the way Myrna pleaded for his attentions with her supplicating manner. When he offhandedly requested that Myrna fetch him a beer, she rushed into the house. By the time she returned, he was describing with gusto his latest writing venture, filled with clever twists.

Myrna sat next to him and hung on every word. "Roman, you should submit that story," she cried with enthusiasm. "I don't know why you keep putting it off. It's so interesting. The trouble is you need more confidence. You don't know how good you are." Roman didn't need more confidence and was quite certain how good he was. Unfortunately, Myrna was of the same opinion he was—they were in the habit of worshiping him together.

The extent of Roman's cavalier behavior grew more evident every time he came to town. Myrna never knew when he would arrive. Sometimes he didn't show up when expected, and he made sure she understood—to be fair to her, Myrna assured me—that he was seeing other women and she'd have to take him when she could get him.

"He calls me whenever he gets the chance. His job keeps him so busy. He does the best he can." She was clearly being taken advantage of by this sheep in wolf's clothing.

Once as we were sitting in the yard, ringed in a half-moon around the barbeque grill, I brought out a photo of Roman slumped in the lawn chair in his oversized shorts that I'd snapped the weekend before. "Oh, you look so handsome," cried Myrna. Roman ignored her. He stood, holding out the 3 x 5 photo, a look of shock on his face. "I can't believe I look like that," he groaned, staring. "I'm not really *that* fat!" He turned the photo over, as if hoping to find a better version on the other side. "Good god, I've really let myself go." It was true, his face was pudgy, his thighs were squeezed together, and a roll of fat hung down in the space between his shirt and shorts. I didn't say anything. An abashed look hung over his face for the rest of the afternoon. For a while I almost liked him.

Rented Southampton Cottage

Kathleen, Ginger and friends
in back yard of cottage

During our second weekend at Southampton, Myrna and Kathleen returned from the grocery store and announced that they had run across a boy at the checkout counter Kathleen had known at Immaculate Heart High. Bill Mahoney was also spending the summer in Southampton, one of nine attorneys who had rented a house up in the hills. They were giving a party that night, could the girls attend?

"You have two roommates? They're invited as well. We're short on girls as pretty as you," Bill urged. He described a sprawling three-story brick house with six bedrooms and a sweeping, landscaped lawn. "Here's the address, grab a taxi, and I guarantee someone will give you a ride home. Don't forget!"

The four of us made ourselves ready, slipping into full-skirted summer dresses and putting on makeup. Nine single attorneys, short on girls? This sounded promising.

We were welcomed at the door by a tall blonde girl in white slacks, a red flowered blouse, and wide leather belt. "Oh yes, the girls from town!" she exclaimed heartily. "Bill told us you were coming. What a coincidence, running into a friend out here in the Hamptons! Do come

241

in. Jim, would you get these girls some drinks? I'm Jeannie. Come, let me introduce you."

We were soon swallowed in a sea of merriment, mingling with young people who crowded the oversized living room and spilled out through the French doors onto a back terrace. I crossed the grey flagstones and stood for a moment on the lawn, which down a steep hill, from which the scattered housetops dipped down out of sight and headed toward the ocean. I could hear a piano ringing out *It Might As Well Be Spring* from somewhere inside the house. The notes breezed past me, clear and enticing, a siren melody. Someone pointed us to the dining room, where we found a spread of hors d'oeuvres laid out on a red and gold cloth. A short, round-faced fellow with sandy hair came up beside me. He said his name was Terry O'Connor, one of the nine attorneys. He lived in Queens with seven siblings, drove an Opel, and would give my friends and me a ride home should we need one.

"It's filled with gin," he told me, referring to the scooped-out watermelon serving as the centerpiece. "You might call it a watermelon sling. Jim fixes it every weekend. We have a party every Saturday night, you know. You're invited to come any time."

"There must be fifty people here. How can you provide all this food and booze every weekend?"

"Every guy on the lease pitches in. We just graduated from Fordham University, so this is our last summer of freedom, you might say." He stuffed a miniature frankfurter wrapped in bacon into his mouth. "The sky's the limit."

By ten o'clock, I was standing with a group around the piano, peering at the sheet music over the shoulder of the piano player. After "I'm Goonna Wash That Man Right Outta My Hair" from *South Pacific*, someone pulled out "Rum and Coco-Cola." For the remainder of the evening the piano was encircled with enthusiastic songsters, belting out tunes from *My Fair Lady, The Sound of Music,* and *Gypsy.* These were followed by Gershwin's "Embraceable You" and "The Hut-Sut Song." I sang full throttle, voice soaring, caught up in the rhythm, the sound of the voices blending, the pleasure of riding with the flow of the silver piano notes.

"Play 'It's been a Long, Long Time,'" someone urged.

"We just sang that!"

"But it's my favorite!"

By the end of the evening, I was seated on the piano bench turning pages for the pianist, an attractive boy in a white shirt, with grey blue eyes and dark hair. He sat upright, dominating the piano with his easy command of the keys, never seeming to tire. From time to time he took long sips from a drink that someone kept refilling. Although I didn't know it yet, I had found my post, a magnetic spot seated next to this tall form, where I remained, singing out full and clear, for the rest of the summer.

I don't think he noticed me sitting beside him, our shoulders touching when someone pushed in next to me. He was intent on playing, and when a request was called out, he obligingly pulled a sheet of music from the pile. When the last of the singers had gone and he finally stood up to close the piano lid, I was aware of his tallness, a good head above me. Now he looked at me with a slight smile, but didn't say anything.

The Big House, Southampton

My roommates were in the kitchen, ready to leave, and Terry offered to drive us to town.

"What a nice party," sighed Kathleen when we got home, falling into a chair. "All those Catholics."

"An endless supply of great supply of goodies, all those homemade canopies," said Myrna flopping on the couch.

"I never drank so much. They can really put it away!" groaned Ginger. "I better hold on to something until I get upstairs."

"I had fun singing," I said. "The piano player sure is good-looking. I guess I'll go to bed."

Every Saturday night I showed up at the big house with one or another of my roommates. Our drinks were never empty. I spent most of the evening seated next to the handsome pianist, who remained intent on his playing. Sometimes he joined the singing, and on the second and third verses he raised his voice so those circling around the ebony piano surface could hear the words. As the evening wore on our voices, supported by never-ending rounds of drinks, became more raucous. The most popular songs were "The Dipsy Doodle," "Johnny Doughboy Found a Rose in Ireland," and Mocking Bird Hill." But the top demand was for the tunes of Bernstein's *West Side Story*. Everyone gathered around for this one:

> *Dear kindly Sergeant Krupke,*
> *You gotta understand,*
> *It's just our bringin' upke*
> *That gets us out of hand.*
> *Our mothers all are junkies,*
> *Our fathers all are drunks,*
> *Golly, Moses, nacherly we're punks!*

Before many weeks had passed, the seat on the bench was considered my exclusive spot. I followed the music and turned pages. Late one night, after the circle of singers had dispersed, the piano player actually spoke to me.

"Want a refill?" he asked. We walked out onto the deserted terrace, drinks in hand. He told me his name was Dave McConnell and he lived in the Bronx with his parents. He had just graduated from Fordham Law School.

"Do you mind playing for the entire evening?" I asked. "You miss the rest of the party."

"The party's right there at the piano," he replied evenly. "I like to play." I could see he relished his role as entertainer and the part it played in the success of the festivities.

"Where did you learn to play so well?" I asked. He turned towards me and smiled. Usually my view of him was from the side as he peered at the music. Now I looked directly into his face, at his dark, arched eyebrows, top-rimmed glasses, and thick black hair framing his head. The smile softened his expression, adding an air of sweetness, and when he looked down at me from his tallness, taking me in fully, I felt a flutter rise in my stomach. I couldn't read his face, couldn't tell what he was thinking. He didn't react to the bustle going on around him as he sat at the piano. It was difficult to interpret such a placid temperament, and I had a strong urge to break through his wall of imperturbability. What was he like? What did he think of me?

He removed his glasses. "I studied at Julliard," he said in response to my question. That was it. He certainly wasn't the chatty type.

"How did that happen?"

"My sixth grade teacher asked who wanted to take piano lessons, and I raised my hand. My mother agreed, if I stuck it out for the entire year. Each year after that the teacher asked again, and each year I raised my hand. This went on for eight years."

"Did you know when you first raised your hand that you had musical talent?"

"I don't have any great talent," he said. "I do have perfect pitch though."

"Give me an A." He hummed a note, and I ran to the piano, calling "Hold that note!" He was right on. I was impressed.

The sound of horseplay, lingerers not yet ready to go home, drifted in from the kitchen. Holding our tall frosted glasses, we settled on a cushioned settee by a row of rose bushes. The voices from the house dimmed as the stragglers began to leave. A door slammed, a car engine gurgled and hummed away in the distance. We sat and gazed at the stars, sipped our drinks, and breathed in the warm rose-scented air.

From then on, the evenings ended up with Dave and me on the garden settee, nursing our last nightcaps. During one of these late-night wind-downs, we wandered into the shadows of the lawn and he took me in his arms and kissed me. I was enraptured. We didn't stray far, since Dave didn't drive and I had to be careful not to miss the last ride to town.

One lazy Saturday my roommates and I lay on the Southampton beach spread out on colored beach towels. Our bodies were smeared with rich-smelling cocoa butter. Ginger and Kathleen had drawn straw hats over their faces, and Myrna lay propped up reading *Look* magazine under a zebra-striped umbrella. I lay on my back, face pointed directly into the sun. By now my skin had turned a deep bronze and I'd started wearing yellow sun dresses and silver link bracelets.

At the sound of gleeful laughter, I glanced over and detected a group of bathers setting up beach chairs not far down the sand. It was the gang from the big house. Dave's tall form stood out among the figures sitting among the towels and coolers, popping open beer cans. I watched their easy camaraderie, longing to be in their midst, but was too shy to make a move.

I turned my face back to the sun. Would he come over? Something about Dave's nonchalance, his unperturbed composure both bothered and infatuated me. I wanted to pierce his remoteness. I wanted him to reach out so that I could feel caring from him and my deep-seated presentiment of rejection would be set at ease.

Without warning, a pair of ankles appeared next to my head and I blinked my eyes open. Terry, one of the attorneys, stood looking down at me.

"Hi," he said. "How're you doing?"

"Good, good." I lifted up on an elbow.

"How'd you girls get here?"

"We walked. It's less than a mile from our house."

Terry studied me for some moments. "So," he said suddenly, "tell me, what are you afraid of?" I looked up at him. What was he driving at?

"Ah—I don't know." I squinted up at his form, backlit by a crescent of sun. "Not much." At this time in my life I thought I could take on anything.

Silence. He glanced at his feet, then chuckled nervously. "See you later," he said and walked off to join his nearby friends.

How weird! Why did he ask me that? I couldn't figure it. He'd looked at me with a sort of tenderness. Could he, in some elusive way, be trying to reach out? What did he know that I didn't know? Why didn't he ask me to join them?

The Gang from the Big House, Southampton Beach

My upper legs were starting to burn.

"People!" I wanted to yell after him. The word popped into my head and I wasn't sure it was the right answer. But he was gone.

Just then I heard Jeannie yelling for me to come over, and I grabbed my towel and walked over to join their party. Dave moved aside to make room for me. From then on I was under the spell of the stories bouncing between the umbrellas, the insistent sun, and Dave's presence beside me.

After one Saturday night party at the big house, the designated driver was nowhere to be found. The downstairs rooms were deserted. Dave and I searched outside. The car that was supposed to drive me home wasn't in the driveway. It looked like I would have to stay the night.

But where?

There was no unused room, no empty spot in the house. Finally, we staggered up to the only available place: Dave's room. From then on a pattern was set. Dave didn't drive and I didn't want to leave early. So we spent the night in his bed on the third floor. When we descended on Sunday morning, Jeannie and Bill Mahoney's girlfriend were already at the stove, swirling eggs in a fry pan. Where and how they had slept I didn't ask.

I soon learned that these boys might be loose with liquor, but they followed the strict protocol of their faith—they did not have intercourse with their girls. The first night we slept together, Dave pulled back and said we would go no further. The boundary was set. I assumed this indicated he was taking me seriously. This was desirable. Or maybe any girl was taboo. We didn't discuss it.

The one exception was Tom McClenahan, the roommate with movie star looks who slept with whoever came along. We could hear groans from his bedroom below ours. "That would be McClenahan," Dave said with a look of disgust. "He's an alley cat." Tom showed up for breakfast robust and cheerful. He was considered a loose screw, and the pun gained some popularity among the boys.

The Sunday brunches served up by Jeannie and Bill's girlfriend were dosed with high-proof flavoring—wine in the pancakes, rum in the fruit cocktail, and Grand Marnier in the coffee. On a side table a shelled-out watermelon or casaba was filled with mix spiked with gin or vodka, with colorful fruit bits and crushed ice floating on the top. These pretty little punches were lethal—one glass would knock the sobriety right out of you—and many of us contented ourselves with an Irish coffee made with Bailey's Cream, which turned out to be not much of an improvement.

We sat out on the terrace, coffee cups in hand, rehashing the hilarious mishaps of the latest party—how Terry had stumbled on a pavestone and sent six bottles of Beefeater gin crashing to pieces on the driveway; how Patrick drove into the wrong driveway at 3:00 a.m. and entered a strange house only to be scared off by sounds of passion issuing from the top of the stairs and the sight of a revolver on the hall table, which sent him stumbling back to his car; how Maureen, a bit wobbly, had mistaken her bedroom and got into bed with Tom, who soon put her straight. Jeannie described how the girls in grade school tantalized the teachers by wearing shiny patent leather shoes, which the nuns believed were used to peek under their habits. Another girl told how she and her classmates padded their uniform sleeves with sanitary napkins to cushion the paddle blows the nuns struck as punishment for incomplete homework.

The tales were greeted with raucous laughter. Dave and I laughed and exchanged confidential glances.

Jeanie told of a luckless Protestant woman who had married a Catholic. Their two children, a girl and a boy, returned home from parochial school one day, announced that their mother was not clean and would not be allowed into heaven, and from then on treated her with an aloof coolness. Everyone rolled their eyes. I appreciated their honesty, their willingness to reveal the shortcomings of a faith they steadfastly adhered to.

Dave was coaxed to relate his experience at All Hollows High. On the first day of his freshman year, the burly teacher stood sternly at his desk until the boys were seated and the class quieted. Then he demanded to know who in the class liked to fight. No one moved.

"Come on, give out, who thinks they would win an all-out donnybrook?" Finally one hand shot up. "Come up here." When the large boy got to the front of the room the teacher shot his fist into the student's face. "That's what you'll get if you try anything in this class." None of the boys ever did.

One day something happened that changed everything. Dave called me at my Manhattan apartment. He'd never called me before. Surprised, I waited to see what he wanted. Could I meet him in Southampton Saturday for dinner before the party? Terry Sullivan and Maureen would be there, along with Jeannie and Jim. It was the top restaurant in Southampton, known for its filet mignon and bananas flambé. He and Terry would pick me up at seven.

From then on he began taking me to dinner every Saturday. Something was afoot. Beyond my just showing up at the big house, we were actually dating. We seemed to be forming a twosome.

†

A postcard arrived from Ward. He was on assignment somewhere in the far east and unable to predict where his work would take him or for how long. I was used to these enigmatic messages, after which I might not hear from him for weeks. Knowing his fascination with the U.S.S.R., I imagined him on some secret reporting quest pertaining to the Cold War, maybe sleuthing in a hidden mountain village in Albania or at clandestine meetings with a British agent à la Kim Philby. His articles in the *New York Times* might originate from in a foreign country, and I was intensely curious about his explorations, about the experiment playing out in the Soviet Union. I wanted to know all I could about a cause that would liberate the world and me with it.

No further word from him. I told myself to wait, uncertain what to expect.

I received a phone call from Dave.

My roommates and I were rummaging in the kitchen as the Southampton sun lifted across the window pane. Dave asked where I had been the night before—at last a personal question! Since Ginger and Kathleen had not been around on Friday to stroll to the nearby Post House for drinks, and Myrna wanted to stay home in case Roman called, I walked across town to grab a movie by myself, something I had never done.

The movie, set in Africa, proved to be highly entertaining. I savored the way Elsa Martinelli won the elusive John Wayne from his romance-free existence with her charming wiles, encouraged by the staff at the Kenyan hunting lodge. By the end of the film she had single-handedly conquered this tall, remote alpha male. Elsa's struggle to dislodge a commanding man from his isolated perch energized me as I strolled home.

I didn't let on I'd been alone. "We went to see *Hatari*, a John Wayne film about big-game hunting in Africa," was all I said. "The animal scenes were terrific."

Dave asked me for dinner the following Friday. From then on we dined with Terry and his date both Friday and Saturday nights. Our weekends were tightening, and so was my fixation on this handsome man and the island life of fun and sunshine.

One late summer evening, after dining on lobster and martinis at an oceanside restaurant in Amagansett, the four of us piled into Terry's car and headed toward the big house. Dave and I were seated in the back seat. Dave turned to me. "You know there're only two more weekends of the summer left. Our lease is up the end of August."

I knew it only too well. I waited. "Do you want to get together in the cities when this is over?"

"Yes, I do," I said calmly. I felt the hairs on my neck tingle. YES!

Then he added, "You know, my father's a policeman." He looked directly at me. I was taken back. This was not a track I had considered, and I wasn't sure how to respond.

"What's the difference?" I tossed off, turning to look out the window. What did I care about things like that? Dave said no more. Neither did I. Talking from the heart was not my habit. Rather I strove to match his indifference. As usual, my feelings were obscure. My immediate desires were not linked in my mind to deeper needs. So much was buried—my emotions, fears, needs—me.

I did know that I was intensely, crazily attracted to him. And I liked being with his fun-loving Irish friends, the singing fests, the constant succession of drinks that transformed me into an outgoing party girl. I envied the close ties created by the group's nationality and religion. Although I was mostly English, I didn't feel connected to any bloodline. When asked about my nationality—which was frequently—I used the term mongrel. I wished I were *something*. There was no advantage in being an undefined nothing. That I was non-Catholic and non-Irish seemed to concern no one, including me. You could be one of us, they said. You even look Irish.

"What's your religion?"

"Nothing."

"You'll do."

I was sold.

Chapter 9　　　　Into The Clouds

A fall wind seeped through the cracks and arches of buildings, pricking the skin with a tease of winter, replacing the lax summer pace of the Southampton beach days. I had received several postcards from Ward postmarked the Soviet Union, no return address. Succumbing to an urge, I tried his usual number only to find it temporarily disconnected. The *Times* could provide no information, nor did I know of any friends to contact. Finally, months later, I received a note informing me that he was living in Moscow, that he had married a Russian woman who spoke fluent French and wishing me the best. Although surprised—Ward had not mentioned such a liaison—I had to admit it seemed a good fit.

Fall brought a continuation of the Southampton parties, now removed to various New York apartments in upper Manhattan or Queens. When we weren't partying, Dave and I dined on steak or lobster accompanied by three or four martinis, then taxied to a movie. It was strange to be together without the surrounding chatter, completely on our own. It felt as if all the furniture had been auctioned off and the stage left empty.

For the first time Dave started meeting my friends. He was in for some novel experiences. The first took place in one of those New York railroad flats consisting of a long, narrow corridor with doors flanking it on either side, ending in a large rectangular living room and kitchen. Dave didn't know anyone at the party except Kerstin and me, but he responded courteously as I introduced him around. When someone discovered he was the only native New Yorker in the room, a group circled in.

"You're actually from New York City?" asked a young man in a brown pullover sweater.

"Yep," Dave smiled with good humor, "I've never been west of Newark."

"We've never seen a native at one of these parties before," someone remarked.

"Ha—now you know how it feels!" I said to Dave, laughing.

"Get his New York accent, you guys!" remarked a skinny man standing next to Kerstin.

"I don't have an accent."

"I would say you do! Listen to him—he says 'pocked the ca in the garawge.' You can hardly understand him." Dave laughed at the exaggeration. No one asked if he was Irish. Nationality was a non-issue.

Over dinner one night at Chester Sewell's Brooklyn apartment, served by Chester's Spanish-born wife, differences between Dave and me surfaced for the first time. Chester's literary-laced conversation and liberal ideas enlivened the table as we discussed politics and Chester described a thesis he'd developed at Cornell on the influence of Noam Chomsky. Dave and Chester couldn't have been more different; they might have sprung from two different planets. I watched Dave's face, hoping he wouldn't be put off. I was aware that my friends tended to be offbeat and liberal, not at all the carousing conservatives Dave was used to. Myself, I was beyond worrying about such discrepancies. It would have taken a lot more to tear me from an attachment that by now absorbed every cell of my being.

A stream of engagements erupted as summer couples became serious and decided to take the plunge into matrimony. First Jeannie and Jim, followed by Terry and Maureen, Tom and his new love, Susheila, and

253

others, which threw the bevy of friends into a tizzy of expectation and generated a new round of celebration parties.

At the end of one of these shindigs I noticed a spunky girl with dark curly hair and flirty eyes squeeze into the seat next to Dave on the couch. After a while, someone put on a record and she tugged at his sleeve. For the next minutes she and Dave floated around the living room to a smoldering Sinatra song, his arm around her waist. I put down my scotch and water. It took forever, but finally the record ended and I slipped up next to Dave. "I need a drink, do you mind?" but before he could leave I was in his arms, clutching him tightly as the swaying voices of The Drifters lifted across the room. Surprised at my own aggressiveness, I looked up at my partner. Dave smiled down at me. As our cheeks touched, I heard the words of the familiar pop song and snuggled closer.

> *You can dance every dance with the gal*
> *Who gave you the eye, let her hold you tight*
> *You can smile every smile for the gal*
> *Who held your hand 'neath the pale moonlight*
>
> *But don't forget who's taking you home*
> *And in whose arms you're gonna be*
> *So darling', save the last dance for me.*

†

Soon after they moved into a spacious apartment overlooking a West Side park, Tom and Susheila threw a splashy housewarming party. By the time Dave and I arrived midnight had struck, and the festivities were raging full force. People lounged in groups telling jokes or sprawled over the couch listening to a story being told simultaneously by several people. Empty liquor bottles lined the tables, and a boy in horn-rimmed glasses dozed sideways on a recliner, mouth open.

Dave waved Tom and Terry over and told them he had an announcement to make. After much shouting and banging of spatulas on the counter tops, the room quieted.

Several hours earlier Dave had appeared at my door, a bottle of J&B Scotch under his arm, so anxious to get inside that he forgot to kiss me. Slipping immediately into the kitchen, he tore open the bottle of scotch and poured it into two tall glasses, then coaxed ice cubes from a freezer tray and added water.

"To us," he said, clinking his glass against mine. When we had seated ourselves on the couch with drinks and cigarettes, Dave turned to me with an air of determination.

"Do," he began, looking me up and down, and I wondered what was coming, but before I could think he went on, "Do you want to get married?" He cared for me, he wanted to get me a ring. "What do you say? I will be transferred soon to California, you could come with me."

The actual event is a blur, partly because at his words my mind stopped. I looked at him for a long time, unable to think. But I didn't have to think. "Yes," I said. I believe he smiled, the rest is lost in the clinking of ice and kisses and running to the phone to make reservations for a celebration dinner.

Soon we were seated at a table overlooking the East River where we consumed a cocktail, glasses of sparkling Dom Perignon, and several Bailey's Irish Creams. By the time we arrived at Tom and Sheila's party, I was in a gripping fog. I felt a swell of excitement and a wide grin fastened crazily on my face. A strip of Dave's hair fell along his forehead and he looked like he was bursting to say something.

At Tom's yell, people in the room turned, others strolled in from the kitchen. The gang would be the first to know. As soon as Dave announced the news, there were shouts and arms lifted the two of us onto chairs and we stood, smiles stretched to our ears, while drinks were poured into sparkling glasses that waved in the air, were drained and waved again. We gazed out over a sea of arms and beaming faces. For the first time, I saw a fire of emotion on Dave's face. He seemed pleased, even exuberant. I was ecstatic.

Did I stop to consider the options, weigh the pros and cons of such a life-changing decision? Not for a second. Nor did I seek council or consult minds that had my welfare at stake. I needed no help. I had until now pretty much followed the course charted by my instincts. Which is another way of saying I usually did what I wanted.

255

The days shifted into high speed. March 16, the date set, was only four months away. Every spare moment was full of preparations and engagements. We taxied to Dave's Bronx apartment to dine with his parents, who treated me with special warmth and not as if I were absconding with their only child. Dave's Aunt Bridie Lenihan entertained us at her house with tales of her stint fighting with the IRA, and we danced the jig in the living room. I talked Kerstin into accompanying us to this party, thinking she might meet an Irish bachelor to her liking, but afterwards she confided that she had no interest in marriage. Anyway, she said, Irish men were too attached to their mothers and didn't marry until their forties.

The reaction in Minneapolis was electric. "You're getting married?" My mother on the other end of the phone was incredulous. "Dave who?" Soon she was squiring me to Saks to select a wedding dress, to Altman's to register for silver and china patterns, and to a salon on Fifth Avenue for hair appointments. Dad booked the Hotel Pierre for the reception. Photographer, cake, invitations, formal wear, dinner selections, flowers, a rehearsal dinner at Luigi's—it was endless.

Mother was continually on the phone with our West Virginia relatives: Granddad Fought, Uncle Holmes, Aunt Mary, my cousin Martha Jane and her husband, Uncle Bert and Aunt Harriet, and others, all delighted at the prospect of an East Coast reunion. Mother sent everyone a list of hotels and booked a two-room suite at the Pierre for entertaining. The air crackled and I walked in a daze on a nimbus bed of diamonds.

In the midst of all this, Mother flew in for Margo and Will's December wedding and hosted a dinner for them and their party at Asti's. One of her friends held a bridal shower for me in Minneapolis, which I was unable to attend, and Dave and I acquired a closetful of household gifts. Mother's days were packed from one end to the other. She was in her element.

Mom and Me

The continual effusiveness of all this took some getting used to. At the bridal shower Margo's mother threw for me in her Manhattan hotel room, I perched on a chair surrounded by smiling, uplifted faces and ribboned boxes. One by one I ripped off the glossy paper, exclaiming with delight and appreciation. I felt rather phony, but tried to follow what I thought was expected. If I played the part, I figured I'd grow into it. Sweet, smiling, optimistic—was this to be the new me?

I threw my introversion to the wind. Whatever was demanded of me, I would handle it.

As I rode up the escalator in Bloomingdale's, I looked with a sense of marvel at my hand sparkling on the railing. The diamond ring on my finger announced that I been chosen, now locked securely into a place of my own. Yet could I really be heading into marriage? How had this happened? My claims that marriage was a purgatory for women, who were promised a vague happiness and found a life of servitude instead, had been whisked away in a swirl of gaiety. My scruples had evidently dissolved, replaced by a confident optimism about the future. I had shed the role of rebellious daughter and threw myself hook, line, and sinker into the arms of the family establishment I had so adamantly renounced in the past.

The path had swung around and returned full circle to traditional beginnings. I had caved. I had bought the standards of my parents after all. I would cook and sew and garden and have babies and join clubs and create a home and family. Life with Dave would create a pattern, a slot to slip into, a definition from which to operate.

I was the luckiest girl in the world.

Mom and Dad (Juanita Fought Bradford and Harold K. Bradford)

After a disappointing internship with a law firm, Dave had rejected the field of law and taken a position in accounting with Colgate Palmolive. The company was transferring him to Berkeley, California, in April, and I would go with him.

I admit I gave up my long-simmering dreams. My desire for Dave had dissolved every residue of resistance. I let myself be led, outfitted, feted, photographed, bejeweled, coiffed, contracted, and sent off to California without a peep. I would have a home of my own, a man I adored, a real sex life, a replacement for a job that was going nowhere. My parents would see a wayward daughter settled and defined. The whole of society applauded. I had finally arrived and fulfillment was just around the corner—it had already begun.

The big question was a hard one: would I join the Catholic Church? That was impossible. No. Would I attend catechism lessons? Yes. Dave accompanied me to the church office for classes in Catholic doctrine. He knew the answer to every question, furnishing details even the priest missed. Second-generation Irish, attendance at exclusively Catholic schools, friends who counted bishops in the family—I had taken on a bastion of the Irish Catholic Jesuit scholarship tradition. It was the beginning of my education in Catholicism.

One night in the back seat of a taxi we narrowed down the options. Dave asked what was, for him, the crucial question: Would I attest to the infallibility of the pope? This drew me up. Here I was an agnostic, with nothing to offer in the spiritual area. Dave's religion, on the other hand, provided stability, precision, and consistency. This felt strong. I could offer nothing of this quality. Dave's opinion of the Methodist church was not improved by my lack of knowledge.

"How many years did you study your religion?" he asked pointedly.

"All the way through high school, every Sunday."

"Who was the founder of the Methodist Church?"

"We studied the bible, not the church." When I couldn't recall the name of John Wesley, Dave shook his head. What kind of an education was that? Too wishy-washy for him. Dave's rock solid stability and what he stood for was appealing, a sane counterbalance to my drifting, amorphous approach.

"The pope—I—don't know," I said at last. "What does the infallibility of the pope mean?" I was willing to agree to anything—almost.

"The pope," Dave explained in a patient voice, "speaks the word of God."

"God speaks through him?"

"Yes."

"Therefore the pope can never be wrong?"

"That's right." It sounded a bit pat.

"I don't really understand that," I said finally. "It's a mystery to me."

"Exactly. It's a mystery."

"Okay," I finally acquiesced. "I guess I can buy that." What did I know? I was swimming in depths of theology I knew nothing about. I agreed, with a sense of compromise.

Dave was satisfied.

My parents didn't mention Catholicism. When I told them we would be married in the Catholic Church, but because I was a non-Catholic, Dave and I would have to stand at the low altar during the ceremony, they said not a word. Dave was a decent sort, smart and educated. The two sets of parents got on well. After the six of us spent an evening together at dinner and a Broadway play, my parents were complimentary. Kate was lovely, with a clear white complexion, beautiful white hair, personable, with good common sense. Her husband, Jack, gruff, with a heart of gold, was something of a softie. These were good people. It was time I settled down. Catholic, the California coast—so be it.

As the March date got closer, Dave's mother Kate approached her parish priest. A non-Catholic! The priest assured her that it would be all right, that the marriage sacrament provided the purification of grace. Have faith.

There was one more hurdle. When Dave and I arrived at the church to sign the prenuptial papers, I looked at the sheet the priest pushed in front of me. The words "promise to raise all ensuing children in the Catholic faith" stood out in big red letters. We had not discussed this. For a moment I was blinded in a sea of confusing red shapes, then looked over at Dave and his countenance, steady and non-pressing, brought me back to a colorless reality. I looked down at the sheet, up at the priest who sat stiff-lipped and unmoved. I closed my eyes and signed.

Relatives at Pierre Hotel: Harold, back to camera;
clockwise: Susan, Judy, Aunt Mary Holland,
Mother, Dave, Dottie Bradford

The wedding over, the guests dispersed, Dave and I ambled slowly along the sidewalk towards the airport hotel. It was late, the airport lobbies were nearly deserted, runway lights flashed red and blue in the distance, occasional headlights bobbed by at our side. We were too exhausted for small talk. Early the next morning, we would catch a plane for San Francisco and a two-week honeymoon at the Fairmont Hotel.

The realization that I now had the makings of my own family overwhelmed me. A new life with a sweet, taciturn, substantive man who smiled down at me in all his handsomeness, who was now the center of my world. Nothing could surpass that.

Susan, Judy, Mother, Dad at Pierre Hotel

I mulled over the events of the day: the last hours at the hairdressers, the hair dryer cradled around my head like a helmet; nervously getting dressed in the Pierre suite, adjusting the pearl necklace and matching earrings Mother had bought in Australia; the taxi ride to St. Patrick's with Dad fretting in the front seat that we would be late and me fretting in the back that we would be early; and the ceremony, a blur of marble, black robes, and Latin chanting; then the dinner-dance at the Pierre.

The booze was starting to wear off and the strain of so much display and merrymaking was beginning to tell. Princess for a day, a dream day of fun and acclaim that I relished while it was happening and fell into exhausted relief when it was over. Now as I strolled along, Dave at my side carrying a black duffle bag, a white carnation still lodged in his buttonhole, my mind felt groggy and the outlines of passing faces were beginning to dim.

The drone of a departing airplane rose above our heads, a reminder that the next morning we would fly off to our new life. Ahead loomed the airport hotel, a tall tower of rectangular glass. Reaching the entrance, we mounted the steps and pushed through the swinging doors. Inside, an open bar was filled with late-night customers scattered in couples among the darkened tables. The words of a familiar Bob Dylan song drifted from the depths of the bar in soft, lugubrious tones:

> _How many roads must a man walk down,_
> _Before you can call him a man?_
> _How many seas must a white dove sail_
> _Before she sleeps in the sand?_
> _Yes, and how many times must the cannon balls fly_
> _Before they're forever banned?_
> _The answer my friend is blowing in the wind_
> _The answer is blowing in the wind._

The image of a winged bird, soaring above the clouds, beyond the orbit of the earth and out into the cosmos to be lost forever shot through my mind. So many passionate songs I knew by heart, voices yearning for a better world, voices that touched my heart in a place that mattered. The sensation was bittersweet, like a parting whose time had come. Then the words disappeared into the dark night, blowing, with the song, into the wind.

I drew a deep breath, aware of Dave's hand warm in mine and his form beside me, tall and broad-shouldered in his smart worsted jacket, his presence closing the space around me. As we approached the marble counter of the front desk, Dave turned to look at me, his grey eyes soft and tender. I looked up and held his gaze. "We're on our way," he whispered, tightening his grip on my hand.

At this point all activity in my brain ceased, and a smile drew over my face and floated like a water lily. Nothing else mattered except the assurance of a fruitful tomorrow with a man of my choosing. I experienced the inevitability of the present moment, where I existed to the exclusion of all else and where at last I was sure I belonged.

Dave and Judy leaving wedding reception, 1963

CPSIA information can be obtained
at www.ICGtesting.com
Printed in the USA
LVOW04s1341260916

506239LV00025B/480/P

9 780692 665978